Black Exodus

Yale Publications in American Studies, 17

Published under the direction
of the American Studies Program

Black Exodus

Black Nationalist and
Back-to-Africa Movements, 1890-1910

by Edwin S. Redkey

**New Haven and London,
Yale University Press**

Library of Congress catalog card number: 77–81427
ISBN: 0–300–01138–5 (cloth), 0–300–01139–3 (paper)
Designed by Helen Frisk Buzyna,
set in Times Roman type,
and printed in the United States of America by
The Carl Purington Rollins Printing-Office of the
Yale University Press, New Haven, Connecticut.
Distributed in Great Britain, Europe, and Africa by
Yale University Press, Ltd., London; in Canada by
McGill-Queen's University Press, Montreal; in Latin
America by Kaiman & Polon, Inc., New York City; in
Australasia by Australia and New Zealand Book Co.,
Pty., Ltd., Artarmon, New South Wales; in India by
UBS Publishers' Distributors Pvt., Ltd., Delhi; in
Japan by John Weatherhill, Inc., Tokyo.

To the Memory of
Malcolm X

Contents

On a hot summer night in 1962, riding through the West African savannah on a Nigerian train, I talked long and earnestly with the several Nigerians who shared the compartment with me. After I had answered many questions about the United States, all but one of the Nigerians then left for supper in the dining car. The one remaining was a young college-trained journalist from Kano. When we were left alone he leaned toward me and asked in a confidential tone, "Really, now, why does not the American government let the Negroes come back to Africa?"

It was not hard to answer his immediate question, but its deeper implications intrigued me. Why, indeed, did the question of African emigration for Afro-Americans keep recurring long after the American Colonization Society and Marcus Garvey were gone? Why have most Afro-Americans remained in the United States despite their disabilities here? What conditions in the past had spawned "back-to-Africa" movements, and why had they never succeeded? Were they sponsored by blacks or whites? What ties existed between Afro-Americans and Africa after the end of the slave trade, and after the end of slavery itself?

Answers to some of these questions were easily found. Others came harder. The present study is an attempt to discover some of the unknowns; in particular, it links the American Colonization Society and the Garvey movement. It demonstrates, furthermore, that black nationalism, a rejection of white American society, was widespread during the period when Booker T. Washington dominated the Afro-American scene. By dealing with only one phase of the question, it shows that Afro-Americans have kept constant ties with Africa, be they ever so romantic or tenuous. Essentially this is a story of lower-class blacks, people on the "mud sill" of American society, not of the black elite who ardently supported either Booker T. Washington or W. E. B. DuBois at the turn of the century. It portrays their frustration with racial oppression in the United States and their attempts to do something about their problems.

For most of those who wanted to emigrate during the years of this study, a "black exodus" was only a dream. But it was a widespread dream of economic and political power, of independence and manhood. For clear historical reasons, the exodus did not become a reality, but the dream persisted. It became manifest in the Garvey movement of the 1920s. Recently, the late Malcolm X gave clearest voice to the same resentment and frustration, the same hope and vision, the same independence and manhood. Although no longer dreaming of an exodus, Malcolm X asserted the same pride and the same call for black unity. His life and teachings, more than any other factor, helped me understand the black nationalism of the 1890s. And they gave me a new understanding of the American race problem in our own time.

Many people helped me in the research and writing of this study; I owe thanks to them all. I am grateful to the staffs of the following libraries: Sterling Memorial Library and the Divinity School Library at Yale University; The Moorland Collection at Howard University; the Schomburg Collection of the New York Public Library; the Manuscripts Division of the Library of Congress; Drew University Library.

I gratefully acknowledge a grant from the Behavioral Sciences Research Fund of Yale University which facilitated the preparation of the manuscript. The *Journal of American History* graciously permitted the inclusion of material which originally appeared in its pages.

Among the many individuals who helped at various stages in this study were Timothy H. Breen, John O. Campbell, Josephus R. Coan, John Moore Crossey, Lawrence O. Kline, Mrs. Elsie M. Lewis, Miss Hattie Gay Little, Rayford W. Logan, Mrs. Caroline Minter, Mrs. Dorothy B. Porter, Joseph Sullivan, and Paul B. Worthman. For special indulgences and assistance beyond the call of duty I am indebted to Mrs. Ann H. Garden, Louis R. Harlan, Svend E. Holsoe, George A. Shepperson, and Robert M. Zemsky. I am much obliged to Professor C. Vann Woodward for his help, encouragement, and example of scholarship. Norman Holmes Pearson made it all possible. My wife, Nancy, not only helped with the research but gave aid and inspiration at every stage of discovery and writing. Despite good advice and welcome assistance from teachers, friends, and family, I alone, alas, am responsible for any errors of fact or interpretation.

Knoxville   E.S.R.
May 1969

Introduction

Most black slaves brought to America would gladly have returned to Africa. Descendants of the slaves knew little of Africa, but whenever problems in the United States overwhelmed them some wanted to emigrate to their fatherland. So it was between 1890 and 1910, an unhappy period in Afro-American history.

The African emigration movement of those years was not a unified campaign dominated by one group or institution, although the venerable American Colonization Society played a role in it. Nor was it a flashy urban mass movement like that led by Marcus Garvey in the 1920s. Instead it was a sporadic, untidy affair involving mainly Southern black farmers and only occasionally attracting the notice of the white public. Blacks led the movement and espoused a form of black nationalism as an answer to the American race problem. Emigration to Africa in the 1890s was not a new idea; rather, it drew on a long tradition of colonization plans. The particularly difficult economic, political, and social conditions of the period provoked some blacks to revive the old dream of a happier life in Africa.

During the period between the Civil War and 1890 the United States had struggled with the question, "What role should blacks play in American life?" During Reconstruction white Americans had answered on sectional grounds: Southerners wanted blacks to remain a subservient laboring class while Northerners wanted them to help assure Republican control of the federal government. In the Compromise of 1877, Southerners surrendered the federal government to the Republicans in return for, among other things, the right to deal with Southern blacks without Northern interference.[1] In the years that followed Reconstruction, there was no unanimity among Southern whites about how to treat the ex-slaves. Some wanted to keep the blacks totally subjugated and used violence to implement that goal. Others were more lenient, especially while they were uncertain whether Northern politicians would abide by the compromise. But in the late 1880s, as the South grew politically bolder, the Southern answer to the race question became increasingly clear: Blacks were to remain a dependent, nonpolitical, and landless laboring class. After 1890 Northern whites took little exception to this solution, and the Southern racial attitude spread northward.[2]

Afro-Americans, by necessity, defined their roles within the limits set by the white majority. They wanted, naturally enough, to be equal in all respects with whites, but the discrepancy between the goal and the reality was immense. How to bridge the gap was the concern of all black spokesmen. Differences among them were more of strategy than what the final result would be. Optimistic blacks may have argued among themselves whether accommodation or protest, economic or intellectual achievement, would best break down the racial barriers, but all such groups were certain that the walls eventually would tumble down. Pessimists, on the other hand, also wanted equality but despaired of gaining it in the United States.

1. C. Vann Woodward, *Reunion and Reaction* (rev. ed. New York, 1956), pp. 229–33.
2. C. Vann Woodward, *The Strange Career of Jim Crow* (2d rev. ed. New York, 1966), Chapters 1–3.

Following American tradition, Southern blacks had eagerly embraced politics after 1865, voting Republican, holding public office, and trying to exert their influence on local and national government. Long before the official end of Reconstruction in 1877, however, Southern whites, by fraud, intimidation, and violence, had effectively reduced black political power. Although some blacks continued to vote and hold minor offices, most became disillusioned with politics as a means of advancing their welfare. In the 1880s they increasingly looked to education and economic progress for success.[3]

Between 1890 and 1910 two prominent black leaders emerged: Booker T. Washington and W. E. B. DuBois. Washington, a Southerner, taught his followers to accept, rather than protest the segregation, disfranchisement, and inequality enforced by whites. This was, in Washington's view, only a short-range tactic which would avoid trouble and enable blacks to live morally, work hard, accumulate money and eventually win the respect and equality they sought. It was a black version of the same "gospel of wealth" which guided most white Americans. In essence, Washington wanted Afro-Americans to follow the economic path to middle-class virtue and its rewards.[4]

DuBois, on the other hand, was a Northern black intellectual. Degrees from Harvard and Berlin certified his accomplishments. Believing firmly that only active protest would gain for blacks the rights and opportunities they wanted, DuBois opposed Washington's accommodation to white oppression. Rather than win respect through economic gain, DuBois insisted that blacks should use education and culture to bridge the chasm between the races. "The talented tenth," he said, would win the respect of

3. August Meier, *Negro Thought in America, 1880–1915* (Ann Arbor, 1963), pp. 26–41.
4. Ibid., pp. 85–118 and passim.

the whites, and the gulf between whites and blacks of lesser achievement would then gradually be overcome.[5]

Different as these tactics were, bitter as were the struggles between the advocates of acommodation and protest, they shared not only the same optimistic goals but the same basic strategy. Each ideology expected a black elite to win the dignity sought by all Afro-Americans. Both factions believed that once the elite had led the way, upper-class American attitudes would change and the lower classes of whites would imitate their betters and overcome their prejudice against blacks. Each alternative was primarily a middle-class plan and reflected the middle-class optimism of American culture.[6]

Both Washington and DuBois won wide support for their ideas, the first after his 1895 "Atlanta Compromise" address, the latter increasingly after his 1903 challenge to Washington. Support came from the middle-class blacks who identified themselves with the elite model projected by the leaders. Even more important, support from white spokesmen and philanthropists was crucial to the popularity of both men. Washington appealed to conservative businessmen and officials, North and South, while DuBois won endorsement from a few wealthy white liberals in the North. White money and prestige helped each leader, in turn, publicize and institutionalize his ideas.

White support thus enabled the two leaders to extend their influence over lower-class blacks—Washington through Tuskegee Institute and DuBois through the *Crisis* magazine and the National Association for the Advancement of Colored People. Both ideologies remained, how-

5. Ibid., pp. 171–247; Francis L. Broderick, *W. E. B. DuBois, Negro Leader in Time of Crisis* (Stanford, 1959), pp. 73–74 and passim; Elliott M. Rudwick, *W. E. B. DuBois, Propagandist of the Negro Protest* (Philadelphia, 1960), pp. 54–76 and passim.

6. Cf. E. Franklin Frazier, *Black Bourgeoisie* (New York, 1962), pp. 65–71.

ever, essentially middle class. Given the slow advance even of wealthy and educated blacks into white society, the ideologies remained as remote from the vast majority of blacks as that middle-class status of wealth or culture. Nevertheless, in the grim racial climate of 1890–1910, many black peasants adulated the two giants, partly because they admired any black who seemed to hold the respect of whites, partly because they desperately needed hope of some kind, and partly because they had absorbed the American cultural dream of success over impossible obstacles. But neither gospel, of black wealth or black talent, could help the tenant farmers who had neither money, education, nor faith in America. During the years after 1890—years of violence, depression, segregation, and disfranchisement—a considerable number of Southern blacks lost the basic optimism shared by Washington and DuBois. Lower-class blacks, remote from middle-class status and pessimistic about gaining equality in middle-class America, formed the popular base of a black movement that advocated emigration to Africa. Causes for this black unrest in the 1890s were many, but the most pressing burden, and the problem that made those people think that emigration was the only solution, was economic. Indeed it was probably true, as Carter G. Woodson has written, that "since the Civil War race troubles have never been sufficient to get in motion a large number of Negroes. The discontent resulted from the land-tenure and credit systems, which had restored slavery in a modified form."[7]

Land tenure in the Southern states had changed in several respects since the Civil War. Especially in the "black belts," the rich alluvial cotton lands, large plantations had predominated before the war. By 1890, much of that land was still held in large tracts but the owners no longer had

7. Carter G. Woodson, *A Century of Negro Migration* (Washington, 1918), p. 130.

slaves to work the soil. The landowners' accommodation
to the new labor system took various forms. Some hired
workers for wages; others rented parts of their land for
money; but most seem to have rented their land for shares
of the crop raised. This "sharecropping" began as a makeshift solution to the problems raised by the destruction of
the Southern economy by the war. Neither the worker nor
the planter had much cash and sharecropping bypassed
the need for ready money. Black and white farmers alike
farmed for shares but, because they had always worked
the plantations, blacks predominated. By 1890 the system had become a fixed part of the Southern economy,
despite problems in the allocation of the proceeds. The
sharecropper paid up to half the annual crop for use of the
land and the remaining portion provided him barely
enough for subsistence. For most blacks this was little
improvement over slavery.[8]

Another outgrowth of postwar agricultural adjustment
in the South was the crop-lien system. Like the sharecrop
system, it evolved as a circumvention of cash money. The
farmer mortgaged his crop, or crop share, against the food
and supplies he needed for the year. The merchant who
made the arrangement charged high prices to cover his
risks, for with such a mortgage it was the merchant who
absorbed losses due to poor crops and fluctuating prices.
At the end of the year, when the crops were gathered and
sold and the credits and debts accounted, the merchant
frequently informed the farmer that the crop had not
earned enough to pay his bill. Thus the farmer was often
forced, under penalty of law, to mortgage the next year's
crop to the same merchant, and the farmer was in virtual
slavery insofar as profits were concerned. Like share-

8. C. Vann Woodward, *Origins of the New South, 1877–1914*
(Baton Rouge, 1951), pp. 175–80; Vernon L. Wharton, *The Negro
in Mississippi, 1865–1890* (Chapel Hill, 1947), pp. 58–73.

cropping, the crop-lien system applied to both white and black, but the black was the chief debtor in the black belt.[9]

Both the sharecropping and crop-lien systems resulted in the growing dependence of the Southern economy on a single cash crop—cotton. As these systems became more widespread and regularized in lines of credit, merchants increasingly accepted only cotton as collateral. They believed, perhaps correctly, that only cotton could be sold outside the South. Despite the fact that Southern states imported great quantities of corn, wheat, and other staples from the North and West, cotton continued to reign in the South. There were exceptions, of course: tobacco, rice, and sugar flourished in some areas; but even these were single-crop areas and they suffered from the vagaries of weather and blight. When whole states depended upon one crop, drops in market price could cause widespread economic distress. Falling prices encouraged farmers to raise more crops, and glutted markets drove prices further down. The cycle was not only possible—it actually happened. When cotton production increased greatly after the Civil War, the price fell. By 1890 many farmers could no longer make a living from cotton.[10]

A growing number of blacks wanted to migrate rather than stay to fight these apparently insoluble economic problems. The number of inquiries received at the American Colonization Society offices rose as cotton prices fell. Many letters cited economic hardship as the basis of their discontent. From Arkansas came the complaint that drought-stricken crops brought almost no return: "Money being so scarce in our vicinity we cannot sell of nothing at all."[11] Mississippi and Alabama blacks complained of

9. Woodward, *Origins of the New South,* pp. 180–85.
10. Ibid.
11. B. Campbell to William Coppinger, 13 August 1890, American Colonization Society Papers, Manuscript Division, Library of Con-

virtual slavery to the landowner and storekeeper. A
Georgia man summed up the situation: "We have little or
no voice here & our wages are so small we scarcely have
enough means to subsist upon. Taxation is so pending
[heavy] that we cannot hold any real estate worth men-
tioning." He concluded: "We feel like children away from
home and are anxious to get home. We are quite sure that
the U.S. of America is not the place for the colored man."[12]

As cotton prices fell in the 1890s, Southern political
unrest rose. Both black and white farmers were hard hit
and both found ways to register their discontent; Populism
and farmer agitation spread across the South. There were
attempts in some states to organize biracial farmers' alliances, and separate black farm groups cooperated with
all-white farmer alliances in calling for political and economic reforms. This breaking of the color line by Populist
politicians gave hope to some blacks, but it also gave the
ruling Conservative Democrats a strong weapon for dis-
crediting the farmers. By 1894 black Populism had
reached its peak,[13] but many blacks still distrusted the
movement. The "farmers' Alliance," wrote one Alabama
black, "is nothing but the Root of Confederacy—the same
old Copper-belly party, changed from grangers to farmers'
Alliance."[14]

As rural unrest grew in the South, an increasing number
of whites wanted to remove blacks from politics. Mississippi was the first state to try official disfranchisement; in
1890, a new state constitution made literacy and understanding of the state constitution requirements for voting.

----

gress, Washington, D.C. Hereafter, unless otherwise noted, all refer-
ences to correspondence will refer to that collection.

12. E. Jackson to C. T. O. King, 16 June 1891 (enclosed in King
to Coppinger, 25 July 1891).

13. Woodward, *Origins*, pp. 235–63.

14. J. B. Blevins to Coppinger, 7 August 1890.

As administered by registrars committed to reducing black voting power, this rule effectively disfranchised all but a handful of Mississippi's blacks.[15] One man wrote to the Colonization Society: "The new constitution and oppressive laws is the reason we want [to] emigrate."[16] Another pleaded: "We as a people are oppressed and disfranchised we are still working hard and our rights taken from us times are hard and getting harder every year we as a people believe that Affrica is the place but to get from under bondage are thinking of Oklahoma as this is our nearest place of safety."[17]

Another feature of the early 1890s was the violence employed against Southern blacks. Violence had always been a constant threat, but as economic decline reduced more whites to the subsistence level, to competing with blacks, and as demagogic politicians used the race issue for gain, persecution of blacks increased. Lynchings were frequent and beatings commonplace. Fear dominated most black communities.[18] A Mississippi black preacher reported that violence awaited any black man who talked of going to Africa. Of the seventy-two members of his proposed emigration group, the local whites "caught to or three of the mens and whip them badly and talked about killing all of them that they could find out was going and they had all the collered people in Cohoma affraid to meet at my church."[19] From Alabama came a similar report: "Some of my collered friends are whip in the county very regular. They whip 2 men [and] 1 woman not long since

15. Wharton, *Negro in Mississippi,* pp. 199–215.

16. R. L. Flagg to Coppinger, 4 May 1891.

17. A. G. Belton to Coppinger, 22 July 1891.

18. Gunnar Myrdal, *An American Dilemma, 1* (New York, 1944), 560–62; Woodward, *Origins,* pp. 351 f; Rayford Logan, *The Negro in American Life and Thought, The Nadir: 1877–1901* (New York, 1954), passim; Wharton, *Negro in Mississippi,* pp. 224–27.

19. H. E. Ellis to Coppinger, November 1890.

and kill one man dead."[20] Such treatment of those who
thought of threatening the labor supply by emigrating
epitomized the prevailing climate of physical violence.

Such were the economic, political, and social conditions that gave rise to black unrest in the early 1890s.
Little wonder, then, that some blacks considered their
plight no better than slavery. They could not accumulate
wealth. They could not use politics for relief. Many could
not even leave their plantations without danger. "Down
here on the Gulf Coast, La. & Miss.," wrote one black,
"the negroes there isn't anything but slaves there and got
them there and cant get out. . . . oh yes they run the negroes
with Hound dogs now days and times as did before 1865.
Oh may God help us to get out from here to Africa."[21]
Because so many of the black peasants who wrote to the
Colonization Society were only semiliterate, their labored
letters seldom detailed their grievances or their hopes. It
was enough for them that they could find someone to
answer their questions about going to Africa. Conditions
in the South had made them lose hope of success in the
United States. In their pessimism they were willing to leave
the country to seek their own nation, a black nation.

Black nationalism is more easily described than defined.
W. E. B. DuBois once wrote: "Here, then, is the dilemma.
. . . What, after all, am I? Am I an American or a Negro?
Can I be both? Or is it my duty to cease to be a Negro as
soon as possible and be an American?"[22] Throughout
most of his life DuBois tried to hold both alternatives.
Nationalists, on the other hand, resolved the question by
grasping only one horn of the dilemma and answering:
"Above all else, we are Negroes."

20. R. L. Davis to Coppinger, 31 August 1891.
21. Ibid.
22. W. E. B. DuBois, *The Conservation of Races* (Washington,
1897), pp. 16–17.

Black nationalism shared many attributes of other nationalisms—elements that John Stuart Mill cited as "identity of political antecedents; the possession of a national history, and a consequent community of recollections; collective pride and humiliation, pleasure and regret, connected with the . . . past."[23] Afro-Americans had a political past of slavery, oppression, and isolation by whites who took special pains to exclude them from American life. As a result, blacks had overflowing recollections of collective humiliation and regret. It may have been harder to find the positive aspects of that heritage, but black nationalists stressed the glories of their African ancestors and the American rhetoric which claimed that all men are equal.

Nationalism in the United States, unlike most European nationalisms, has always been expressed not in terms of race, language, or culture but in universalist terms. The Declaration of Independence declared that *all* men, not just Anglo-Saxon Americans, were created free and equal. Accordingly, the American nation was to be composed of all who lived on its land and pledged allegiance to its government and principles. But there have always been assumptions and reservations behind the universalist words. Thomas Jefferson, for example, who wrote the Declaration of Independence, believed that blacks were incapable of fitting into American life. He advocated the simplest of all nationalist formulas: removal of the black aliens from the United States.[24] Other proposed solutions to the problem of the blacks' presence in America varied from per-

23. John Stuart Mill, *Representative Government* (1861), quoted in Karl W. Deutsch, *Nationalism and Social Communication* (Cambridge, Mass., 1953), p. 5.

24. Winthrop D. Jordan, *White Over Black, American Attitudes toward the Negro, 1550–1812* (Chapel Hill, 1968), pp. 542–69; Dumas Malone, *Jefferson the Virginian* (Boston, 1948), pp. 266–69.

petual slavery to separate communities for them—whites who advocated practical equality and integration were rare in the nineteenth century. As a sense of nationalism gripped Americans, Afro-Americans were excluded from full participation in all the white man's basic national functions as they pertained to voting, education, prosperity, worship, and military service. The quick return to most of the prewar restrictions in the 1890s, after the brief experiments of Reconstruction, demonstrates how deeply ingrained white nationalism had become.

That blacks should react in kind to white nationalism should not cause surprise. Elie Kedourie has observed that if nationalism captures "the intellectual and political leaders of one group, and they proceed to act according to its tenets, then the same doctrine must spread to other groups, who will feel impelled, in the face of threatening claims, to adopt it for their own use."[25] The growing nationalism and white chauvinism of the United States after Reconstruction provided an obvious model for blacks who felt the injustice of their situation. A mirror image of the American nation, a black image with democratic, prosperous, self-sufficient institutions, could have strong appeal to Afro-Americans who might become pessimistic about their prospects in the United States.

White nationalism provided not only a potential model for black nationalism but an oppressive force that was felt by all blacks. The rhetoric that defended slavery clearly identified blacks as aliens, perhaps nonhumans. Those same ideas buttressed the caste system instituted after emancipation. That the United States was a white man's country was continually impressed upon blacks who showed ambition or protested injustice: they were aliens who did not belong. Thus, if Kenneth R. Minogue's insight is valid, that nationalism "is a political movement

25. Elie Kedourie, *Nationalism* (rev. ed. New York, 1962), p. 116.

depending on a feeling of grievance against foreigners,"[26] blacks were primed for a nationalist reaction to white oppression.

If black nationalism was not, however, the predominant black reaction to white nationalism, the reason must be sought in the basic optimism of black Americans. Most blacks were convinced that most white Americans actually believed their rhetoric of equality and therefore could be educated, prodded, or shamed into applying these ideals to their relations with blacks. Blacks who held this optimistic view of American society lacked what Hans Kohn has called "the living and active corporate will" to nationalism. They still saw their destiny in the United States rather than in their own black nation-state. Nationalists saw such a state as "the ideal and only legitimate form of political organization . . . the source of all cultural creative energy and of economic well-being."[27] When circumstances dimmed their optimism, an increasing number of blacks joined the nationalists.

Perhaps the ideas of the black nationalists have been best summarized by E. U. Essien-Udom, as "the belief of a group that it shares, or ought to share, a common heritage of language, culture and religion; and that its heritage, way of life and ethnic identity are distinct from those of other groups . . . that they ought to rule themselves and shape their own destinies."[28] This description applies not

26. Kenneth R. Minogue, *Nationalism* (London, 1967), p. 25.

27. Hans Kohn, *Nationalism, Its Meaning and History* (Princeton, 1955), p. 10.

28. E. U. Essien-Udom, *Black Nationalism, A Search for an Identity in America* (New York, 1962), p. 20. For other studies of black nationalism see Edmund David Cronon, *Black Moses, The Story of Marcus Garvey and the Universal Negro Improvement Association* (Madison, 1955); Harold Cruse, *The Crisis of the Negro Intellectual* (New York, 1967); C. Eric Lincoln, *The Black Muslims in America* (Boston, 1961); Howard Brotz, *The Black Jews of Harlem* (New York, 1964); Robert A. Bone, *The Negro Novel in America* (New Haven, 1958), pp. 1–8; Eugene D. Genovese, "The Legacy of Slavery and the

only to the twentieth-century Black Muslims Essien-Udom
was studying but to the black nationalists of earlier times.

Like other nationalists, black nationalists had political,
social, and cultural goals. They sought political and physical withdrawal into their own society, where they could
control their fate. They stressed a heritage derived from
a glorious past in Africa and a suffering past in America.
Because race was the essential unifying factor, they used
Africa to symbolize the best in black culture. Imbued with
the values of United States civilization, they sought freedom and opportunity to exercise for themselves those
American values. Although they believed all men were
created equal, nationalistic blacks assumed that white
Americans would never recognize their equality. Based
on the rejection of white American society, black nationalism found adherents among blacks who had no hope of
ever joining that society.[29]

Peasant blacks drifted in and out of black nationalism
as their personal and general conditions fluctuated. In the
agrarian South, where whites controlled the economy, nationalism expressed the black man's despair of ever own-
ing his own land or making a decent living. Where violence
and oppression were common, nationalism expressed black
determination to withdraw from the white world into a
black community where no whites could threaten and insult
them. In a society where blacks were not only shunned and

Roots of Black Nationalism," *Studies on the Left, 6* (Nov.–Dec. 1966),
3–26; A. James Gregor, "Black Nationalism: A Preliminary Analysis
of Negro Radicalism," *Science and Society, 27* (Fall 1963), 415–32.
Howard H. Bell, "Negro Nationalism in the 1850s," *Journal of Negro
Education, 35* (Winter 1966), 100–04; Hollis R. Lynch, "Pan-Negro
Nationalism in the New World, Before 1862," in *Boston University
Papers on Africa, II,* Jeffrey Butler ed. (Boston, 1966), pp. 149–79.
    29. William E. Bittle and Gilbert Geis, *The Longest Way Home*
(Detroit, 1964), p. 25 and passim. Cf. Woodson, *Negro Migration,*
passim.

despised but taught to abhor their blackness, nationalism inverted the values and made a virtue of color. By 1890, after a quarter-century of freedom, many Southern blacks were beginning to despair of gaining the good life they believed was their right as Americans. They were entering a period of economic, political, and social hardship that would make the appeals of nationalism quite tempting.

Black nationalism was a rejection of the American status quo, but it remained for circumstances and individual leaders to provide direction and positive goals for unhappy black farmers. The North and the West of the United States provided the most obvious outlet for Afro-American frustrations. Even before the Civil War the North had the aura of a promised land for Southern blacks, but Northern whites were not much more tolerant than Southerners in 1890. Furthermore, black cotton-farmers had little hope of gaining land or jobs in the North. Land was available in the West, but even there the black was an outcast. Nationalist separatism led to the foundation of several all-black towns across the South, and in 1890 a black leader attempted to create an all-black state in what is now western Oklahoma. Migration within the United States, however, was not notably successful for black peasants. They wanted land above all, but whites wanted the same land, and racial prejudice usually assured white predominance. Many blacks who moved to the West became even more unhappy when the change did not improve their status.

The most pessimistic nationalists advocated emigration from the United States. Some wanted to go to the Caribbean, and others moved to Canada, but Africa had a perennial appeal for American blacks.[30] Black nationalists saw the "dark continent" as the natural home of black

30. Cf. Harold R. Isaacs, *The New World of Negro Americans* (New York, 1963), pp. 105–13 and passim.

men, the one place on earth where Negroes might build a nation of their own and escape American oppression. There they could get land, independence and self-respect. The nationalists of 1890, furthermore, drew on a long tradition of colonization and emigration by Afro-Americans.

Colonization and emigration were separate but parallel traditions, occasionally merging but more often mutually exclusive. Colonization was essentially a white man's solution to the race problem and emigration was a black nationalist answer.[31] At times the two combined in a strange marriage of white segregationists and black radicals. The American Colonization Society was the foremost advocate of overseas colonization and its history through 1870 has already been written.[32] But the nationalist tradition of African emigration began long before 1817, when the Society was founded.

Because most slaves were illiterate, few documents tell of their desire to return to Africa. Some Africans, however, had been educated in the Muslim tradition before being enslaved and sent across the Atlantic, and several such men left autobiographies in Arabic. Each of them considered Africa his true home and a promised land of freedom from slavery.[33]

31. Howard H. Bell, "A Survey of the Negro Convention Movement, 1830–1861" (unpublished doctoral dissertation, Northwestern University, 1953).

32. Philip J. Staudenraus, *The African Colonization Movement, 1816–1865* (New York, 1961); Willis D. Boyd, "Negro Colonization in the National Crisis, 1860–1870" (unpublished doctoral dissertation, UCLA, 1953). A "bibliographical essay" by Staudenraus (pp. 305–10) surveys the vast literature on the American Colonization Society.

33. Elizabeth Donnan, *Documents Illustrative of the Slave Trade, 2* (Washington, 1931), 420–27; *African Repository, 13* (July 1837), 203–05; "The Autobiography of Omar ibn Said, Slave in North Carolina," *American Historical Review, 30* (July 1925), 787–95; "Autobiography of Abou Bekir Sadiki, Alias Edward Doulan," *Journal of Negro History, 21* (January 1936), 52–55; Douglas Grant, *The Fortunate Slave: An Ilustration of American Slavery in the Early Eighteenth*

Few ties with Africa persisted among later-generation slaves and free blacks. Color was their most obvious inheritance from the fatherland. As Afro-Americans developed their own culture, it became a variation more American than African in content;[34] nevertheless, black and white Americans insisted on calling blacks "Africans" or "Afro-Americans." These terms, coupled with the prejudices of race and culture, continually reminded blacks that they were not part of the basic American nation. They further reminded blacks that, although they thought themselves entitled to the privileges of the United States, Africa was their peculiar heritage.

Vestigial emigration sentiment lay close enough to the surface that, when emancipation came to the slaves in the Northern states after the American Revolution, back-to-Africa schemes quickly appeared. In 1787 in Boston, eighty free blacks petitioned the Massachusetts government for financial aid in getting to Africa. The group promised to preach Christianity and open commerce with the United States; nothing, however, came of its efforts.[35]

White philanthropists also became interested in colonizing the ex-slaves in Africa. As early as 1773, Samuel Hopkins, a New England theologian who advocated the ethics of "disinterested benevolence," proposed sending free Christian blacks as missionaries to Africa. Religious philanthropists, both American and British, made plans for establishing a colony of freedmen in West Africa,

---

Century (New York, 1968); Philip D. Curtin, ed., Africa Remembered: Narratives by West Africans from the Era of the Slave Trade (Madison, 1967).

34. Cf. E. Franklin Frazier, The Negro in the United States (New York, 1957), pp. 4–21; Melville J. Herskovits, The Myth of the Negro Past (New York, 1941); Charles Keil, Urban Blues (Chicago, 1966), pp. 1–34.

35. Benjamin Quarles, The Negro in the Making of America (New York, 1964), p. 96.

which the British were the first to do. Under the leadership of Granville Sharp, a group of reformers in 1787 transported a number of ex-slaves from London to Sierra Leone, where they founded a city.[36]

Among the Americans who watched the Sierra Leone experiment with interest was Paul Cuffee, a black ship captain from Massachusetts. Cuffee, a devout Quaker, decided to open trade between the new colony and the United States. He believed that such commerce would lead to the repatriation of many free blacks from the United States and the consequent evangelization of West Africa. The War of 1812 delayed Cuffee's project, but he spent considerable time and money trying to convince free blacks and the federal government that his project was wise and practical. Even though he died in 1817, after conducting only one shipload of settlers to Sierra Leone, Cuffee had spread an idea among blacks and whites that soon grew into an organized colonization movement.[37]

The American Colonization Society (ACS) was founded in 1817, just before Cuffee died. With funds from white philanthropists and support from the federal and some of the state governments, it founded Liberia, adjacent to Sierra Leone, in West Africa. The society's primary object, it maintained, was to put free blacks where they could best use their civilized talents for the benefit of themselves and Africa. Before the Civil War the society transported 13,000 Afro-Americans to Liberia, most of whom were ex-slaves whose masters had freed them specifically on

36. Staudenraus, *African Colonization*, pp. 1–11; Christopher Fyfe, *A History of Sierra Leone* (London, 1962), pp. 112 f.

37. Staudenraus, *African Colonization*, pp. 9–11; Henry N. Sherwood, "Paul Cuffee," *Journal of Negro History*, 8 (April 1923), 153–229; idem, "Paul Cuffee and His Contribution to the American Colonization Society," *Proceedings of the Mississippi Valley Historical Society*, 6 (1913), 370–404; idem, "Early Negro Deportation Projects," *Mississippi Valley Historical Review*, 2 (March 1916), 484–508; Fyfe, *Sierra Leone*, p. 112 and Chapters 1–5.

condition that they leave the United States. But relatively few free blacks volunteered to join the colony. Despite many difficulties within and outside the organization, and in the United States and in Africa, the society remained in existence into the twentieth century, sending blacks to Africa annually.[38]

Opposition to the society came from several sources. Most free blacks, considering the United States their home, refused to leave; even Paul Cuffee had spoken out against the new organization. ACS sponsors found Cuffee's statements paradoxical and disappointing, but his reasons are not hard to discern. Cuffee wanted emigration for the purpose of opening trade with Africa, enriching the settlers, and spreading civilization and Christianity. Although these goals were also affirmed by the society, the difference was that Cuffee was black and his efforts could be considered self-help. In no way did he insinuate that black men were inherently inferior to whites, nor did he suggest that they could not achieve success in the United States—he was himself an exemplary and successful businessman. Blacks feared that the society's efforts to secure federal aid for colonization assumed that they could never live happily among whites and that the government might eventually deport them by force. In short, Africa could be a valid option for free blacks only as long as it did not exclude the possibility of their remaining in the United States. Neither Cuffee nor the Colonization Society appears to have harbored black nationalist ideas.[39]

Opposition to the society also came from whites. Some Southerners saw the society's promise of freedom in Africa as a threat to the institution of slavery. More seriously, the abolitionists, who were indeed trying to destroy slavery,

38. Staudenraus, *African Colonization,* passim.
39. Ibid.; Sherwood, "Paul Cuffee and His Contribution," pp. 400–04.

saw colonization as a plan to rid the nation of free blacks
so that slavery would be more secure. Opposition from
abolitionists increased in the 1830s and led to a decline
in the income and operations of the society.[40]

Articulate free blacks, equating colonization with deportation, continued to oppose the society; they even organized national conventions to condemn colonization.
During the 1850s, however, amid growing tension over
the slavery issue, emigration found new encouragement.
Fugitive slave laws made blacks so uneasy that many mi-
grated to Canada while others went to the Caribbean or
Liberia. Even some of the most ardent black abolitionists,
hitherto optimistic, began to think that emigration might
be better than enduring "freedom" in the United States.
According to the foremost historian of ante bellum black
thought, "Leaders, including the great Frederick Douglass,
who had championed staying at home, shifted eventually
to embrace the belief in the 'reflex influence' of a Negro
nation. By April 1861—and the outbreak of war—virtually all [articulate blacks] had accepted emigration as
a legitimate route to progress and nationalism as rightful
doctrine."[41]

Although the Colonization Society thrived again in the
pre-Civil War years, black support for emigration did not
necessarily mean black support for the society. Among
others, Harvard-trained physician Martin R. Delany attempted to start his own African emigration scheme. His
ideal African colony would not be like Liberia, "a poor
miserable mockery—a burlesque on a government . . . a

40. Staudenraus, *African Colonization,* Chapters 9–17.
41. Bell, "Negro Convention Movement," p. 272; Bell, "Negro Nationalism in the 1850s," pp. 101–03; Hollis R. Lynch, Pan-Negro Nationalism in the New World, Before 1862," in *Boston University
Papers on Africa, II,* pp. 149–79; Staudenraus, *African Colonization,*
pp. 32–33; Leon Litwack, *North of Slavery* (Chicago, 1961), pp. 24–27.

mere dependency of Southern slaveholders."[42] Instead, he visited what is now known as Nigeria to sign a treaty with the Yoruba king of Abeokuta in preparation for Afro-American settlements. By the time he returned to the United States, however, the Civil War—with its promise of freedom for the slaves—had started. Although nothing more came of his emigration scheme after Delany accepted a commission in the Union army, the incident demonstrated that blacks still had strong emotional ties to Africa, and were willing to consider emigration, but only on their own terms.[43]

The advent of the Civil War diverted the energies of the Colonization Society and the subsequent emancipation of the slaves made blacks more reluctant than ever to sail for Africa. President Abraham Lincoln's schemes to settle freed slaves in the West Indies also failed to get black support. But after the war ended, the blacks found themselves harassed by Southern whites and bound by stringent "black codes." Between 1865 and 1870 the Colonization Society flourished again as unhappy freedmen sought more genuine freedom. The emigration cycle again touched bottom after the federal government gave citizenship and voting rights to blacks. As the freedmen found new privilege and power in the United States, Africa had less appeal.[44]

Not until 1877 did another significant emigration movement occur. Although the Colonization Society was still

42. Martin R. Delany, *The Condition, Elevation, Emigration and Destiny of the Colored People of the United States Politically Considered* (Philadelphia, 1852), pp. 168, 211; idem, *Official Report of the Niger Valley Exploring Party* (New York, 1861), pp. 10 ff; "Frank A. Rollin" (Frank R. Whipper), *The Life and Public Services of Martin R. Delany* (Boston, 1883), p. 80.

43. Delany, *Official Report*, p. 57; Bell, "Negro Convention Movement," pp. 238–45.

44. Staudenraus, *African Colonization*, pp. 246–49; Boyd, "Negro Colonization," passim.

functioning, South Carolina blacks decided to take matters into their own hands. The collapse of Republican Reconstruction had demoralized many who believed, with much justification, that the violence and economic oppression that had threatened them throughout Reconstruction would soon become intolerable. The discontent that grew from political and economic changes proved fertile soil for black nationalism. Martin Delany and other Charleston blacks launched the Liberian Exodus Joint Stock Steamship Company to provide for emigration to Africa. With "Africa fever" at full flame in the spring of 1878, the company's ship, "Azor," made its first—and only—voyage; because of inexperienced planning and incompetent operation by the ship's white captain, the company lost the "Azor" in debtor's court. The significance of the South Carolina experiment, however, lay not in its small accomplishment or rapid demise; rather, it was the first of many all-black African emigration schemes to arise after the Civil War. It marked the shift of black agitation from the North to the South where most blacks lived.[45]

The African emigration movements of the 1890s, like that of 1878, grew in direct response to difficult racial conditions. America's race relations by 1890 were on the edge of a steep decline, starting to pitch downward toward a long, low valley which would extend well into the twentieth century. The white people, mostly Northern, who had urged equality for men of all races, grew tired of their uphill struggle. Other whites, mostly Southern but with many Northern allies, who had urged a caste system with blacks as peons to replace slaves, grew confident of success. They determined to force blacks to remain subordinate in all things social, political, and economic. For blacks the results were disheartening; they increasingly found them-

45. George Brown Tindall, *South Carolina Negroes, 1877–1890* (Columbia, S.C., 1952), pp. 153–68.

selves socially outcast, politically disfranchised, and economically subjugated. Searching for ways to ease their burden, many swallowed their pride and accommodated themselves to their low position; others protested and worked for integration into American society. In such a period of changing conditions and ideologies it is not surprising that still other blacks heeded suggestions that they emigrate to Africa.

When the long history of black emigration met the troubled conditions and the peasant pessimism of the 1890s, the scene was set for an outpouring of African emigration excitement. To focus such unrest in a practical movement, however, required leadership and organization and the narrative of African emigration from 1890 to 1910 is a story of the search for effective leadership and organization for the many unhappy blacks who despaired of making a home in the United States. During the early years of the period the American Colonization Society played an important role, but was succeeded by other organizations. Leadership came from several sources, but one man clearly stood out as the foremost agitator for African emigration. The words and actions of Bishop Henry M. Turner, more than any other factor, gave direction and enthusiasm to black nationalism in the 1890s. He appealed directly to the Southern blacks and thus influenced all the organizations interested in the movement. Throughout the entire period his relentless barrage of emigration propaganda provided the foundation for all that happened.

2

Bishop Turner's African Dream

Bishop Henry McNeal Turner (1834–1915) was, without doubt the most prominent and outspoken American advocate of black emigration in the years between the Civil War and the First World War. By constant agitation he kept Afro-Americans aware of their African heritage and their disabilities in the United States. Turner possessed a dominating personality, a biting tongue, and a pungent vocabulary which gained him high office and wide audiences, first in Georgia's Reconstruction politics and later in the African Methodist Episcopal (A.M.E.) church. In his bitter disappointment with the American treatment of blacks, the bishop evolved an all-consuming nationalism which demanded emigration to Africa. To understand his forceful agitation in the years following 1890, one must know Turner's background and the nature of his vision of Africa.

Bishop Turner's life of nationalist agitation was founded on the frustrations of great energy and talent by the prejudice of white America. In South Carolina, where he was free-born, Turner experienced that prejudice from the beginning. He ran away from the cotton fields, where he had been apprenticed to work beside slaves, and found his own job sweeping out a law office. When the young law clerks observed his quick mind and eagerness to learn, they surreptitiously taught him to read and write, for legally no black was allowed to become literate. When he was twenty years old he was ordained a traveling evangelist in the white-dominated Southern Methodist church. Turner visited towns and cities throughout the South, preaching to both black and white. The prejudice he continually encountered made him ill at ease—resentful that he, a free man, should be prevented from doing all that his drive and ability suggested. His nascent nationalism found its first outlet in New Orleans, where, in 1858, he discovered something new to his experience—a church governed solely by blacks, the A.M.E. church. Without hesitation he joined it, partly as an act of defiance against whites and partly from attraction to an autonomous black organization in which he could realize his ambition for status and power.[1]

During the Civil War years Turner found new scope for his energies and new hope for the Afro-American. When he had finished his training as a pastor in Baltimore, he was assigned to an important parish in Washington, D.C., on Capitol Hill. After the general emancipation he became openly belligerent and urged the newly freed slaves to defend themselves vigorously when attacked or insulted. Believing, furthermore, that blacks had not only rights but obligations, Turner agitated for the use of black troops by Union forces. After that became national policy, the first companies of black troops from Washington were mustered in his churchyard. As a reward for his recruiting efforts and in recognition of his leadership abilities, Turner was appointed chaplain to the black troops. His intense pride in his people had led him to dizzying new heights of personal achievement.[2]

1. Mungo M. Ponton, *The Life and Times of Henry M. Turner* (Atlanta, 1917), p. 33 and passim; Thaddeus E. Horton, "A Black Moses," in James T. Haley, ed., *Afro-American Encyclopedia* (Nashville, 1895), pp. 35–38; *New York Globe,* 21 April 1883; *Christian Recorder,* 17 July 1884, 6 September 1888.

2. *Washington Star,* 22, 26 April 1862, 4, 6 February, 5, 8, 19 May, 10 June 1863; "Military Records of Henry M. Turner," U.S. Archives, Washington, D.C.

Turner's glory collapsed at the end of the war. Assigned to duty in Georgia as a chaplain with the Freedmen's Bureau, he soon found it impossible to remain in that government organization, which discriminated against him because of his color. Turning to church organization he devoted his energies to establishing the A.M.E. church in Georgia where it had never before existed. Only in the black man's church, he thought, could he find freedom to lead and people to direct.[3]

The Republican party, however, soon gave Turner another outlet for leadership and race pride. Because he was well known throughout the state and was already familiar with Republican officials in Washington, Turner was an obvious choice to become a party organizer among the freedmen of Georgia. He called the first Republican state convention and later was elected to the 1867 Georgia Constitutional Convention and the 1868 legislature. By organizing Loyal Leagues and Equal Rights Associations, he won the respect of the blacks. By his participation in party and governmental affairs, he believed that at last he had also won the respect of whites.[4] But like Adam cast out of the garden, Turner had tasted the forbidden fruit of political power, and no sooner had the state legislature convened that it sought to disqualify blacks from holding elective office. In a strong speech on the house floor, Turner protested the pending dismissal and demanded his rights as a free citizen of the United States. To his fellow black

3. Horton, "A Black Moses," pp. 35–38; *Augusta Colored American*, 13 January 1866. E. Merton Coulter, *The South During Reconstruction, 1865–1877* (Baton Rouge, 1947), p. 99; idem, "Henry M. Turner: Georgia Negro Preacher-Politician During the Reconstruction Era," *Georgia Historical Quarterly, 48* (December 1964), 371–410.

4. Coulter, *Reconstruction*, pp. 59–60; *Christian Recorder*, 6 September 1888; *Augusta Loyal Georgian*, 13 January 1866; Clarence A. Bacote, "William Finch, Negro Councilman and Political Activist in Atlanta During Reconstruction," *Journal of Negro History, 40* (October 1955), 341–64.

delegates he proclaimed: "White men are not to be trusted. They will betray you. . . . Don't fight for a country that refuses to recognize your rights. . . . Black men, hold up your heads. . . . This thing means revolution."[5] But his fall was ordained and Turner was cast out.

Hoping to recover some of his prestige, he applied for the office of United States Minister to the black Republic of Haiti, but, failing in this, he asked for and received appointment as postmaster at Macon, Georgia. As the first black postmaster in the state he became a *cause célèbre,* but pressure mounted on the federal government for his dismissal, and Turner was charged with fraud, counterfeiting, and theft. After only two weeks in office he was dismissed. Thus, after three years of attempting to gain political power through the Republican party, Turner had to settle for an appointment as customs inspector for the "back waters around Savannah." Frustrated and without political power, he retreated into work for his black church, concluding that the United States was a white man's nation and that blacks must leave, preferably for Africa.[6]

Turner had long been fascinated by Africa, especially when he was most pessimistic about the future of blacks in the United States. During his days of training in Baltimore for an A.M.E. pastorate and during the dark months just before the Civil War, he was one of many free blacks who had been temporarily convinced that emigration was the only answer to the dilemma of being a black in white America. Later he recalled preaching a sermon, titled "The

5. *Atlanta Constitution,* 4 September 1868.
6. James Atkins to William A. Richardson, Secretary of the Treasury, 25 November 1873, "Treasury Department Appointments and Recommendations for Office, 1873–1877, re: H. M. Turner," in U.S. Archives. *Testimony Taken by the Joint Select Committee to Inquire into the Condition of Affairs in the Late Insurrectionary States,* 42d Congress, 2d sess., 1871–72, Report 41, part 7, pp. 1034–42, 1184 f., 1196.

Redemption of Africa and the Means to Be Employed,"
that advocated conversion of the heathen by Afro-American missionary settlers.[7] In 1862, while the war was under
way but before President Lincoln had issued the Emancipation Proclamation, Turner heard an address by Alexander Crummell, a black missionary to Liberia who advocated emigration. Turner wrote that Crummell's address
made him a convert to African repatriation.[8] Perhaps in
the years following emancipation, when the future of
Afro-Americans looked brighter and Turner was serving
in a victorious army, he wavered in his emigration convictions. But each time his own fortunes reached a new low,
he returned to the idea, like the sinner who is "saved" at
every revival meeting. Turner wrote again, during the disappointing days of early Reconstruction, "I became a convert to emigration five weeks ago. . . . I expect to advocate
it hereafter, as much as I can."[9]

Whether or not he stayed converted during his days of
political ascendancy in postwar Georgia, Turner spoke
strongly for emigration in the gloomy days of later Reconstruction and thereafter. When the United States considered annexing Santo Domingo, Turner wrote to Senator
Charles Sumner, the chief opponent of the annexation,
that he agreed with Sumner's position. Turner viewed the
island, with its black Republic of Haiti, as "the only relic
of negro nationality on the American continent" that had
been kept as a "resting place for blacks in the event of frus-

7. *Washington Star*, 26, 27 April 1862.

8. Turner to *Washington Post*, 25 January 1895. Crummell's
changing views on emigration can be traced in his *Relations and Duties
of the Free Colored Men in America to Africa* (Hartford, 1861) and
his *Africa and America* (Springfield, Mass., 1891). See also W. E. B.
DuBois, *The Souls of Black Folk* (New York, 1903 and 1961), Chapter 12.

9. Turner to Coppinger, 18 July 1866. See also Willis D. Boyd,
"Negro Colonization in the Reconstruction Era, 1865–70," *Georgia
Historical Quarterly, 40* (December 1956), pp. 358–82.

trations in the United States."[10] But Africa, not Haiti, was
first in Turner's heart. As a circuit preacher and A.M.E.
district superintendent, he urged his people to follow the
"voice of a mysterious providence, saying, 'Return to the
land of your Fathers.' . . . There is no more doubt in my
mind that we have ultimately to return to Africa than there
is of the existence of God."[11]

As he entered the prime of life, Turner was a bitter,
disillusioned man. He had tasted the things he wanted
most in life—political power and prestige—only to have
had them snatched away by the prejudice of white men.
Most blacks reacted to the loss of their rights and privileges
either by protesting through the Republican party or by
acquiescing to their situation—by trying to get along with
the least amount of agitation or trouble. Turner, however,
had tried politics and found it wanting, and he was too
energetic and ambitious to follow the path of least resistance. Instead, he found himself a black nationalist with
a burning desire to see his people do well. If white men
would not let blacks perform to their highest abilities in the
United States, Turner reasoned, then black men must establish their own nation and civilization to bring respect
and dignity to their race. Having made this decision in his
early forties, Turner proceeded on his nationalistic career,
working within his all-black church and urging his people
to emigrate.

Turner quickly rose to power in the church. Throughout
the Reconstruction period he had built a strong base in
Georgia by bringing thousands of black Methodists out of

10. Turner to Charles Sumner, 1, 5 January 1871, in Charles Sumner Papers, Harvard University Library, Cambridge, Mass.
11. Turner to the editor, *African Repository,* 28 November 1874
(published in ibid., *51* [April 1875], 39); Turner to the editor, ibid., *52*
(July 1876), 83–86. Cf. *Birmingham Iron Age,* 10 December 1874. So
ardently did Turner proclaim black emigration that the American
Colonization Society made him a lifetime honorary vice-president in
1876.

the white-dominated Southern Methodist church into the
A.M.E. denomination. His prodigious energy and fiery
manner, in and out of the pulpit, were well known throughout the South. He contributed frequently to the church's
national weekly newspaper, and his sermons were often
quoted in the white press. By 1876 he was sufficiently
prominent in his church to be appointed manager of its
publishing concern. The duties of manager carried Turner
to every A.M.E. district convention in the nation to sell
books and Sunday school materials, but also to make himself known to every local pastor. During his four years as
publications manager he acquired such a following, especially among young ministers and the new churches in
the South, that in 1880, despite opposition from older,
Northern churchmen, Turner was overwhelmingly elected
one of the dozen bishops of the church.[12]

Long before his election to the episcopacy, Turner's
emigration ideas were widely known throughout the
church. Not only did he not try to conceal them, wherever
he traveled, especially in the South, he proclaimed his
gospel of the mutual redemption of Afro-Americans and
Africans. When emigration excitement swept South Carolina in 1877 and Charleston blacks organized their own
exodus to Liberia, Turner gave the ship his benediction in
a well-publicized speech.[13] Although many of his race admired him for his appeal to racial pride, many others disliked his rejection of the United States. Middle-class blacks
had made progress since emancipation and had reason to
hope for further success. American individualism had
begun to bear fruit for them and, despite their belonging to
the black caste, they had risen in wealth and education
above the masses of plantation workers. By 1883, black
churchmen and secular leaders who were optimistic about

12. *Christian Recorder,* 20 May 1880.
13. Tindall, *South Carolina Negroes,* pp. 153–68.

the United States began to attack Turner's emigration schemes in the A.M.E.'s weekly *Christian Recorder,* probably the most influential black newspaper in the land. In answer to such criticism, Bishop Turner publicly formulated his African dream, the dream he had nourished for many years and would carry with him through the rest of his life.

At the root of Turner's angry, bitter dream of black nationalism lay a vision of the racial equality of all men. He believed that "the great Jehovah, in his allwise providence, had made a distinction in the color but not in political or social status of the human race."[14] It had become evident to the bishop, at the end of Reconstruction, that despite American rhetoric and Radical Republican laws, the whites of the North as well as the South were loath to see blacks as their social equals, although most articulate Afro-Americans remained optimistic in the face of declining conditions and argued that black men need only work harder. But the equalization of the races, which Turner and most blacks sought, became less likely as American political and social barriers grew. According to the bishop, the sequel to the increasing oppression would be "war, efforts of extermination, anarchy, horror and a wail to heaven," for he observed that 'whoever the white race does not consort with, it will crush out."[15] Equality was an individualistic idea in the United States, but Turner transformed it into a racial concept because the practice of inequality, in contrast to the rhetoric of equality, was racial and collective. This vision of equality, born in Turner's youth as a free black, would not die when prejudice made equality impossible in America. Therefore he rejected the nation that had sired the vision and looked

14. *Atlanta Constitution,* 4 September 1868.
15. Turner to *Christian Recorder,* 22 February 1883; editorial in *Christian Recorder,* 4 January 1883.

to Africa where his color would not limit his social aspirations.

Most articulate Afro-Americans considered emigration too great a price to pay for social equality. The aging abolitionist hero, Frederick Douglass, reminded *Recorder* readers that blacks had been in America for 250 years and owed no allegiance whatever to Africa. In his view, the United States provided as good a place as any for achieving equality. Another critic reminded the bishop that a man's color was no evidence of his nationality and accused Turner of treason.[16] But Bishop Turner viewed his American citizenship as all the more reason for objecting to his subordinate status. "We were born here," he wrote, "raised here, fought, bled and died here, and have a thousand times more right here than hundreds of thousands of those who help to snub, proscribe and persecute us, and that is one of the reasons I almost despise the land of my birth." Turner would have claimed the United States if this had not meant relinquishing his ideal of equality and achievement. He would rather surrender his birthright than his dream.[17]

Prejudice against the black man was as strong in the North and West as in the South, according to the bishop, and he believed that, although blacks might escape violence, they could not really change their status by moving from the South to another part of the country.[18] Turner reported that many Southern blacks were restless and prepared to leave for Africa rather than sit and listen to the theoretical solutions to racial problems offered by middle-class Northern blacks. "There never was a time when the colored people were more concerned about Africa in every

16. Frederick Douglass to *Christian Recorder,* 1 February 1883; John P. Sampson to *Christian Recorder,* 18 January 1883.
17. Turner to *Christian Recorder,* 22 February 1883.
18. Ibid., and ibid., 4 January 1883.

respect than at present. If the Northern Negro is satisfied with matters and things, we of the South are far from [so] being."[19]

Benjamin T. Tanner, the editor of the *Recorder,* was skeptical of Turner's followers. Because Tanner knew "the thoughts of those Negroes who read and write," he claimed that "what one thoughtful man among us writes outweighs in value the whole Niagara of eloquence common to our people [who] talk in the vein that we know our hearers desire us to talk," and that Turner heard only what he wanted to hear.[20] Whatever the truth of Tanner's analysis, there was considerable interest in Africa among the Southern blacks, and letters of inquiry about Liberia arrived steadily at the headquarters of the American Colonization Society.

If emigration showed cowardice, as Tanner charged, Turner would answer "What of it?" At a time when many Europeans were leaving their ancestral homes and known dangers for unknown risks in new lands, emigration was not dishonorable, and the bishop exclaimed: "Yes, I would make Africa a place of refuge, because I see no other shelter from the stormy blast, from the red tide of persecution, from the horrors of American prejudice." Claiming that self-interest, self-preservation, and "self in all its aspects" had motivated every migration since the Tower of Babel, Turner saw no more shame in Afro-American emigration to Liberia than in the Pilgrims' move to Plymouth Bay. But Editor Tanner pointed out that men from all over the world were seeking out the United States as the main chance for achieving their dreams and that even African students stayed on in America after their studies were finished. "The idea of a people leaving a country like America to go anywhere to better their condition . . . is like

19. Ibid., 4 January 1883.
20. Editorial in ibid.

running from the sun for both light and heat." Turner rejoined that all was different for the black man, who had
once been a slave in the "land of opportunity." He believed
a revolution was necessary, and it must take the form of
emigration to Africa. The only redemption for the victims
of white American nationalism would be black African
nationalism.[21]

But Africa was to be much more than a refuge for per-
secuted Afro-Americans. Turner saw the "fatherland" as
a great symbol for the entire race, and he saw it primarily
as a political symbol, for he was essentially a political man.
In a time when blacks were being divested of political
power and office in the United States, and when some black
leaders were settling for subordinate patronage offices and
personal economic gain rather than true political power,
Turner still linked the fate of the Afro-American with politics. "I do not believe any race will ever be respected, or
ought to be respected," he wrote, "who do not show themselves capable of founding and manning a government of
their own creation."[22]

Responsible black nationhood would be not only a symbol to the entire race, it would provide models for the advancement of black individuals. Turner asked his chal-
lengers in the *Recorder* whether they knew of a race that
had "amounted to anything" as long as it had been "shut
out from all honorable positions, from being kings and
queens, lords, dukes, presidents, governors, mayors, gen-
erals?" Answering his own question, he proclaimed:
"Till we have black men in the seat of power, respected,
feared, hated and reverenced, our young men will never
rise for the reason they will never look up." Tanner reminded the bishop the blacks had governments and nations in Haiti and Liberia and that many black men were

21. Ibid.; Turner to *Christian Recorder,* 22 February 1883.
22. Turner to *Christian Recorder,* 22 February, 21 June 1883.

doing well in the United States, but Turner obliquely discounted such gains as incapable of producing the desired results. What was needed, he said, was "an outlet, a theater of manhood and activity established somewhere for our young men and women," a state "that the world will respect and [whose] glory and influence will tell upon the destinies of the race from pole to pole; our children's children can rest securely under [its] aegis, whether in Africa, Europe, Asia, America or upon the high seas."[23] Thus Turner recognized that a powerful and independent African nation would redeem the self-respect of black men everywhere and provide the national identity without which Afro-Americans were made easy victims of white oppression.

Turner's symbolic African nation embodied most elements of nationalism and the classic American dream. He echoed the old chorus of the American colonials and immigrants: hope for a fresh start in a place where men had self-government and freedom from persecution and aristocracy; where land was available and economic opportunity beckoned; where every man was judged on his merits, and could even become president; where there was freedom from the old proscriptions; where there was the challenge of a land to the subdued by the democratic process and civilized by Christianity. All these things the bishop saw in his ideal state. Like the early nationalist leaders of Europe, he took the prevailing ideas of national greatness, tailored them to fit the needs of his people, and rejected the multinational United States.

Turner saw God's hand in history, ordaining a great destiny for his black people. The bishop explained that God had allowed white men to bring black men to America

23. Ibid., 25 January, 21 June 1883. Cf. Harold Isaacs, *The New World of Negro Americans* (New York, 1963), esp. pp. 325–49, for a discussion of the effects of recent African independence on the thinking of Afro-Americans.

because the African needed the civilization and Christianity of the United States, a nation supposedly consecrated as a sanctuary from persecution and peonage. Not that God endorsed slavery as such—he permitted it as a test of the white man's obedience, Turner claimed, for the two races were to embrace one another and work out the problem of civilizing and redeeming Africa. But the white man had defaulted on his obligation to God and to the black man by forbidding his servants to improve themselves. "We gave the white man our labor, yes! In return he should have educated us, taught us to read and write, at least, and seen that Africa was well supplied with missionaries."[24] Instead, the ex-slaves themselves must assume the task of redeeming Africa.

Turner saw the mission of the black emigrant not only as converting the African but helping him stand on his own feet against white invaders. The European scramble for African colonies had begun by 1883, and Turner feared that Europeans, who had once stolen Africans from Africa, would now steal Africa from the Africans. He chided his opponents for merely meditating and for wanting to "wait till the whites go over and civilize Africa, and homestead all the land and take us along to black their boots and groom their horses. Wait till the French or English find some great mines of gold, diamonds or some other precious metal or treasures, so we can raise a howl over it and charge the whites with endeavoring to take away our fathers' inheritance, and lift a wail for the sympathy of the world." Turner would take the initiative to make Africa the black man's preserve.[25]

Contrary to some of the misinterpretations by his critics, the bishop did not urge a wholesale migration of all Afro-

24. Turner to *Christian Recorder*, 22 February 1883. See also Turner's speech in the *Augusta Colored American*, 13 January 1866.
25. Turner to *Christian Recorder*, 22 February 1883.

Americans to Africa; he recognized the impossibility of unloading millions of black paupers into a new land. "Such a course would be madness in the extreme and folly unpardonable," he wrote. "Five or ten thousand a year would be enough." Half a million civilized, Christian blacks would be enough to build a nation of which Turner could be proud. But these half-million repatriates would have to be well chosen, for "all the riffraff white-men worshippers, aimless, objectless, selfish, little-souled and would-be-white Negroes of this country" would be useless in Africa because they had no confidence in themselves or in other black men. Only the proud and resourceful might contribute to his symbolic state, for brave, ambitious, and educated young men and women would be necessary to raise a nation worthy of respect. "All this jargon about 'Bishop Turner trying to get all us colored people out of the United States' is not only nonsense, but absolutely false," the bishop claimed, "for two-thirds of the American Negroes would be of no help to anyone anywhere."[26]

Unfortunately for the bishop's plans, those who came closest to meeting his specifications were the ones least likely to forsake the gains they had made in the United States. Furthermore—as George T. Downing, a wealthy black man from Rhode Island, reminded Turner—the most cultured, experienced, energetic, and moral Afro-Americans were "the very persons we are most in need of at home. . . . We are not sufficiently represented in the needed character to upbuild Africa; we have not sufficient of it for home needs; this is our great misfortune; certainly we have not a scholar or businessman to spare."[27]

Then too, black Americans had many questions about the suitability of the dark continent, questions based upon ignorance, misinformation, and the grim accounts of some

26. Ibid., and ibid., 25 January 1883.
27. George T. Downing to *New York Globe,* 27 January 1883.

disillusioned emigrés and travelers. Chief among these
threats to Bishop Turner's nationalistic dream was the
complaint about the climate and the fevers. Some emigrants had returned to the United States with accounts of
how a tenth of their group had died soon after arrival off
the African coast, and letters from those who had remained in Liberia told of more death and disease in the
fever swamps. Some white men, moreover, who feared the
loss of their labor supply, had magnified the stories of
horror and death and slavery in Africa. Those blacks who
were disposed to stay in the United States did little to
brighten this African image.[28]

Turner vigorously answered the "nonsensical jargon
that the climate of Africa is against us, we can't live there,
the tropics are no place for moral and intellectual development." God had created Africa, and to deny that it was
good "charges God with folly," wrote the bishop, for man
is "cosmopolitan [and] his home is everywhere upon the
face of the globe." Turner admitted that there would be
problems in adjusting to a new climate, but even suffering
the fever, he asserted, was better than dying at the hands of
lynch mobs in America; so why should blacks balk at the
risks of undertaking a divine errand into the wilderness?[29]

The bishop had two ready answers to the practical questions of money and transportation. First, he believed that
the American government should appropriate money to
assist blacks who volunteered to settle in Africa. For services rendered during slavery, the nation owed the ex-
slaves some 40 billion dollars, according to Turner's cal-
culation, "estimating one hundred dollars a year for two

28. J. C. Embry to *Christian Recorder*, 1 February 1883. Tindall,
South Carolina Negroes, pp. 156 f. Afro-Americans generally shared
the view that West Africa was the black man's as well as the white
man's graveyard. Cf. Philip D. Curtin, *The Image of Africa: British
Ideas and Actions, 1780–1850* (Madison, 1964).
    29. Turner to *Christian Recorder*, 22 February 1883.

million of us for two hundred years." But if government funds were not forthcoming, he had a second plan. Turner followed with great interest the development of commerce and exploration in Africa, often citing the statistics of growing European trade there. He urged and cajoled American businessmen, white and black, to enter that profitable trade and to establish regular links with Liberia. Because there was "a general unrest and a wholesale dissatisfaction" among his people, Turner promised that "if a line of steamers were started from New Orleans, Mobile, Savannah or Charleston, they would be crowded to density every trip they made to Africa."[30]

Bishop Turner was politely civil to white men but less accommodating to blacks. Like other black nationalists he called for a virtual separation of the races, a segregation approved by many whites, although most articulate Afro-Americans—the black middle-class—would rather have integration into American society. Turner's blunt evaluation of "scullion" blacks who opposed his emigration scheme won him many enemies. He accused three-fourths of the Afro-Americans of "doing nothing day and night but cry: Glory, honor, dominion and greatness to White." Believing that self-respect and race pride were essential qualities for greatness on any continent, Turner charged that even the "so-called leading men worshipped white." To achieve either the American dream or its dark reflection, the African dream, Turner demanded a basic change of heart in black men, for "a man must believe he is somebody before he is acknowledged to be somebody. . . . Neither [the] Republican nor Democratic party can do for

30. Ibid., and ibid., 26 July 1883. The *African Repository,* in *59* (April 1883) and regularly thereafter, carried this notice inside the front cover: "So numerous have the applications [for passage to Liberia] become that . . . the Society will hereafter give preference . . . to those who will pay a part of the cost of their passage and settlement to Liberia."

the colored race what [it] can do for [itself]. Respect
black!" To stress the point he proclaimed that "God is a
Negro: Even the heathen in Africa believed that they were
'created in God's image.' But American Africans believed
that they resemble the devil and hence the contempt they
have for themselves and each other!" All the more reason,
the bishop urged, for a "Negro nationality where black men
can be taught to respect themselves."[31]

The newspaper debate had tapered off by the summer of
1883, for Bishop Turner was deeply involved in church
business. However, because of the wide circulation of the
Christian Recorder and the prominence of the principal
voices in the debate, considerable interest had been aroused
in the black community. Most of those who wrote about
the issue opposed emigration in any form, but several men
spoke out in support of the African dream. Among them
was another A.M.E. bishop, R. H. Cain, who had been a
Reconstruction congressman from South Carolina; he predicted that, like Israel in the wilderness for forty years,
Afro-Americans might have to wait until the old generation
had died out before the new generation would follow
Bishop Turner to the promised land. More cautiously, T.
Thomas Fortune, the young editor of the *New York Globe,*
reserved judgment. "Emigration may yet play a very important part in the solution of the question of our position
in this country," he acknowledged. "We will say this much,
that Dr. Tanner may speak, in his view, the prevailing
opinion of northern colored men, while Bishop Turner may
speak that of the South. [But] whatever may be the wishes
of the thoughtful men of the race, the masses of our people
in the South are growing fearfully restless."[32] Whatever the
impact on others, the debate had led Turner to formulate

31. Turner, quoted in *A.M.E. Church Review, 1* (January 1885),
246; *Voice of Missions,* November 1895.
32. R. H. Cain to *Christian Recorder,* 12 July 1883; *New York
Globe,* 13 January 1883.

his nationalist ideas, which had been ripening for years, and there would be little change in that nationalism throughout the rest of his long and active life.

In the years that followed the emigration debate of 1883, Turner found little in the American scene that lessened his disappointment with the United States or changed his mind about Africa. Indeed, a major blow was suffered by Afro-Americans, later in 1883, when the United States Supreme Court ruled that the Civil Rights Act of 1875 was unconstitutional—that the federal government could not prevent racial discrimination by private parties. To Bishop Turner, always hypersensitive to the question of social equality, this civil rights decision symbolized all that was wrong in the American attitude toward blacks. In a widely circulated pamphlet and in press interviews, he attacked the decision, the court, and the American people. Everything about the court's decision, he claimed, "seems to indicate that [it] was made in the interest of party politics."[33] He predicted that the decision would put the race issue back into national politics, where eventually it would have to be fought again—if blacks lived through the storm. He concluded that the Supreme Court had effectively absolved Afro-Americans of all allegiance to the United States: "If the government that freed him cannot protect that freedom," the black man would no longer "enlist in the armies of the government, or swear to defend the United States Constitution." That Constitution, he said, "is a dirty rag, a cheat, a libel and ought to be spit upon by every Negro in the land." In Turner's view the civil rights decision marked a new high (or low) in the white nationalism of the United States, and it was clear to him

33. *Memphis Appeal,* 6 November 1883, quoted in *Christian Recorder,* 13 December 1883; *St. Louis Globe,* n.d., quoted in *Christian Recorder,* 8 November 1883. See also H. M. Turner, *The Barbarous Decision of the Supreme Court Declaring the Civil Rights Act Unconstitutional* (Atlanta, 1883).

that there was no room for blacks in a white man's country. "If the Court's decision is right and is accepted by the country, then prepare to return to Africa or get ready for extermination."[34]

Despite this grim prediction Turner remained in the United States, working within the A.M.E. church which gave him wide range for his nationalist activities. His episcopal assignments covered most of the deep Southern states and the Indian Territory. Traveling annually to each state conference he regularly made his plea for emigration and attacked the United States. He also wrote frequently for church publications and his blistering statements on the race question kept him in the limelight. Known as a strong leader, a fiery preacher, and an effective administrator, Turner attracted a widespread and loyal following. Thus church work proved a useful if not entirely satisfactory substitute for his political urges and gave him a wide audience for his emigration ideas.

Although ecclesiastical business dominated Turner's activities in the late 1880s, the events of the 1890s stirred him to renewed emigration efforts. The general deterioration of race relations, the attempts to disfranchise blacks in Southern states, and the rapid increase in violence again convinced the bishop that America was no place for the black man. On his tours through the South he found increasing evidence of Afro-American willingness to emigrate. In response, Turner stepped up his agitation, urging that blacks must emigrate or perish under the onslaught of white nationalism.[35]

If any reinforcement of his solution to the race prob-

34. Turner in the *Memphis Appeal,* 6 November 1883, quoted in *Christian Recorder,* 13 December 1883.
35. Richard R. Wright, Jr., *The Bishops of the African Methodist Episcopal Church* (Nashville, 1963), pp. 336 ff.; J. Minton Batten, "Henry M. Turner, Negro Bishop Extraordinary," *Church History, 7* (September 1938), 231–46.

lem were needed, the bishop found it when he obtained a firsthand glimpse of his long-promised black utopia. In 1891 the A.M.E. Council of Bishops authorized Turner to visit Africa. He had long wanted to travel to the fatherland, but his church was financially weak and could not afford merely to send its bishops on tour; its small missionary effort was confined to a few workers in Haiti and British Guiana. Nevertheless, because several pastors had emigrated to Africa with their people, a few A.M.E. congregations functioned in Liberia and in neighboring Sierra Leone. Without substantial support from the home organization, the African churches struggled along, ministering to the emigrants, converting a few natives, and attracting dissident members of white-operated missions. Although officially Turner was sent to organize the A.M.E. churches for better supervision and financial support, the bishop viewed his trip as a pilgrimage and a chance to compare the real Africa with his dream Africa. Before he left the United States he announced that he planned to "look over the ground with reference to [his] plan" and he promised to let the nation know his verdict. Despite unfavorable reports from other travelers, Turner was sure he would "see or hear nothing that would change [his] convictions."[36]

Committed to discovering much good in Africa and Africans, Bishop Turner wrote to the *Christian Recorder* that he had found encouragement for his African dream. His first contacts with Africans on board the ship headed toward Africa brought ecstatic reports from the bishop. According to his letters, moreover, he received a tumultuous welcome in Sierra Leone; when the people of Freetown heard of his arrival they streamed to the waterfront

36. Lewellyn L. Berry, *A Century of Missions of the African Methodist Episcopal Church, 1840–1940* (New York, 1942), pp. 71–72; Turner, quoted in the *Illinois State* (n.d., n.p.), quoted in *Christian Recorder,* 23 July 1891; *Atlanta Constitution,* 15 September 1891.

to meet and behold this splendid black bishop. He wept
as he set foot on African soil and he was enraptured with
its geography and people. Instead of reporting miasmic
swamps, he sent back exaggerated descriptions of a clean,
sanitary city built on hills that rose from the harbor and
of black men standing erect and proud. He spoke to the
British governor of the colony, visited prosperous homes
and businesses owned by black men, and worshiped with
natives "right from the bush, with a mere cloth over them,
[but] full of the Holy Ghost." All that Turner saw he
pronounced good.[37]

Moving on to Liberia, Turner recorded similar impressions, with one major addition: Liberia was a free republic,
not a colony, and it boasted a black president and government—the ultimate in political and social achievement.
"One thing the black man has here," he wrote, "and that
is manhood, freedom and the fullest liberty; he feels like
a lord and walks the same way." Turner traveled about the
country, visiting the immigrant settlements, mission stations, and native villages and reporting the great promise
of the coffee plantations, the coal and iron deposits, and
the general potential for rapid economic growth. If other
travelers spoke adversely of the weather and fever, the
bishop mentioned them only briefly, for he visited during
the dry, healthy season. In any case, he wrote, the interior
highlands were always healthy; if white missionaries could
safely live there, so could Afro-Americans.[38]

African people impressed Turner as much as the geography, and he praised the well-educated Muslim teachers
who were active throughout West Africa—preparing the
way for Christianity, as he saw it, by forbidding the terrible
liquor traffic by which white traders debauched the people.

37. Turner's letters were collected in the *A.M.E. Church Review, 8*
(April 1892), 446–98.
38. Ibid.

Among the inhabitants, he differentiated between the various tribes of natives who lived in Liberia. Furthermore, an ancient citizen told Turner that in the slave days they never "used to sell 'big blood' Africans to white men except we catch him in war," which convinced Turner that most American blacks (especially those who disagreed about emigration) were descended from the weaker people, who had always been slaves, even in Africa. (Turner claimed descent from African royalty.) But most of the people in Liberia were worthy inheritors of the bishop's dream, and his glowing accounts encouraged Afro-Americans to repatriate themselves and take advantage of the opportunities in trade, mining, and agriculture, but most of all in equality and self-respect.[39]

Like other nationalists in other times, the bishop held a romantic vision of his great black nation of the future. That Liberia was still a greatly underdeveloped country did not bother him; it was an independent black nation, and that was all that mattered. Its romanticized future, in Turner's mind and therefore in the minds of black Americans, would be glorious. Africa was all Turner dreamed it could be, and more. "I get mad and sick," he wrote, "when I look at the possibilities God has placed within our reach, and to think that we are such block-heads we cannot see and use them." The native Africans, doubtless following Turner's lead, could not understand why "the black man is at home across the sea." By the time he left for the United States, after a month in the fatherland, the bishop was more convinced than ever that the status of black men in America was closely tied to Africa. "I see the wisdom of my position now as I never dreamed before. If the black man ever rises

39. Ibid. Turner claimed that his grandfather had been freed under a British colonial law that forbade the enslavement of African royalty in South Carolina (Ponton, *Life and Times*, p. 33). It is more likely that Turner's free status at birth derived from a white maternal grandmother *(New York Globe,* 21 April 1883).

to wealth . . . he will never do it by trying to be white or snubbing his native country." And for Turner that country was Africa.[40]

Returning to the United States in February 1892, Bishop Turner was ready to move heaven and earth to get Afro-Americans to Africa. He found, on his return, a heightened interest among rural blacks, who said they would do almost anything to escape the economic and social problems that beset them. Turner's letters from Africa, published weekly in the *Christian Recorder* and later printed together as a pamphlet, attracted great attention. But even before the bishop had made his African journey, a debate in Congress had generated emigration excitement in the United States.

40. Turner letters in *A.M.E. Church Review*, 8 (April 1892), 446–98.

3

Blyden and the Butler Bill

Bishop Turner's persistent nationalist propaganda notwithstanding, the event that brought national attention to
African emigration in the 1890s was a congressional debate. The bill in question would give federal aid to blacks
who wished to leave their Southern homes and settle anywhere outside the South. Although the measure did not
specifically name Africa as the proper place for blacks,
there was no doubt in the minds of the debaters or the
colored people that Africa was the issue. Closely related to
the introduction of the emigration bill was the American
visit of an African, Professor Edward W. Blyden of
Liberia, whose avowed purpose was to stir up interest and
aid for repatriating the blacks. His reputation as a learned
African, his widely reported speeches for emigration, and
his friendship with the senators who sponsored the emigration bill made the visitor an integral part of the back-to-
Africa story.

Blyden came to the United States at the request of the
American Colonization Society, which had long encouraged unhappy blacks to seek new homes in Africa. Despite
the problems that had beset it, especially since the emancipation of the slaves, the society in the late 1880s still sent
about a hundred colonists each year to Liberia. As race
relations deteriorated and many blacks grew restless, there
was hope in the society for a new emigration boom. Firmly
believing that emigration was the best solution to Ameri-

ca's race problem, and hoping to capitalize on black dissatisfaction, the Colonization Society summoned its most illustrious emigrant, Blyden, back to the United States to stir up interest in colonization.[1]

A statesman and intellectual who had helped found Liberia College and had served as his adopted country's Minister to Great Britain, Blyden was at ease anywhere, including the United States. On his arrival he went promptly to Chicago, where the Colonization Society had arranged for him to attend the convention of the American Missionary Association, an organization of churchmen, mostly white, who had given much energy and money to the welfare of blacks since before the Civil War. Blyden hoped to interest these gentlemen in the work of African colonization, and perhaps in giving money and prestige to the scheme. He planned to tell them about himself, about Africa, and about his dream of conquering that continent for Christianity by means of black settlers and missionaries. Although he did not address the convention formally, Blyden talked individually with many of the churchmen.[2]

Of all the lectures about Africa that Blyden might have given the convention, none could have been more impressive than his own life story. Blyden was not a native Liberian, nor was he originally from the United States. Born free in the Danish West Indies in 1832, he had received his basic education from an American missionary, who discovered that the boy was brilliant, hard working, and had a gift for languages. When Blyden decided to become a preacher, his missionary teacher took him to the United States in 1850 to study at Rutgers Theological College in New Jersey, but because Blyden was black, the son of

1. Coppinger to Blyden, 26 January, 3 May 1889; Hollis R. Lynch, *Edward Wilmot Blyden: Pan-Negro Patriot, 1832–1912* (London, 1967), pp. xv–xvi, 124–31.
2. Blyden to Coppinger, 2 November 1889; Minutes of the Board of Directors of the ACS, p. 263, in ACS papers.

pure African parents, Rutgers refused him admission. The
New York Colonization Society, an auxiliary of the ACS,
heard of his plight and offered to send him to Liberia, an
offer he accepted. In Africa, after completing his education
under a Presbyterian missionary, Blyden became a teacher
and a Presbyterian pastor. Since the 1850s he had written
and traveled widely. He was a scholar, widely read in many
languages, especially Arabic, the language of Islam and
the black Mohammedans in the interior of Africa. He had
visited European statesmen and American presidents, and
it could truly be said that he was a distinguished man. As
such, he was an excellent advertisement for black emigration to Africa.[3]

To black and white audiences alike, Blyden spoke about
Africa's people and religions. Chicagoans learned how
white missionaries had invaded Africa with little respect
for the people or their traditions and no understanding of
either the pagan or Muslim religions, intending only to
uproot and destroy all this in the name of Christ. Black
Christians, Blyden reasoned, would have more respect for
African culture and would not incur the wrath of the
Africans. He urged whites to appoint and support black
missionaries, and he exhorted Afro-Americans to volun-
teer for service in the continent of the future. His hearers
easily perceived from Blyden's words and manner that he
was happy to be black, proud to be African.[4]

He lectured frequently on "The Koran in Africa."
Blyden was not a Muslim, although he knew the Koran and
Islam well, the latter being the dominant religion in the
interior parts of West Africa. Blyden respected the learned
and devout Muslims who traveled to the coastal ports, and

3. Lynch, *Blyden,* Chapter 1.
4. Edward W. Blyden, *The African Problem and Other Discourses
Delivered in America in 1890* (London, 1890), pp. 64–69. Blyden to
Coppinger, 4, 5 November 1889.

he admired their scriptures. Blyden told his Chicago audiences how, in Chapter 31 of the Koran, Mohammed paid tribute to a wise black man. He concluded that the reason many Africans chose Islam over Christianity was that the Koran protected the black man from "self-deprecation in the presence of Arab or European." By contrast, the black Christian was "taught by the books he reads, by the pictures he sees, by the foreign teachers who attempt to guide him, by the systematic ignoring of his talents in Church and State" that black is bad and blacks inferior.

What were American Christians to do about this religious tragedy? How could they prevent Islam from winning all Africa? Blyden resolved the problem in favor of Christianity and the black race. The only way to establish the religion of Jesus in Africa, he declared, was to create an "African Church" led and populated not by "foreigners" but by black men who could show that black was good and black men honorable. American blacks must lead the movement, said Blyden, and soon, for Islam was marching.[5]

Blyden did not win many disciples in Chicago although he considered the visit "profitable," and his sponsor, the Colonization Society, was pleased. Neither the American Missionary Association nor the local blacks endorsed his ideas although they welcomed Blyden himself. He had not expected much response in the North, however; compared to the South, Northern Negroes were few in number and relatively satisfied. Therefore Blyden eagerly anticipated his forthcoming visit to the South.[6]

5. Blyden, *The African Problem,* pp. 90–104, esp. pp. 99 f. and 102.
6. See Meier, *Negro Thought,* pp. 19–82, for a discussion of blacks' ideas on the race problem in 1890. According to the Bureau of the Census, *Bulletin Number Eight: Negroes in the United States* (Washington, 1904), p. 11, 89.7 percent of American blacks lived in the South in 1900.

After brief calls at Philadelphia and Washington, he went to Charleston, a major center of Negro population, when he was given a royal welcome. Blacks and whites alike were eager to hear about the South Carolina blacks who in previous years had emigrated to Africa. With such a reception Blyden was confident that Charleston would provide a rich harvest for emigration.[7] Blyden spoke more openly of his Negro nationalism in the South. An important facet of his ideology was an intense dislike of mulattoes—Afro-Americans of part-white ancestry. In the North he said little about the issue because so many Northern blacks were of mixed descent. In the old slave states, however, the ratio of pure blacks to mulattoes was much higher, according to Blyden, and he believed he could further the cause of emigration by dwelling on racial differences among the American blacks. Having spent most of his youth in the West Indies, where the social differences between black and brown were rigid, Blyden gained his distrust and dislike of mulattoes early. There had been little in his subsequent experience in Liberia to change his mind, for there had been recurring friction between pure blacks and mixed-bloods for control of the country. Because of his criticism of mulatto Liberians, Blyden had been forced on several occasions to leave Monrovia for the neighboring British colony of Sierra Leone to escape persecution.

Blyden saw a deep division between pure blacks and part-backs. True blacks, descendants of unmixed African parents, he asserted, were eager to return to Africa. Their mulatto half-brothers, however, wanted to inherit the power and prestige of their white ancestors in America. Blyden accused whites of wrongly stereotyping all blacks and missing the differences in heritage. To Blyden, skin color and love for Africa were two indicators of racial

7. Blyden to Coppinger, 29 November 1889. Tindall, *South Carolina Negroes*, pp. 153–68.

purity. He told his listeners not to be ashamed of their black skins and woolly hair: "As a race you are independent and distinct, and have a mission to perform."[8] In an age of nationalism, Blyden adapted the current racial ideas of the German philosophers—Hegel, Herder, and Fichte —to his own people and continent, urging the unification of all true Africans and rejecting interlopers. He was convinced that, in the United States, the blacks who opposed his repatriation plan were all mulattoes, people who, if given the opportunity, would spoil Africa as they were spoiling the United States.[9]

Evidence indicates that there has always been a subtle discrimination between Afro-Americans of light and dark complexion, between those of all-African and those of part-white ancestry. Blyden undoubtedly had good grounds on which to base his charges against the mulattoes in the United States, who often used their lightness of color and their white ancestry to claim leadership privileges over their darker relatives. In the United States, however, blacks and those of mixed blood were forced together by white prejudice, and most American state laws and customs considered any person even of part African ancestry to be a Negro. Because of such strong pressure for unity, it was difficult for Blyden to drive a wedge between mulatto and black.[10]

In Charleston, even the mulattoes had welcomed Blyden with open arms, for he was indeed one of the most distinguished black men in the world. Most of his listeners spoke favorably of Liberia, and many praised Blyden himself, who tolerated the mulattoes. But he relished the opinions of the pure blacks, who, he said, assured him that there was

8. *Chicago Inter-Ocean,* 5 November 1889.
9. Lynch, *Blyden,* pp. 60 f. and Chapter 6.
10. Blyden to Coppinger, 3 December 1889; *Charleston World,* 3 December 1889. Cf. Myrdal, *American Dilemma, 1,* 695–700.

an intense longing for Africa among the blacks of South Carolina and throughout the South.[11]

One of the white men who greeted him was the editor of the Charleston *News and Courier*, James C. Hemphill, who called on Blyden for an interview. Blyden found Hemphill a sympathetic and willing listener; so he went on at length about Liberia, about America's racial problem, and about his theory that pure blacks should proceed forthwith to Africa. The *News and Courier* gave a prominent place to the interview and invited Blyden to write an editorial about emigration. Through the press services that carried the story of Blyden's visit, his ideas received widespread publicity throughout the South.[12]

Blyden was pleased but not surprised to receive a warm welcome from influential white men; it was part of his racial ideology that wise men, black and white, would endorse emigration. In Charleston, conservative white politicians were interested in helping blacks leave the South. Indeed, Senator Wade Hampton, a leader of conservative Democrats in the state had previously suggested that the federal government grant money to transport blacks out of the South, and out of the United States if need be.[13] In addition, an anonymously written book, *An Appeal to Pharaoh*,[14] which had been published shortly before Blyden's arrival in the United States also distinguished between black and mulatto and urged the repatriation of true blacks to Africa. Speculation about the author's identity was widespread, and eventually the public learned that the author was Carlyle McKinley, assistant editor of Hemp-

11. Blyden to Coppinger, 29 November 1889.

12. Ibid., and ibid., 16 December 1889; *Charleston News and Courier*, 1, 16 December 1889; *Atlanta Constitution*, 30 November 1889.

13. *Congressional Record, 21* (30 January 1890), 971–72.

14. Carlyle McKinley, *An Appeal to Pharaoh* (New York, 1889). Cf. interview with James C. Hemphill in the *New York Times*, 25 April 1892.

hill's *News and Courier.* Perhaps Blyden had known of
this and chose to come to Charleston because of its white
friends of emigration. In any case, Blyden was greatly encouraged by his welcome.[15]

Trouble was not long in coming, however, for Blyden,
Liberia, and black repatriation all had their enemies. One
attack came from Atlanta where the *Atlanta Constitution,*
a prime spokesman for the "new," industrializing South,
reported Blyden's views and commented editorially, "He
is entitled to a hearing. There is something startling in this
voice from Africa."[16] The trouble came next day when the
Constitution published a letter from Charles H. J. Taylor,
a mulatto and former United States Minister to Liberia.
(Taylor had stayed in Africa only four months in 1887,
never leaving Monrovia, and even the Liberian government had complained of his shallow reports, calculated
to dissuade Afro-Americans who considered settling
there.[17]) Taylor's letter accused Blyden of inviting blacks
to go where—because mulattoes were in power—Blyden
himself could not go. He called the Liberian visitor a
Muslim, a fetish-worshiper, and a hypocrite who advocated
emigration solely for mercenary reasons. Taylor urged a
"law to place in the penitentiary for ten years any man who
by word or activities encourages individuals to leave here
for the 'Black land of snakes, centipedes, fever, miasms,
driven encuga, ignorance, poverty, superstition and
death.' " After making various charges of weakness and
corruption against Liberia, he challenged Blyden "to meet

15. Blyden to Coppinger, 29 November 1889.
16. *Atlanta Constitution,* 30 November 1889.
17. Edwin J. Barclay to Charles Hall Adams, 29 December 1887.
Cf. Meier, *Negro Thought,* Chapter 2; C. H. J. Taylor to T. F. Bayard
(U. S. Secretary of State), 8 June, 31 August 1887. Cf. Taylor's 115–
page resignation, addressed to President Grover Cleveland (c. 11 November 1887), in dispatches from U. S. ministers to Liberia, U. S.
Archives.

me in a joint debate throughout the United States concerning Liberia, and I will prove in his presence that there is no penitentiary . . . as mean in every way as Liberia. . . . Let Blyden meet me if he dares."[18]

When a newspaper reporter confronted Blyden with Taylor's blast, the Liberian responded as might be expected. "I won't answer him," he replied. "If he were a white man I should reply to him; if he were a Negro I should endeavor to convince him, but he is neither, and is not concerned with the work which I have undertaken." When Taylor came to Charleston to attack Blyden publicly, the latter wrote that such attacks helped him "open the eyes of white and black to the animus of the mulatto."[19]

The attacks by Taylor and others notwithstanding, Blyden spoke often and vigorously in favor of Liberia. Despite its very real diplomatic, financial, and political problems, he glossed over the demerits of Liberia, choosing to stress the simple fact that it was a civilized African state, a home for all black men.[20]

If his version of Africa was challenged by men like Taylor, Blyden's descriptions of the racial situation in the South and the restlessness of the blacks struck home. He told his audiences of the providential pattern for the African in the modern world, in which the slavery phase took the black man out of Africa for service to the wider world. Then, after emancipation, the black man entered the education phase, in which he could learn to support himself and compete in the world's markets. The final stage would be emigration and repatriation, when the true sons of

18. *Atlanta Constitution,* 1 December 1889.
19. *Charleston World,* 3 December 1889; Blyden to Coppinger, 3 December 1889.
20. Blyden to Coppinger, 10 December 1889; Staudenraus, *African Colonization,* pp. 59–65, 240 f.; Raymond W. Bixler, *Foreign Policy of the United States in Liberia* (New York, 1957), pp. 15–19. Cf. Daniel F. McCall, "Liberia: An Appraisal," *Annals of the American Academy of Political and Social Science, 306* (July 1956), 89–90.

Africa would lead the natives into the modern era, into
civilization and Christianity. "Well, we are now passing
through the second stage of the problem," he told his audiences, "and the indications on every hand are that the third
phase is now approaching. These indications are seen in
the restlessness of the Negroes, thousands of whom are
anxious to go." Moreover, he said, white men like the
writer of *An Appeal to Pharaoh* were beginning to see a
need for the complete separation of the races. Another
"indication" was the fact that Africa was beginning to be
exploited by Europeans and "it is not to be supposed that
the Negro will not awake to a sense of his privileges and
rights and advantages there, and to his disadvantages
here." For these reasons, Blyden was certain that blacks
would soon begin a steady exodus to Africa. The only ob-
jective evidence for this, the increasing number of inquiries
and applications received at the Colonization Society
offices, indicated that indeed many blacks considered African emigration a valid option.[21]

Blyden wrote a long editorial for the *News and Courier*
in which he again praised *An Appeal to Pharaoh* and other
Southern white calls for black emigration. "The question
is not simply between the white man and the Negro," he
wrote, "but between the white man on the one side, and
the Negro *plus* the mulatto or mixed man, on the other
side." If Blyden was aware of the growing political, social,
and economic divisions among Southern white men, he
never mentioned them, even though blacks were soon to
be sacrificed to those divisions. He had seen too much
treachery by mulattoes at the expense of blacks, even in
Africa, where white men were a smaller factor, and he
relished each opportunity to divide South Carolina's blacks
along color lines. "The Negroes now have their eyes open,"

21. *Charleston News and Courier,* 3 December 1889.

he wrote to William Coppinger, the secretary of the Colonization Society, "and the recent articles in the *Courier* have roused them to a sense of their rights and privileges. . . . In the future the blacks say they will send from the Negro [congressional] districts either a Negro or a white man—no more miscegens." No wonder the white conservatives endorsed the ideas of a man who labored so valiantly to split the black community and separate the races.[22]

From Charleston Blyden headed south to Jacksonville, Florida, where he was awaited by other white politicians. On his trip to Florida he had to ride in the "Nigger Car, but it was very comfortable," he wrote. "I was very glad for it gave me an opportunity of conversing freely with those sturdy working men who came in at various stations. . . . I found that they are all very anxious to go [to Africa]. They say they see no chance here for their children and matters are getting worse."[23]

His welcome in Jacksonville was similar to that at Charleston, and the *Florida Times-Union,* a conservative newspaper, waxed enthusiastic about his emigration ideas. An editorial written to oppose a federal aid-to-education bill concluded with ringing praise for Blyden. "[He] seems to be the heaven-appointed medium for helping to solve the [race] problem. We wish him well in his great mission and approve his purpose to visit and address both races in every state and city of the South."[24]

But instead of remaining in the South to speak to blacks and influential whites, Blyden returned to the North early in January 1890. He could have stayed in the Southern states, capitalizing on his support there, and he might have

22. Ibid., 16 December 1889; Blyden to Coppinger, 16, 17, 20 December 1889.
23. Blyden to Coppinger, 22 December 1889.
24. *Florida Times-Union,* 28 December 1889.

asked for financial backing from wealthy whites or tried to organize Southern blacks for emigration, but instead he went to Washington, which was soon to become the center of an emigration debate. Ostensibly Blyden went there to speak at the annual meeting of the American Colonization Society; a more important attraction, however, was a bill that had recently been introduced into the Senate, which called for federal aid to emigration. Blyden was fully aware that the Colonization Society was not able to transport and support the thousands of black emigrants he envisioned. He therefore welcomed the prospect of government assistance.[25]

The race issue was high on the nation's agenda for political action. President Benjamin Harrison, a Republican, had set the scene with his first annual address to Congress on December 3, 1889, while Blyden was in Charleston. A major point in Harrison's message was the call for passage of a federal law to prevent white terrorists from depriving (Republican) blacks of their votes in federal elections. Discussing the role of the blacks in American life, he said: "They have as a people shown themselves to be friendly and faithful toward the white race under temptations of tremendous strength. . . . Their sudden withdrawal would stop production and bring disorder into the household as well as the shop." The President acknowledged that, generally, blacks "do not desire to quit their homes, and their employers resent the interference of the emigration agents who seek to stimulate such a desire." Blyden, who was nothing if not an emigration agent, wrote to his sponsors at the Colonization Society that he was relieved the President had not condemned emigration as such, only "sudden" withdrawal.[26]

25. Lynch, *Blyden,* p. 129.
26. James Richardson, ed., *Messages and Papers of the Presidents,* 9 (New York, 1917), 55 f. Blyden to Coppinger, 4 December 1889.

Southern white politicians were dismayed by the President's recommendation that the national government control federal elections in each state. They saw the speech and the "elections bill" or "force bill" (designed to carry out the recommendation) as an attempt by the Republicans to gain perpetual control of the federal government by guaranteeing the black vote. Southerners reacted strenuously, the most notorious reaction being the Mississippi Constitutional Convention of 1890, which succeeded in restricting the right to vote through rigorous literacy and comprehension tests that were designed to remove blacks from the voting lists. This response from Mississippi took time, however, and was not complete until September 1890. A more immediate Southern response occurred in Congress itself, where several bills were introduced calling for federal aid to assist blacks in moving from the South to Africa. Preeminent among these was the bill offered by Senator Matthew Butler of South Carolina.[27]

The Butler bill was simple. It would provide transportation for every black who wanted to move out of the Southern states if the applicant certified that he wished to become a citizen of the country of destination. Butler requested that five million dollars be appropriated to start the exodus. Although the bill did not mention Africa, it was interpreted by the blacks and by the senators who debated it as an African emigration plan. In addition to Butler's bill, a resolution by Senator R. L. Gibson, a conservative Democrat from Louisiana, asked the Senate to investigate the practicality of acquiring or setting aside territory on which to settle emigrant Afro-Americans. Another resolution, by Senator John T. Morgan, a conservative Democrat from

27. Richard E. Welch, Jr., "The Federal Elections Bill of 1890: Postscripts and Prelude," *Journal of American History*, 52 (December 1965), 511–26; Rayford W. Logan, *The Betrayal of the Negro* (New York, 1965), pp. 65–76; Vernon Lane Wharton, *The Negro in Mississippi, 1865–1890* (Chapel Hill, 1947), pp. 208 ff.

Alabama, asked the Senate to inquire into new ways to improve American trade and relations with the people of the Free State of the Congo. Taken together, these bills and resolutions, all offered within a few days after the President's message, brought national attention to the idea of colonization as a solution for America's race problem.[28]

Endorsement of black emigration by conservative Southern Democrats was in part a racial move, in part political. From the Southern point of view, the threat of the Republican elections bill was serious, for there was growing dissension between the conservative and radical factions of white voters. The possibility that a black Republican party, revitalized by federal protection, might capitalize on white divisions alarmed both white factions. Not only was this true in South Carolina, where the schism took the form of a fight within the Democratic party, it also was true in other parts of the South, where opposition to conservative control took the form of third-party movements. In view of this dissension, the white politicians considered that action against the elections bill was absolutely necessary. If some whites, like Hemphill and McKinley, thought emigration was a feasible way of reducing racial tension, others were more interested in pleasing the electorate. If indeed a large number of blacks wanted to emigrate, as Blyden said, Butler's bill would enlist their support for the conservative side. In any case, rural and small-town whites should be pleased at the prospect of reducing the black population. Opposition came from large landowners who, as President Harrison remarked, were disturbed at the efforts of emigration agents to draw away their black labor force. Even if the plan for African emigration was not feasible, the political move—capitalizing on Southern fear of Republicans and distrust of blacks—could be a useful tool in rallying support for the conserva-

28. *Congressional Record, 21,* 125, 155–57, 338, 802.

tives. Butler's main purpose was to provide an alternative for the elections bill, against which all white Southerners and Northern Democrats would vote. Butler's bill and the elections bill, along with Senator Blair's aid-to-education bill, provided the basis for an extensive national debate on the race question.[29]

The first to speak for Butler's bill was Senator J. T. Morgan of Alabama, the senior Democrat on the Senate Committee on Foreign Relations, who had long been interested in opening relations with Africa, especially the Congo. The Congo basin had come into public attention after the explorer Henry M. Stanley had crossed the continent in 1876 while tracing the course of the Congo River. European nations had then begun scheming to establish control over the vast Congo valley, but King Leopold of the Belgians succeeded in outmaneuvering the other powers and established what he called "The Free State of the Congo" in 1883. A primary factor in the survival of Leopold's "free state" was the early recognition of the Congo flag by the United States, the first nation to do so. The man who introduced the resolution for recognition and who argued most strongly for it was Senator Morgan. Among the reasons for recognition that Morgan had cited was the right of the Afro-American to return to Africa, to his own nation. Since 1883 Morgan had maintained his concern for the Congo, and a few days before Butler introduced his emigration bill, Morgan had asked the Senate to "inquire and report upon the best method of encouraging trade, commerce and intercourse between the people of the Free State of the Congo and the United States." The intent

29. See C. Vann Woodward, *Origins of the New South,* Chapter 9, for a discussion of rural white discontent with the Conservative Democrats. Cf. V. O. Key, Jr., *Southern Politics* (New York, 1949), pp. 533–41, for a discussion of the black political threat in the period of white schism. Cf. Stanley P. Hirschson, *Farewell to the Bloody Shirt* (Bloomington, 1962), pp. 190–92.

of his resolution, he added, was to encourage a general
migration by American blacks to the Congo. In light of
this background, few senators were surprised when
Morgan rose on January 7 to speak for Butler's bill.[30]

The senator's long, rambling speech urged deportation
of the blacks for essentially four reasons.[31] First, he maintained that wherever two races live together, a strong "race
aversion" grows between them. "The most cultivated
Negro is constantly armed with inveterate suspicions toward the white race," Morgan said. Furthermore, those
suspicions had increased rapidly since emancipation. Second, travelers' accounts demonstrated that Congo natives
suffered greatly from the Arab slave trade and Islamic
missionaries, from which fates it was America's duty to
rescue the Congolese. Third, Morgan brought forth a
parade of commercial information about the economic
value of the Congo. (Through his efforts the United States
had posted a "commercial agent" in the Congo to report
on investment opportunities. The senator included the
agent's optimistic report in the speech.)[32] Finally, to mini-
mize "race aversion," to help the suffering Congo natives
and to develop the wealth of the country, the senator pre-
scribed the settlement of Afro-Americans in the Congo,
where they would work wonders for the native population
by abolishing slavery, raising the level of education, and
establishing representative government. "Christianity will
find a door opened by her hand-maiden Commerce,
through which the heart of Africa will be entered in tri-

30. Paul McStallworth, "The United States and the Congo Question, 1884–1914" (unpublished doctoral dissertation, Ohio State University 1954), pp. 1–20; *Congressional Record, 21*, 125; *New York
Daily Tribune,* 11 December 1889. Cf. Ruth M. Slade, *English Speaking Missions in the Congo Independent State, 1878–1908* (Brussels,
1959), pp. 104–06, 254–56.
31. *Congressional Record, 21,* 419–30.
32. See McStallworth, "The Congo Question," passim, for the names
of numerous American investors in the Congo Free State.

umph by the Prince of Peace," followed by "civilization, wealth . . . and political manhood." Such a plan, he declared, would provide a way for the black man to be free from the restraints that American life had placed on him. Best of all, according to Morgan, emigration and settlement, based on commercial development of the Congo, would free the United States from a "general amalgamation of races."

Senator Butler was next to speak for his bill and his reasons for advocating emigration differed considerably from those of Senator Morgan.[33] Butler, neither a doctrinaire racist nor a supporter of King Leopold's Congo, carefully pointed out that his bill called for the blacks' voluntary departure from the Southern states and that the rights of the black citizens of the United States must always be protected. "Would it be an unreasonable demand," he inquired, "if the negro should ask his guardian to supplement his allowance of citizenship and civil rights by transportation to the Free State of the Congo or Liberia if he wanted to go there?"

Butler appealed to the blacks themselves for evidence that emigration would be good. Among others, he cited his friend Blyden, whose writings were strong texts for black repatriation. The Liberian's most recent book, *Christianity, Islam and the Negro Race,* contained several essays that provided ideas and long quotes for Butler's address, and he summoned the ghosts of Thomas Jefferson, Daniel Webster, and Abraham Lincoln to bless the colonization idea and sanctify the scheme for redeeming Africa with black settlers. The senator omitted Blyden's attacks against mulattoes, but the main thought in the speech was Blyden's.[34] From other blacks the senator ob-

33. *Congressional Record, 21,* 622–30.
34. Edward W. Blyden, *Christianity, Islam and the Negro Race* (London, 1887).

tained statements that favored emigration, statements intended to convince the Senate that Africa was the desire
not only of Southern senators but of most black Americans.[35]

Republican senators rose to challenge Butler. Senator
George F. Hoar of Massachusetts, the Senate sponsor of
the elections bill, scolded Butler for even dreaming of
asking the Afro-American to leave the country until he
had received every right and opportunity of citizenship.
Senator Henry W. Blair, also of Massachusetts and the
sponsor of the aid-to-education bill, noted wryly that there
were so many blacks in the country it would be easier for
the federal government to "export to Africa 10,000 judi-
ciously selected white people," and the whole problem
would be settled.[36] Senator John J. Ingalls of Kansas,
widely known for his colorful oratory against Democrats,
gave a dramatic oration against Butler's bill. Despite his
statement that it was impossible for the two races to live
together, Ingalls was hailed by blacks and Republicans
around the nation. The senator's primary purpose was
electioneering, but his flamboyant speech attracted even
more attention to the idea of emigration.[37]

There was little chance that the Democratic bill would
pass the Republican Congress, and there was little surprise
when Hoar, Blair, and Ingalls opposed emigration. But
Senator Butler was disappointed when Southern Democrats also spoke against the measure. Senator Edward C.
Walthall of Mississippi was more concerned with stopping
the steady influx of blacks into his state than with the prospects for sending them to Africa. Senator Zebulon Vance
of North Carolina, the senior Democrat on the Finance

35. *Washington Post,* 21 November 1889; *African Repository, 66*
(April 1890), 53–54.
36. *Congressional Record,* 21, 628–30.
37. Ibid., pp. 802–06; cf. *New York Times,* 24 January 1890.

Committee, believed it was impractical to pay for the removal of millions of people to Africa. He wanted the federal government to "just leave the South alone" to deal with the naturally "ignorant and evil" but "gentle" blacks. Walthall and Vance spoke for the Southern planters, who realized the value of black labor but wanted to avoid giving the blacks political power proportional to their numbers.[38]

Senator Wade Hampton, Butler's compatriot from South Carolina, answered Vance's criticisms with a gentle speech. He added little to the fund of ideas favoring the blacks' removal, but he drew public attention to *An Appeal to Pharaoh,* which estimated that governmental appropriations of 32 million dollars each year for ten years could transport every Afro-American to Africa. With this thinly disguised appeal to the Republicans to use the Treasury surplus, Hampton ended what proved to be the last speech on the emigration bill.[39]

The bill never came to a vote. Although its exact fate in committee is unknown, it clearly had little chance of passage for it was a partisan measure that divided even the minority party. Possibly its sponsors might have agreed with the Republicans to drop the emigration proposal in order to allow the Blair education bill to be debated and voted down, as indeed it was. Had the emigration bill not been dropped, its sponsors could have kept it before the Senate and thereby stalled consideration of tariff legislation, which was important to the Republicans. Indeed, it was the Republicans' desire for the new "McKinley Tariff" that later led to the sacrifice of the elections bill.[40] Whatever the reason for the death of Butler's bill, it was never mentioned again in the Senate. The importance of the

38. *Congressional Record, 21,* 857, 966–71.
39. Ibid., pp. 971–74; McKinley, *Appeal to Pharaoh,* pp. 164–94.
40. Logan, *Betrayal of the Negro,* pp. 70, 75–81; Welch, "Federal Elections Bill," pp. 516 ff.

measure, so far as this study is concerned, was not its legislative fate but the widespread public attention that was generated by the Senate debate. Among blacks especially, there would be repercussions for years to come.

The immediate reaction of prominent blacks to the emigration issue was predictably negative. The black press, especially in the North, vigorously attacked the principle advocates of emigration. Some editors chose party labels to smear the senators. T. Thomas Fortune of the *New York Age* assailed Senator Morgan, who "through a singular mockery of fate has found his way into the U.S. Senate which he besmirches with his presence and attempts to inoculate with Democratic virus and colorphobia through the agency of his wagging, poisonous tongue." Another black editor claimed that Senator Butler would find "that his ancestors had a much easier task in stealing from their humble homes and bringing to these shores our ancestors than he and his posterity will have to remove them." The *Huntsville Gazette* merely stated that the senators did not speak for the majority of Southern people, black or white. The strongest attacks were saved for Blyden, who was called "the most loathsome and hated West Indian African who ever visited these shores," a "spy, hireling and firebrand," an "enemy of the race," and "a learned old zip." Several newspapers urged him to go back to Africa himself.[41]

Objections to the repatriation scheme were, of course, motivated by more than mere partisan politics or personality conflicts. Black people had labored long and hard to help make the United States a success, and many of them bitterly resented attempts to deny them the fruit of their labor, whether by terrorism, segregation, or deportation.

41. *New York Age*, 11, 18 January 1890; *Kansas City American Citizen*, 20 December 1889, 17 January 1890; *Huntsville Gazette*, 18 January 1890; *Cleveland Gazette*, 15, 22 February 1890; Indianapolis *Freeman*, 15 February 1890.

During the debate on the Butler bill, two major black conventions met to discuss the race problem. The Afro-American League, which met in Chicago to protest violence and segregation, decided on self-help and race pride as the primary avenues for advancement. One spokesman drew uproarious laughter from his audience when he proposed, as had Senator Blair, that the federal government finance the removal of certain dissatisfied white men from the South and that Senator Morgan, Butler, or Hampton be the "Moses" for his race. The convention called for the migration of blacks to the North and West but would have nothing to do with Africa. At another convention, which met in Washington a few weeks later to support Blair's education bill, black leaders had nothing good to say about African repatriation and believed that education could lift their people into the mainstream of American life.[42]

The black press had more to say about the Butler bill and why African emigration was wrong. The *Savannah Tribune* pointed out that because the "Liberia experiment" had been a failure, it would be a crime to send loyal Afro-Americans there. The white race, claimed the *Tribune,* had an obligation to care for the "weaker race" and compensate for the wrongs of slavery. Another paper pointed out that total deportation would be impractical because the black population was increasing at a rate of more than 800 per day. Still another declared that so many blacks had white blood in their veins that few would leave the United States. The *Christian Recorder* warned its readers not to become bewitched by the "African fallacy" because of Blyden. "Dr. Blyden is at liberty to think and reason about America from an African standpoint, but Americans should think and reason from the standpoint of Ameri-

42. Meier, *Negro Thought,* pp. 70 f., 128–30; *New York Age,* 25 January, 1 February 1890; *Indianapolis Freeman,* 8 February 1890.

cans." Several writers echoed President Harrison's opinion that the black man was the economic backbone of the South and that Southerners could not afford to see their laborers depart. A correspondent of the *Christian Recorder* pointed out that the fate of Africa was even then being decided by the great powers of Europe. "A handful of American Negroes . . . along the banks of the Congo," he concluded "will hardly gain serious attention in the international councils which are to settle the geography of Africa."[43]

The opinion of many articulate blacks was expressed by Benjamin F. Lee, the new editor of the *Christian Recorder*. Because Africa was coming to the attention of the world through men like Livingstone and Stanley, he thought the Afro-American was being forced to think about his relationship to the land of his ancestors. Many blacks, he wrote, had considered going to Africa, but there was no unanimity among them despite pressures from Blyden, Turner, and some Southern whites for emigration. If the whites were mystified because blacks were divided in their opinions, it was because the whites had too rigid a stereotype of the American black man. The difference between those who want to stay and those who want to go, Lee said, "is not the line between any two of the grades of color that mar [us] despite all the sneers of Dr. Blyden on this subject." Lee protested that he was as concerned as any man about Africa and its people, but that did not mean he wanted to live there. The desire to "move, move, move" was squandering the meager wealth of the blacks, he said, and sooner or later they must settle down and face life. Lee believed that, for most Afro-Americans, the United States would always be home. Even if many wanted to

43. *Savannah Tribune,* 21 December 1889; *Topeka Capitol,* 10 January 1890; *Christian Recorder,* 23 January, 6 February 1890.

leave, he wrote, it was best for them to remain and make things better at home.[44]

Public opinion among white Americans also was one-sided against the blacks' emigrating; and the handful of responsible papers that endorsed Butler's bill had few new ideas to substantiate their arguments. The editors of most journals agreed with the reasoning advanced by the black newspapers. Even though partisanship and sectionalism were evident in the editorials, most of them cited the economic and logistic problems and concluded that mass emigration was not feasible. Many Northern whites considered the whole scheme to send citizens away from their homes grossly immoral. Some opposed Butler's bill because it left the possibility that blacks would move into the North, and, as the *New York Times* editorialized, "the communities to which it is proposed to send the negroes will refuse to receive them." The prejudice against blacks was nationwide, but few whites, North or South, wanted the blacks to go to Africa.[45]

Blyden, however, did not seem disillusioned by the difficulties encountered by the Butler bill when he spoke to the seventy-third anniversary meeting of the American Colonization Society in Washington. "It may take many years before the people come to these views, and therefore before legislation upon them may be possible," he said, "but there is evidently movement in that direction." He proclaimed that sentiments for emigration were not yet ready in the United States among either whites or blacks, and decided, moreover, that "the industrial condition of the South is not prepared for it," nor were conditions "yet ready in Africa

44. *Christian Recorder,* 24 April 1890.
45. *Public Opinion, 18* (1890), 371 ff. (24, 31 January, 7, 14 February 1890); *New York Times,* 21, 26 January 1890; *Atlanta Constitution,* 18 December 1889.

for a complete exodus." He concluded with a lament that
the whole matter of black repatriation was being handled
as a partisan political issue when "there are millions whose
life is bound up [with Africa]." Despite his disappointment in Congress and the reduced prospects for immediate
action, Blyden lost none of his conviction about eventual
emigration.[46]

The loudest and most enthusiastic black response to the
Butler bill came from Bishop Turner, whose fullest statement on the measure appeared in an open letter he addressed to former Senator Blanche K. Bruce, a respected
black elder who had written against the bill. The bishop
ridiculed the common supposition, echoed by Bruce, that
Butler's bill required all blacks to go to Africa. "Thousands
and hundreds of thousands of us are no more fit to go to
Africa than we are fit to go to Paradise," wrote Turner.
The unfit, according to the bishop, were those who "worship white gods . . . who are fools enough to believe that
the Devil is black and therefore all who are black are con-
sanguinely related to him . . . who pretend to be serving
God and have no aim higher than to get to heaven to be
white." Such people would be a curse to Africa. Butler's
bill, Turner pointed out, although a substantial start, was
altogether too modest; it would take much more than a
mere five million dollars to help the million Southern rural
blacks who wanted to emigrate. Turner claimed to know
the mind of the black peasant in a way that Northern and
middle-class blacks could not; and he reported great unrest
in the countryside.[47]

Bruce had suggested that the Butler bill was bad because
Butler and the other proponents were Democrats and there-
fore worthy of automatic opposition. Acknowledging that
Butler had no great love for the black race, Turner asserted

46. *African Repository, 66* (April, July 1890), 40, 72, 74, 80.
47. Turner to *Washington Post,* 17 March 1890.

that help would be accepted even from the hand of an enemy. "I care not what animus prompted Senator Butler," he wrote. "Immortality enthroned his brow from the moment he offered that bill. . . . If it passes—and grant, O my God, that it may—it will enable at least a hundred thousand self-reliant black men to go where they can work out their own destiny." If Congress should fail to pass this bill, "sooner or later," Turner predicted, "God will raise up a thousand Butlers, black and white, and hundreds of millions [of dollars] will be appropriated" for emigration to Africa. Turner wrote eloquently and his open letter to Bruce was widely quoted and discussed. It was, however, a lonely cry against a storm of protest from articulate blacks who were offended as much by Turner as by the thought of emigrating.[48]

Thus the Butler bill to aid black emigration died in the Senate with only a few conservative Southern whites and some radical blacks on hand to mourn it. Although the bill never had a chance of enactment, it stirred up a nationwide discussion of emigration that became even more important in the decade to come. Throughout the 1890s, as the troubles of Afro-Americans increased, the suggestion planted by the Butler bill debate and nurtured by men like Blyden and Turner flowered from time to time in a kind of "African fever," a burning desire on the part of some blacks to leave the United States. The American Colonization Society took on signs of new life and other organizations sent agents and propaganda through the South to stir up excitement. For several years to come, in letters of inquiry to the Colonization Society, blacks who were eager to escape oppression would ask about the Butler bill.

Blyden remained in the United States for several weeks after the Senate debate ended. Although he knew there would be no immediate government support for emigra-

48. Ibid.

tion, he could be satisfied that his visit had produced its desired result. If his stay at Charleston had not actually produced the Butler bill, he had given Senator Butler the words to advocate emigration. Newspapers and opponents had attacked Blyden, Butler, and Morgan in the same phrases, and Blyden's name was spread throughout the nation. When he stepped aboard the ship in New York to return to Africa, Bishop Turner was there to wish him godspeed.[49]

49. Blyden to Coppinger, 24 March 1890; *Christian Recorder,* 13 March 1890.

4

The American Colonization Society, I:
Organization and Operation, 1890

Blyden's visit and the Butler bill had stimulated discussion and drawn out ideas, pro and con, about black emigration. Bishop Turner, the chief American advocate of emigration, publicized Africa and agitated among blacks. But in 1890 the only way interested people could get to Africa was through the venerable American Colonization Society. To understand the African emigration movement of the 1890s it is necessary to look at the society, its history, personnel, policies, operations, and its offspring, the Republic of Liberia.

In the fifteen years or so before Blyden's 1889 visit the Society had drifted along without much encouragement from either blacks, merchants, or wealthy whites. Occasionally a legacy would be left it from a long-time supporter, but new benefactors were few and old sponsors were dying off. Using income from endowments and slowly liquidating its capital, the society continued to send annually from fifty to a hundred emigrants to Liberia. The society asked the would-be emigrants to contribute toward the cost of their passage on the one small sailing vessel still engaged in American trade with West Africa. (For a time after the Civil War the society had owned its own ship, but it proved too costly to operate.) The American merchant fleet had declined drastically after European steamships

captured much of the transatlantic trade, and there was little commerce with West Africa to entice American skip-
pers. Liberia shipped some coffee to the United States and
the settlers preferred American manufactured goods, but
most goods arrived in British or German ships. With only
two or three sailings each year from New York to Liberia
the society did well to send as many emigrants as it did. By
1890 it had settled over 15,000 Afro-Americans in Liberia, but only 1,130 since 1872. Despite encouragement
from Bishop Turner during the 1880s relatively few blacks
wanted to go to Africa. Fewer still could actually emigrate
because the Colonization Society was so nearly destitute.[1]

Two trends in those years had served to sustain the hopes
of the society: the growing racial tension in the United
States and the opening of Africa to European exploration.
Racial oppression led a small but increasing number of
blacks to apply for emigration, but the scramble for Africa
was an even more important factor. European explorers
had been tramping through the interior of Africa, especially West and South Africa, for many years, but it was not
until the 1860s that American public interest had been
excited by reports from David Livingstone. When Livingstone became "lost" in Central Africa, it was an American
newspaper that sent Henry M. Stanley to dramatically
"find" the explorer in 1872 and report his whereabouts to
the world. Stanley later set out to explore Central Africa
and in 1877 completed a pioneering cross-continent trek
in which he had traced the course of the Congo River. Immediately thereafter European powers, mutually suspicious of one another's expansion plans, began maneuvering for African territory. Senator Morgan's friend, King

1. No detailed study has been made of the Colonization Society
for the years after 1870 but the *African Repository* and the society's
annual reports for those years provide a sketchy history. The statistics
are from *Liberia Bulletin, 16* (February 1900), 28.

Leopold of the Belgians, scored a major coup by establishing the internationalized Congo Free State. Soon the scramble was on, with the other nations of Europe sending explorers and claiming territory in other parts of Africa. To avoid direct conflict in Europe and to "stabilize" Africa, the great powers met at the Berlin Conference on the Congo in 1884–85.[2] At Senator Morgan's insistence even the United States sent representatives. Ever since John Quincy Adams had insisted to President James Monroe that the United States should never become a colonial power, Americans had shunned colonies. But times were changing and the world was shrinking. Some Americans wanted the United States to claim overseas colonies, and others stressed the great potential of African commerce. These internationalists would soon awaken the United States press and public to the existence and desirability of Africa, and only a few years later the United States would embark on its own brand of imperialism in the Caribbean and the Pacific.[3]

The Colonization Society hoped to capitalize on this interest. Its *African Repository* began running stories about trade and commerce with all Africa, not just Liberia. It also told of the work of missionaries and explorers who were invading the continent. By 1890 a new excitement stirred the few remaining members of the society, which at that time consisted mostly of Northern whites, who had been members for many, many years. According to the society's constitution, anyone who paid a dollar could become a member for a year. Thirty dollars bought a life membership and for a thousand dollars any American citizen could become a "life director." Its Board

2. Roland Oliver and John Fage, *A Short History of Africa* (Baltimore, 1962), Chapter 16; Ruth Slade, *King Leopold's Congo* (London, 1962), pp. 37–43.
3. McStallworth, "The Congo Question," passim.

of Directors also included the members of the executive committee and representatives of the various auxiliary societies. The Board met each January to discuss policy and hear anniversary speakers like Professor Blyden. When Blyden spoke in 1890 the public meeting was attended by many dignitaries and interested Washington residents, but of the twenty directors only eleven were present. The only auxiliary societies that contributed $200 that year and thereby earned representation on the Board were from Pennsylvania and New Jersey. The New York and Massachusetts Colonization Societies still functioned, but the New York group was at odds with the policies of the parent society and the Massachusetts group was moribund.[4]

In 1889 the ACS had received a total of $17,144, mostly from legacies and interest, which was administered primarily by the executive committee. This committee, with the permanent secretary-treasurer, directed the day-to-day affairs of the society from its headquarters building in Washington. The committee consisted of the secretary-treasurer and seven members appointed by the committee itself. The members were Washington-area citizens of a philanthropic bent if not of great wealth; most were clergymen, the chairman was a federal judge. Members were empowered not only to appoint their successors but to select the secretary-treasurer, to hire agents in the United States and Africa, and to decide which applicants for passage to Liberia should go. To all intents and purposes these seven men, with the secretary-treasurer and president, were the American Colonization Society in 1890.[5]

For many years the president had been John H. B. Latrobe, a wealthy lawyer and member of a prominent Baltimore family. At an early age he had become interested in colonization and in 1827 had helped organize

4. *African Repository,* 66 (April 1890), 33–44 and back cover.
5. Ibid.

the Maryland Colonization Society. In the years that followed, Latrobe urged the ACS to expand its Liberian colony and thus corner as much as possible of what he hoped would develop into a rich African trade. Under his leadership the Maryland Society, after splitting from the parent group in 1833, founded the colony of "Maryland in Liberia." The Maryland colony at Cape Palmas survived, but only through many hardships. It even gained "independence" in 1847 under Latrobe's urging, but within ten years it had united with Liberia. After the demise of the Maryland Society in 1853, Latrobe rejoined the ACS and soon became its president. His enthusiasm for colonization continued strong in his old age. In 1889, after reading *An Appeal to Pharaoh*, he wrote glowingly to the secretary of the society: "I admit that I can see no other solution to the so-called 'Negro question' than by their separation, nor can I see how this can be brought about unless there shall grow up in Africa a civilized black nation that shall become as attractive to the negroes of the United States as this country is to the Europeans." Despite failing health, Latrobe continued to provide a spiritual drive for the society.[6]

Latrobe's prominence notwithstanding, the man who actually operated the ACS was its secretary-treasurer, William Coppinger, who had literally spent his life in the colonization movement. At the age of ten, shortly after immigrating with his parents from Britain, he became an office boy in the Pennsylvania Colonization Society. Twenty-six years later, in 1864, he was appointed secretary of the parent society. After the Civil War he traveled through the South, speaking to newly freed blacks and per-

6. Latrobe to Coppinger, 25 October 1889, 25 January 1890; John E. Semmes, *John H. B. Latrobe and His Times, 1803–1891* (Baltimore, 1917), pp. 139–72; Staudenraus, *African Colonization*, pp. 110–12, 157–61, 190 f., 232 f.

suading several thousand of them to sail to Liberia. When the emigration tide ebbed in 1872, Coppinger retreated to Washington, where he administered the society's affairs. Among other duties, he edited and circulated the quarterly *African Repository* and corresponded with the blacks who wanted to leave the United States and those who had settled in Liberia. Completely loyal to the society as the years progressed, he increasingly personified the organization; he was convinced of its mission to Africa and America, oblivious to criticism, and forever confident that a new departure was just around the corner.[7]

The policies of the Colonization Society during the late 1880s reflected this optimism as Coppinger and his allies took positive steps to counter the main problems of the society: lack of transportation between the United States and Africa, dearth of funds, and want of black support. A campaign for increased American trade with Africa took first priority; if more ships sailed to Liberia, it would be easier and cheaper for the society to send emigrants. To impress merchants with the possibilities of African trade, the *African Repository* carried stories and statistics of the increasing value of the trade to European ships that plied the African coast. European governments, moreover, were exploring for new riches. Gold in South Africa, rubber in the coastal and Congo regions, coffee in Liberia, and timber, hides, palm oil, cocoa, and minerals from other parts of the continent were some of the known resources, and there was promise that other products would be discovered. In addition, the Africa promoters suggested there were immense potential markets for American goods among the natives and the Liberian settlers.[8]

The society tried to secure new money by sending its

7. *Liberia Bulletin, 1* (November 1892), 1–3; Boyd, "Negro Colonization," passim. *Washington Post,* 12 February 1892.
8. *African Repository.*

agents among philanthropists and by attempting to rejuvenate the state auxiliary societies. One of these agents was Blyden; another was Henry W. Grimes, a former Attorney General of Liberia, who traveled to the United States in 1889.[9] Between them, Blyden and Grimes spoke to audiences from Florida to Boston and as far west as Chicago. They contrasted the glories of Liberia with the difficulties of America's race problem and tried to convince their hearers to support emigration. They spoke to church societies and missionary groups, black and white alike. At the Colonization Society's request, they attempted to organize local auxiliaries, as the society had done in its heyday seventy years earlier. Despite the efforts of the agents, receipts remained low and actually decreased in 1890. No new auxiliary societies were organized, but the established auxiliaries took on new life and interest, especially when Grimes told of the great potential of African trade. Nevertheless, their financial aid to the parent society did not increase. Many of the funds held by the Pennsylvania, New Jersey, New York, and Massachusetts Colonization Societies were reserved for education in Liberia and thus were not available for direct emigration expenses. But it was difficult to convince most people who had money to give to charity that colonization was the answer to the race problem. Nevertheless, the society and its agents persisted in their campaign.[10]

9. Minutes of the Board of Directors (1869–1912), 16 June 1889, 22 January 1890, ACS Papers; H. W. Grimes to Coppinger, 12 February, 10 March 1890. ACS Executive Committee Journal (1886–1912), 2 May 1889, 5 December 1889, 6 November, 4 December 1890, ACS Papers.

10. *Philadelphia Ledger,* 14 October 1890; Grimes to Coppinger, November 1889 to November 1890, esp. 10 March 1890; Blyden to Coppinger, 15 March 1889, 3, 5, 12, 14 March 1890; Coppinger to Blyden, 26, 28 January, 16 April 1889; ACS Executive Committee Journal (1886–1912), 2 May 1889 and thereafter. Annual receipts were summarized in *Liberia Bulletin, 16* (February (1900), 28. Detailed

The third problem of the American Colonization Society in 1890 was recruiting blacks for Liberia. Although the number of applications for passage was increasing, most of the letters came from semiliterate peasants who could neither help pay their passage nor contribute anything to Liberia other than labor. Consequently, the society strove to convince educated and enterprising young blacks to emigrate, and this task also was assigned to traveling agents. In addition to Grimes and Blyden, the society employed the Reverend Ezekiel E. Smith to travel through the South addressing students and church and business groups. Smith, a North Carolina educator, having served ably as United States Minister to Liberia for two years, was well qualified to describe its virtues. Like Grimes, Smith centered his work in North Carolina but traveled as far afield as Dallas and Kansas City to address church conventions. Despite their efforts, there is little evidence that these agents made any more impact on educated blacks than did Bishop Turner.[11]

A major drawback to their recruiting efforts was the oft-repeated report from returned emigrants that Liberia was uninhabitable; indeed, returnees had plagued the society from the beginning. Especially after the Civil War, emigrants from almost every shipload, had defected, and when the defectors arrived back in the United States, their stories of hardship and illness received wide publicity. The attack of C. H. J. Taylor against Blyden was typical of those who had visited Liberia. Furthermore, the mate of the ship that carried ACS emigrants to Liberia declared that scarcely a single Afro-American in Liberia would not return to the

---

receipts were published in each annual report and each issue of the *African Repository*.

11. The Executive Committee Journal listed the inquiries by state until a flood of letters in 1891 made such listing unwieldy. E. E. Smith to Coppinger, 26, 29 November 1890, 1 September 1891.

United States if he had the money. Even testimonial letters from recent settlers, old citizens, government officials, and society agents in Liberia could not overcome the apprehensions of educated blacks who, in addition to wanting to stay in the United States, saw Liberia as a failure.[12]

In 1890 the Colonization Society devoted as much of its attention to Liberia as to Afro-Americans. The black republic was still heavily dependent on American help for moral and diplomatic support as well as for new settlers. To attract American blacks to Africa, propagandists (like Bishop Turner and Secretary Coppinger) had to refute unfavorable rumors and dispel general ignorance about Liberia. Many Americans had grave suspicions about the country because of its reputation for an unhealthy climate, feeble economy, and bad government. In 1890, furthermore, it was rumored that Liberia might soon lose its independence either to Britain or France. Because Liberia was the goal of most American emigration movements, the state of its affairs was of great importance to blacks who wished to emigrate.

The true condition of Liberia in 1890, if fully known by Americans, would indeed have given little encouragement to emigrationists. The little republic had struggled since the time of its independence in 1847 to maintain its nationhood despite its marginal subsistence economy, indebtedness to European powers, inability to police the natives in the hinterland, and impotence to resist encroachments on its borders. At no time had these struggles been satisfactorily resolved.

Liberia's most persistent problem, at least in the eyes of would-be settlers, was its unhealthy climate. Located in "the white man's grave," Liberia's coast was low and swampy, a seat of various fevers and plagues. Like the rest of West Africa, it was considered unfit for white habitation

12. *New York Herald,* 20 January 1890.

because many explorers, missionaries, and traders had died shortly after arrival. But the prevalent racial ideology in the United States maintained that blacks, having originated in Africa, were by nature able to live there. This thinking lingered among colonizationists long after experience had shown that blacks born in America were equally susceptible to African fevers. In truth, malaria, the chief killer in Liberia, also took a dreadful toll among the natives, especially children; those who survived to maturity acquired immunity only by suffering and surviving the disease as infants. Despite increasing medical knowledge about tropical fevers and the utilization of quinine as a remedy, the death rate among new arrivals from America remained high. There were few physicians in the country and drugs cost money the settlers did not have. The "acclimating fever," an initial attack of malaria, was almost universal. If settlers could not afford to rest for several weeks after their apparent recovery, new attacks of fever could quickly be fatal. There was agitation for settlement inland, away from the coast, to avoid the fevers, but most immigrants wanted to stay close to the ports, the centers of government and commerce, with the result that numerous horror stories of disease and death reached the United States through letters and returnees.[13]

Those who emigrated to Liberia also faced the prospect of farming at a subsistence level for several years. Most newcomers were settled on land donated by the government, but it was covered with trees or scrub that had to be cleared before cultivation could start. Once the land was cleared, the settlers planted coffee trees, which took five years to produce their first crop. Meanwhile the farmer and his family had to build a shelter, raise foodstuffs, and endure the fever. At the start, most of the new houses imitated

    13. Curtin, *Image of Africa,* Chapter 14; Staudenraus, *African Colonization,* p. 102.

the native huts; the foodstuffs were also African, unfamiliar products such as yams and cassava. The Colonization Society provided settlers with basic food for their first six months in Liberia but the supply was seldom sufficient, and six months soon elapsed. Little wonder that so many left or wished to leave soon after their arrival. When coffee farms reached production the farmer could count on some cash income, but he suffered from fluctuations in coffee prices and paid high prices for American or European products. Not all immigrants became farmers, of course, but because almost all of them had been farmers in the United States there was little prospect for them as merchants or government officials. Merchants could make a comfortable living but they were few in number and could do little toward building the nation. Essentially Liberia was a land of poor farmers with a thin class of businessmen who were well off only by comparison to the peasants and natives.[14]

Liberia desperately needed development capital. Efforts to attract wealthy American blacks failed, however; first, because there were so few wealthy American blacks, and second, because those few wished to remain in the United States. White American capitalists were able to find better investment opportunities in the Western Hemisphere. Europeans, on the other hand, with business in Africa and with shipping lines available to handle trade, were more interested in Liberia's resources. Rubber, for example, attracted a British syndicate in 1889, and the Liberian Legislature awarded this "Liberian Concession Company" exclusive rights to collect and export rubber. In return the syndicate paid $100,000 in gold. India Rubber Estates Company soon took over the concession, and Lord Raglan, an important investor in the company, visited Liberia to view his holdings. His report on the potential for rubber, railroads, and banks being enthusiastic, Liberians and

14. Harry H. Johnston, *Liberia, 1* (London, 1906), 340–74, 398–431.

their overseas supporters were excited. The Colonization Society saw a new day ahead and appealed for more emigrants. In 1890 it looked as though Liberia might recover from its financial distress.[15]

From the beginning of its nationhood Liberia had suffered from inadequate financing and inefficient management of its treasury. Revenues were small and the people refused to tax themselves. When the "bonus" from the rubber syndicate arrived in 1890, officials used some of it to buy a gunboat for customs enforcement, but most of the money went into private pockets as payment for "back salaries" of government officials. None, apparently, went to bondholders in Britain.[16]

One reason Liberia collected very little customs duties was that the Monrovia government had little control over the indigenous tribes. Failure to control the tribes also cost Liberia part of its territory. As originally settled, Liberia bordered only Sierra Leone to the northwest and native territory to the east, but once the European scramble began, the French claimed the eastern territory. The borders had never been explored and the exact extent of Liberia's domain was never clearly known. As a result, the British and the French began to "squeeze" Liberia, victim —along with the native Africans—of the Anglo-French competition. Because Liberia's claims to land were usually based on treaties with local chiefs, the Europeans frequently found it easy to challenge those pacts, offer greater rewards to the tribes, and negotiate new treaties that deprived Liberia of title. When Blyden visited the United

15. Blyden to Coppinger, 9 April 1890; C. T. O. King to Coppinger, 8 July, 20 October 1890; "Lord Raglan's Report," in ACS domestic letters received in May 1890; *Acts Passed by the Legislature of the Republic of Liberia in the Session of 1888–1889* (Monrovia, 1889); *Acts, 1889–1890* (Monrovia, 1890); *Acts, 1890–1891* (Monrovia, 1891); *African Repository, 66* (July 1890), 87 f.

16. Johnston, *Liberia, 1*:258–76; George W. Brown, *The Economic History of Liberia* (Washington, 1941), Section E.

States in 1889–90, the French were pressing Liberia for new boundaries, lines that would detach more land from the republic.[17]

Because of the pressure from its European neighbors, Liberia was eager to attract new settlers from the United States. Although the Liberian government maintained that the natives were Liberian citizens, neither the Americo-Liberians, the Europeans, nor the natives themselves gave much credence to the idea. The French, in particular, asserted that, because there were no settlements of "civilized" people in the hinterland, Liberia had no valid claim to the area. Even if the Liberian claim were allowed, the French argued that raids by Liberian natives against tribes in French territory created a local state of war, giving French troops the right to invade Liberian territory. Furthermore, the Liberian claim to certain inland areas was based on questionable explorations of the interior in 1869.[18] By 1890 the French had sent their own explorers into the region and were claiming the land for themselves.

Liberia, therefore, hoped to counter this pressure by settling newcomers from the United States in the interior. Such settlements would establish Monrovia's control over the hinterland, put "civilized" people in the way of French advance, and thus protect Liberia's territory. The Government also hoped that such concessions as the rubber monopoly and the railroad grant given to a Pennsylvania businessman would help hold the frontier. Liberian Secretary of State Ernest J. Barclay expressed great hopes for this latter venture. "Emigrants could be sent right through to

17. Johnston, *Liberia, 1*:241–57; Hanna A. Jones, "The Struggle for Political and Cultural Unification in Liberia, 1847–1930" (unpublished doctoral dissertation, Northwestern University 1962); George Peter Murdock, *Africa, Its Peoples and Their Culture History* (New York, 1959), pp. 64–100, 259–64.

18. Benjamin Anderson, *Narrative of a Journey to Musardu, Capital of the Western Mandingoes* (New York, 1870).

form [a] chain of posts . . . along the banks of the Niger," he wrote Coppinger. "The intervening territory would thus be saved from absorption by parties to the 'scramble' and secured as a future home for thousands in the United States who are now turning their eyes toward the land of their forefathers."[19] The Liberian legislature passed an act in 1890 "making provisions for the inducement, encouragement and maintenance of Negro Immigrants to the Republic of Liberia"; and part of the act provided for boundary surveys. Thus the pressures of imperialism and the inherent needs of Liberia helped create a receptive nation, eager for all the Americans the Colonization Society could send.[20] The flow of emigrants, however, was disappointingly small. Although the society received an increasing number of inquiries, it could send only about fifty people two or three times each year, and some of them would return to the United States.

The operations of the Colonization Society and the problems of Liberia affected each group of emigrants who traveled from the United States to Africa. A typical group sailed from New York in June 1890 aboard a small sailing bark owned by Yates and Porterfield, the only American merchants still trading directly with West Africa. On board were fifty-four people, half of them children. They came from seven different states. Monroe County in northeast Mississippi was home for half the group. It seems that one Isham Quinn had gone from Monroe County to Liberia in the spring of 1888 and the blacks around his home town of Amory had been excited about his prospects. As soon as Quinn left, a number of requests for information came to the Colonization Society; but it was not easy for people, especially poor people who had often been conned into various schemes by sharp operators or naïve dream-

19. Barclay to Coppinger, 25 March 1890.
20. *Acts, 1890–1891*, pp. 7–10.

ers, to give up their homes for Africa. To be sure of this move they wanted to hear directly from Quinn about Liberia. When the Society sent them application blanks and the latest issue of *African Repository*, Wallace Smith cautiously replied, "Mr. Isham Quinn is gone to Liberiy & he was to write as soon as he land in that Republic & let me know from ther so I will keep this blank & send it in as soon as ready to go."[21]

When Robert Wicker and his brother Thomas wrote to the society, they were concerned about money. The society had long since decided to give preference to applicants who could contribute something toward their passage, which would not only aid the society but would presumably eliminate applicants who were either not serious or improvident. "i have Got 7 in my family. pleas tell me how much money to the head will i have to send," Tom Wicker inquired. The Colonization Society estimated that it cost about $100 to send each adult to Liberia and support him for six months, but it accepted whatever the applicants would or could pay as evidence of good faith. For Wicker and the others from Monroe County the cost of moving was compounded because emigrants had to pay their own rail fare to New York. If they were not to arrive penniless in Africa, they would have to save a considerable amount —considerable for poor black farmers in Mississippi in the 1890s. Tom Wicker eventually sent six dollars to the society.[22]

Daniel Hill worried about how to dispose of his property. Although most black farmers in the South rented or sharecropped their farms, a few owned their own land, and Hill asked Coppinger if the Colonization Society would buy his 80-acre farm or lend him money against it.

21. W. W. Smith to Coppinger, 19 May, 2 June 1888.
22. T. W. Wicker to Coppinger, 26 September 1889, 4 January 1890.

The society declined, of course, because it had little money to tie up in real estate and even less to pay an administrator. In some areas of the South, when it became known that a man was going to Liberia, white bankers would give him almost nothing for his land, thereby forcing him to remain or to surrender his farm at a minimum price. But Hill was fortunate. He reported to Coppinger that "we have all sold out & now we are paying rent for hose room We are E. X. Spense."[23]

Disposing of property, arranging affairs, and saving money all took time and the group from Monroe County was not ready to go for almost two years after Quinn had departed. Perry Broadnax, meanwhile, went to work as a railroad laborer to earn enough money to pay for his family of nine. Nelson Coombs delayed going because his wife was ill. The reports from Quinn were encouraging—he seemed to be settled and happy in Liberia—and by January 1890, Coombs, Broadnax, Hill, Smith, and the Wicker brothers were ready to leave for a new country. They had contributed about a dollar each for thirty-seven people and had enough money to buy their rail tickets to New York. All that remained was for the Colonization Society to accept them for passage.[24]

Coppinger had kept account of the people from Monroe County and had watched their interest in Liberia grow and become definite. It had always been society policy, whenever possible, to send groups of neighbors to Liberia, for it was believed such groups would find it easier to work together in a new settlement in a new country. The six families from Mississippi, therefore, would be a good nucleus for a shipload of emigrants, and Secretary Cop-

23. D. Hill to Coppinger, 18 September 1889, 2 February 1890; Coppinger to Hill, 21 September 1889, 20 January 1890.
24. P. Broadnax to Coppinger, 17 October, 3 December 1889, 9 May 1890; N. Coombs to Coppinger, 16 March 1889.

pinger began in January to write to them about leaving in May.[25]

In addition to those from Monroe County many others wished to go to Liberia. The task of Coppinger and the Executive Committee was to select the most promising of the current applicants for passage. Many who had inquired did not actually apply, while many who applied could not raise enough money or courage to leave home. Some went to New York for the ship but settled permanently in the city. Strangely, perhaps, Coppinger—who did his best to select emigrants who would get to Africa and stay—seldom asked for reference letters; but most of the semiliterate blacks with whom he dealt would probably have had difficulty getting such letters from their white creditors. At any rate there usually seemed to be enough likely candidates to fill each ship, and so it was in 1890.

From Morrillton, Arkansas, Anthony Lipscomb had written Coppinger in August 1889: "There are a great many of us after would make a trip in the Spring and we would. Be thankful to have as much information about it as you are willing to give us we are a Nation of people with out much edgucation."[26] After receiving completed application forms for Lipscomb and his family (the "great many" decided to wait a while before going), Coppinger assured him that the executive committee would consider his request but warned that "thousands of people are applying and we can help only a few."[27] Lipscomb wrote earnestly and frequently of his desire to go to Liberia and his sincerity and importunity must have impressed the committee, for Coppinger soon wrote that the society planned

25. The *African Repository's* inside front cover for all issues in the late 1880s stated the society's policy on emigrants' contributions for passage. Coppinger to P. Broadnax, 9 January 1890; Coppinger to W. W. Smith, 4 February 1890; Coppinger to D. Hill, 8 February 1890.
26. A. M. Lipscomb to Coppinger, 20 August 1889.
27. Coppinger to Lipscomb, 27 November 1889.

to help him.[28] As soon as his crops were gathered, Lipscomb prepared to leave; his wife and five children closed their rented farm in Morrillton and the family moved to Little Rock in January. Lipscomb wrote Coppinger: "I hired for the perpose of cumulating all I can for to defray my expenses the wages are verry low here but they were nothing were I cam from." He promised to send every cent he could spare to the Colonization Society, but there is no record that he could spare anything.[29]

Henry Johnson came from Halifax, North Carolina, but he wrote to the society from New York City. He wanted to sail on the next ship to Liberia and to take a group of fifteen people, including his aged parents. Coppinger informed him that the society did not send people as old as Johnson's parents, but the others could apply and await the decision of the executive committee. The secretary did not inquire why Johnson had come to New York. Perhaps like others before him, Johnson had left home for the port city following a rumor that from New York there was free transportation to Africa.[30]

An exception to the rule of poverty-stricken blacks' applying for passage was Joseph James. James wanted to emigrate with his family, and he offered the society the magnificent sum of $85 toward expenses. Coppinger responded immediately and urged James to send the money, saying "I feel sure that the Executive Committee will aid you early in May next."[31] When James received this word, in late March, he quickly left his home in Monticello, Florida, and moved to New York. Coppinger regretted that James had moved to the expensive city so soon, but the latter replied: "Me & wife is anxious to go to libearia

28. Ibid., 27 February 1890.
29. Lipscomb to Coppinger, 7 January 1890.
30. H. J. Johnson to Coppinger, 17 January, 20 February, 20 March 1890.
31. Coppinger to J. J. James, 22 March 1890.

to help build up the country & I would reather be here a little too soon than to be a little too late. I mean to go thar & go to work."[32]

James was the only applicant who wrote about his motivations for leaving home and his hopes for living in Africa. A kind of nationalism, a desire to help the black republic thrive and be a credit to all blacks, seemed to push him. Most of the others had a hard time writing any kind of letter, and apparently did not think it necessary to inform the society about their inner desires; it was enough that they were eager to go. Although the conditions that affected them will never be exactly known, it can be inferred for the group in Monroe County that Quinn's success encouraged them to follow him to a free land and the promise of a new life. Also, Liberian propaganda from various sources must have lured them to Africa. For the would-be emigrants, however, it seems clear that the decline in their farm income, the background of increasing racial tension and violence, and the general conclusion that the United States was a white man's country combined to make them ready to emigrate.

In Washington, Coppinger and the executive committee believed that they had a good list of emigrants for the next ship. When the committee met with Dr. Blyden on January 30, it approved the applications of the people from Mississippi. By letter, Coppinger told them the expected sailing date was May, but he warned them not to leave for New York until they had received an "order for passage." Ships often left late, and experience had shown how expensive a long stay in the port could be. The committee looked for more applicants to add to the thirty-seven from Mississippi. By early April it had accepted Lipscomb, James, and Johnson. When Johnson informed Coppinger that instead of eleven there would be but four in his group,

32. J. J. James to Coppinger, 3 May 1890.

the ACS secretary looked for others to fill the ship, whose sailing date had been delayed until mid-June.[33]

As if by design, three black missionaries applied for passage and completed the emigrant list. From St. Paul, Minnesota, came Mary Louisa Bibbs and her husband Moses, recommended by a Baptist friend in the Pennsylvania Colonization Society. The letter came in early May, and although he usually maintained that the Colonization Society was not a missionary society, Coppinger accepted Mr. and Mrs. Bibbs. Bibbs was a laborer and his wife was experienced in "nursing and helping fallen women." Both could "talk and pray well."[34] From Boston, in late May, came the application of Sarah Gorham. A devout member of Bishop Turner's denomination, she enclosed recommendations from several people, including the eminent Reverend Phillips Brooks. Within two weeks Mrs. Gorham had received her travel orders and begun her journey to Africa to help save the natives.[35]

Fifty-four emigrants converged on New York City to meet the ship in June—the only ship that sailed between the United States and West Africa. Indeed, Yates and Porterfield, who had for many years transported the semi-annual migrations to Liberia, wrote to Coppinger in December 1889 that the company had all but decided to abandon trading with West Africa: "It has not paid to trade there for some time."[36] Part of the reason was that the company could not afford the extensive network of

33. ACS Executive Committee Journal (1886–1912), 30 January, 3 April, 1 May 1890; Coppinger to W. W. Smith, 4 February 1890; Coppinger to J. J. James, 1 April 1890; Coppinger to A. M. Lipscomb, 1 April 1890; Coppinger to H. J. Johnson, 16 April 1890.

34. M. Bibbs to Coppinger, 15 May 1890; W. W. McConnell to Coppinger, 15 May 1890; H. G. Guinness to Coppinger, 30 April 1890; Coppinger to H. C. Mabie, 19 May 1890.

35. S. E. Gorham to Coppinger, 21 May 1890; Coppinger to Gorham, 22, 29 May 1890.

36. Yates and Porterfield Company to Coppinger, late December 1889, quoted in Coppinger to C. T. O. King, 30 December 1889.

agents in Liberia it needed to draw away trade from European merchants. Another difficulty arose from the fact that a number of European-controlled ports in West Africa prohibited American ships from trading there. Yates and Porterfield carried what goods they could pick up in Liberia and Sierra Leone without local agents, and occasionally their ship would return via the West Indies to pick up extra cargo. Such was the case in May 1890, when the "Liberia" stopped at Jamaica, delaying her departure with the emigrants. The farmers from Mississippi and Arkansas were a pitiable sight when they finally stepped off the train and walked across Manhattan to the docks, but the others were better dressed and fed. The Bibbs and Mrs. Gorham arrived late but managed to get abroad before sailing, although part of Bibbs' luggage was left behind. They sailed for their new home on June 14.[37]

In Liberia, meanwhile, preparations were under way to receive the newcomers. The regular practice of the Liberian government was to give land to each settler who would agree to live on it. Each married man received 25 acres, each bachelor received 10. The Colonization Society, chiefly through its Monrovia agent, determined what part of Liberia would receive each cargo of immigrants. The five primary areas in which Americo-Liberians lived were Cape Palmas (the old Maryland colony), Greenville, Buchanan, Monrovia, and Cape Mount. Monrovia and its environs had by far the largest population of settlers and "civilized" natives, especially in the area along the Saint Paul River, which extended inland northeast of Monrovia and to which the fifty-four new immigrants was assigned.[38]

The agent for the Colonization Society in Liberia was

37. Yates and Porterfield Company to Coppinger, 8 May 1890; Robert Manson to Coppinger, 26 June 1890; Coppinger to C. T. O. King, 14 June 1890.
38. Coppinger to J. C. Horton, 19 May 1890.

Charles T. O. King. A member of a prominent Liberian family and a former mayor of Monrovia, King was one of the leading local businessmen. His duties for the society, in addition to arranging for the settlement of immigrants, consisted of managing the society's warehouse in Monrovia, disbursing money to the three or four school teachers supported by the society, and keeping the Washington office informed about conditions in Liberia. Because the country depended upon the Colonization Society for its ties to the United States and the American philanthropists who supported Liberian schools and churches, the agent's role was important for Liberia. And, of course, the position often led to more profitable connections. During the early months of 1890, while the prospective emigrants were concluding their affairs in the United States, King sailed to Britain to join Blyden in negotiating the new rubber concession with the British syndicate. In early July, King announced that he was to be the Liberian agent for the concessionaire, undoubtedly with a substantial increase in his annual income.[39]

While in London, King left the details of planning for the group that was due in July to a subagent. King had appointed a subagent, P. J. Flournoy, well in advance of the arrival date of the settlers. Following King's instructions, Flournoy prepared to settle the new group on land adjacent to "Louisiana" on the Saint Paul River, where it would begin a new community, called Fendall in honor of a long-time member of the Colonization Society. When July arrived, huts had been built and parcels of land set aside for the newcomers.[40]

After forty-one days at sea, the immigrant ship dropped anchor off Monrovia, and King, just returned from Britain

39. *African Repository, 66* (October 1890), 126 f.; C. T. O. King to Coppinger, 8 July 1890.
40. P. J. Flournoy to Coppinger, 22 March 1890; C. T. O. King to Coppinger, 8 July 1890.

with Liberia's "bonus" from the rubber concession, reported to Secretary Coppinger that all was in readiness. Despite the long trip and a delay in landing, the immigrants arrived "all in excellent health and spirits." Because of bad experiences with immigrants who had been corrupted by a stay in Monrovia, a city of about 2,500 souls, King arranged for most of the newcomers to be transported directly from the ship to Fendall. The immigrants, whom Coppinger described as "industrious lilies of the soil," arrived at last in the new homes for which they had worked and dreamed so long.[41]

One would like to know what they thought when they arrived. July was part of the rainy season, and it poured heavily during the trip upstream in Liberia's only steam launch. The wharf at Louisiana was hardly more than a clay bank and the rains had made it a fearful clay slide, from the river bank to the river's edge, along a slope of 40 or 50 feet. There were a few homes near the river but the farms extended several miles inland, and the group had to hike five or six miles, partly through flooded bogs. As the party tramped inland with its baggage, each family was assigned temporary quarters near established farms along the way. Most of the quarters were minimal—thatched native-style huts. In this rainy season of the year, it was little wonder that most newcomers caught fever. This was very much a pioneer country and it would take hardy people to make it into a modern nation.[42]

Within a few days King had sent the official surveyor, Benjamin K. Anderson, to Fendall to survey the farms, which thus far had been only lines on a map and thick bush on the land. In addition to laying out the farms Anderson

41. C. T. O. King to Coppinger, 28 July 1890; Coppinger to King, 13 June 1890.
42. B. K. Anderson to C. T. O. King, 24 September 1890 (enclosed in King to Coppinger, 14 November 1890).

had to ascertain that there were no prior claims to the land. On a number of occasions, old settlers had bought up the land around them in order to speculate on new-comers—they would buy the land cheaply, with bounty certificates awarded for military service. Because surveys were expensive and the land office was either corrupt or incompetent, bounty land claims were seldom surveyed or otherwise attached to the land. Immigrants at other settlements had cleared their land and planted coffee trees, only to have older settlers step forward with a shadowy land certificate and claim prior possession of the farm so laboriously made by the newcomers. Surveyor Anderson, convinced that subagent Flournoy had some such plot in mind, countered it by surveying the new farms well outside the established boundaries of the older farms.[43]

If the new immigrants were apprehensive about their location, there is no record of it. The land was relatively good—better in most respects than the riverfront lands. Its rolling hills were covered with thick underbrush, but native farmers, who cleared a small patch, had farmed it to exhaustion and then moved on, leaving enough open land for each family to begin building and planting immediately. Anderson reported that the new people were industrious and intelligent and had begun working as soon as their land was assigned; they had set about building temporary houses and planting food crops and coffee trees. Mr. Cole, a "civilized" native farmer, visited the homesteads frequently to give aid and advice. All the immigrants were reported "highly pleased with their respective assignments of land." When Flournoy took one of them to dine at Dr. Blyden's nearby home, the newcomer was reported to have said: "We are delighted, but if we don't like it we had better. There is no other country for the black man."[44]

43. Ibid.
44. Ibid.; Blyden to Coppinger, 1 September 1890.

It was not long, however, before dissatisfaction began. For one thing, the Bibbs' luggage, some 650 pounds of it, did not arrive until the next March. Mrs. Bibbs, who "talked and prayed well," also complained well; when the trunks finally arrived, she claimed she was overcharged for storage and shipping. Furthermore, a Mr. Osborn, who had drifted from settlement to settlement since arriving in Liberia several years earlier, came to Fendall to try his luck and sow his discontent. Also, agent King dismissed subagent Flournoy for trying to settle the newcomers on his own land, thereby extracting free labor. After his dismissal, Flournoy accused his successor and King of giving the new immigrants short rations. Because the Colonization Society had promised them free food for six months, it is understandable that the rations could become a subject of quarreling. The monthly dole was also subject to abuse: Mrs. Gorham, who came in the July ship but remained in Monrovia, drew her September rations, sold them, and sailed away to Sierra Leone.[45]

More serious was the defection of Mr. and Mrs. James. They tried farming at Fendall for three or four months, but by November Mrs. James had gone back to Monrovia, and her husband soon followed. When King heard that they were selling their possessions to finance their return to the United States, he withheld their fifth month's rations lest they sell them and leave. Although her husband accepted the decision and thanked King for all his help, Mrs. James threatened eternal vengeance and promised to destroy the Colonization Society when she returned to America. Dr. Blyden was not slow to observe that the James couple was "nearly white," and that "such people cling to the cities in America and wherever they go. They are

45. M. Bibbs to Coppinger, 4 January 1891; R. H. Jackson to Coppinger, 12 March 1891; P. J. Flournoy to Coppinger, 27 September 1890, 20 June 1891; C. T. O. King to Coppinger, 6 September 1890.

not in accord with nature. They are not fit for pioneer work and, moreover, they will never be satisfied to endure privations to build up a Negro state." Too many mulattoes, he concluded, had blighted the prospects for Fendall.[46] The Jameses arrived in New York the next February, having returned via Liverpool, and were added to the list of defectors who complained to the press and made the recruiting task of the society so difficult.[47]

Nevertheless, Fendall survived. One year later more colonists settled there and began their struggle with the land, the climate, and the fever. It was hardly paradise, but the immigrants from Mississippi, Arkansas, and elsewhere had their own homes and land. No white men destroyed their self-respect. Best of all there was hope—hope for solvency, hope for peace of mind, hope for the good life. If some complained, most were content. If some left, most stayed to build.

The experience of the 1890 emigrants was typical of many others in the history of the American Colonization Society. Such was the way Liberia had grown. The process was haphazard, but allowed dissatisfied Afro-Americans a safety valve for their unrest. If few actually emigrated, the symbolic fact of a black man's country encouraged many American blacks in the 1890s. Behind Liberia and its settlers stood the Colonization Society with its sometimes successful past, its aging membership, and its empty treasury. Even as it faced the new decade, the society optimistically planned to help Africa and America by advocating emigration.

46. Blyden to Coppinger, 9 November 1890, 1 May 1891.
47. C. T. O. King to Coppinger, 26 December 1890; Coppinger to King, 21 February 1891.

5

The American Colonization Society, II: The Crisis of 1892

The optimism of the American Colonization Society was rewarded in 1891 by a great increase of interest in Africa among Southern blacks. Arkansas and Oklahoma, in particular, gave birth to emigrations that drew national attention. These movements, though not great in size, reflected black unrest which engulfed the entire South. The places from which the emigrants departed were, paradoxically, places in which many other blacks were settling. The manner in which they learned of Liberia and left their homes was not unique, but the result of their exodus was singularly pathetic. And its impact on the Colonization Society was overwhelming.

Three strands formed this tangled story. The first involved people from the Indian Territory, later Oklahoma; the second involved blacks from Arkansas; the third involved the American Colonization Society. All these met in a snarled skein at New York City late in February 1892.

Oklahoma in the early 1890s was a major attraction for blacks and whites alike. Officially known as the Indian Territory because it had been designated a home for Indian tribes moved from eastern states, Oklahoma had long attracted land-hungry non-Indian settlers. In 1889 the federal government divided the region into the Indian Territory and the Oklahoma Territory and opened the latter to

homestead settlement. The rush to Oklahoma during the
early 1890s drew land-hungry people from great dis-
tances. The propaganda issued by railroads and townsite
speculators fed the imaginations of blacks in Arkansas
and throughout the South who wanted land and independence.

"Oklahoma fever" among blacks was greatly stimulated
by the attempts of some Afro-Americans to establish an
all-black state. Such a plan was proposed by Edwin P.
McCabe, a black politician from Kansas. McCabe, who
planned to settle a voting majority of blacks in each
electoral district of the newly opened territory, sought to
be appointed the first governor of Oklahoma. With Mc-
Cabe's propaganda feeding their own hunger for land and
political independence, thousands of blacks responded to
the appeals of Oklahoma boosters throughout the South.
Over 7,000 blacks entered the territory during the first
year of settlement. In some areas McCabe established all-
black towns where black people could, within limits,
govern themselves and avoid white persecution. The first
of these was Langston City, founded in 1890. Soon Mc-
Cabe was publishing the *Langston City Herald* and circulating it throughout the Southern states, creating great
excitement with its full-page maps of the proposed city
and its accounts of newly arrived settlers. "Oklahoma
Clubs" sprang up across the South and blacks continued
to move into the territory. Thus the African emigration
movement was only one of several resettlement schemes
that competed for the migrating black man.[1]

Even as black people poured into Oklahoma, other
blacks were living there among the Indians. Before the
Civil War the "Five Civilized Tribes" of Indians, who had

1. Mozell C. Hill, "The All-Negro Society in Oklahoma" (unpublished doctoral dissertation, University of Chicago, 1946), pp. 21–30.
Toby Symington, "The Negro Migration to Oklahoma, 1889–1910"
(unpublished paper in author's possession), pp. 23–28.

been transported from the Southeastern states to new homes west of Arkansas, owned African slaves. The lot of the slaves under the Indians had been easier than that of slaves owned by whites, for the Indians considered the ownership of slaves a status symbol rather than an economic factor in their society. As a result, relations between slave and master were easier, and some tribes allowed intermarriage and social equality. After the Civil War the Indians, who had sided with the Confederacy, lost their slaves and were forced to sign new treaties with the federal government. The treaties cut down their land allotment and imposed other burdens on the Indians. As a result, some Indians increasingly blamed their troubles on the blacks, over whom the war was fought. Nevertheless, one of the enforced treaty provisions required that the ex-slaves of the Indians be adopted into the tribes and given full rights. These pacts guaranteed the blacks land and citizenship. As a result, blacks from other parts of the South drifted into Indian Territory and settled among the freedmen already there, sharing their relatively good life.[2]

But Oklahoma was not a black paradise and life among the Indians was not all sweetness and light. Since Reconstruction, some of the tribes had grown increasingly resentful of the blacks in their midst, especially as more blacks from the South settled on tribal lands. In 1891 it was reported that "the Choctaws are driving the Negroes out of that Nation. Anyone employing a colored servant is subjected to a $50.00 fine."[3] Whatever racial prejudices the Indians may have had were reinforced by the many whites who joined the land rush. When the number of

2. Nathanael J. Washington, *Historical Development of the Negro in Oklahoma* (Tulsa, 1948), pp. 19–37 and passim. Woodson, *Negro Migration,* pp. 143–46.
3. *Lexington Leader,* 28 November 1891, quoted in Hill, "All-Negro Society in Oklahoma," p. 25.

black settlers began to alarm whites in the newly home-
steaded parts of the territory, blacks were ordered to
leave.[4] There were even disturbances in all-black Langston City, when whites tried to frighten the blacks away.[5]
As a result, some of the blacks who had just arrived in the
territory began thinking of going elsewhere. And Africa
had its advocates. Bishop Turner and the Colonization
Society were well known in the territory; and a few Oklahoma blacks had gone to Liberia and their reports on
Africa had been encouraging. Some of the dissatisfied
blacks therefore thought Africa was the answer to their
problems.[6]

This was particularly true in parts of the Cherokee nation. Around Muldrow and Redland, just west of Fort
Smith, Arkansas, there was a large settlement of blacks,
and because of the special privileges granted freedmen in
the tribes, most of them owned farms and raised cotton.
Aside from their land, however, their worldly possessions
were few. Prices for cotton were low, but generally the
blacks lived comfortably among the Cherokees. Many
had Indian wives and their children were treated as Indians. Nevertheless, as the influx of outsiders increased,
even the Cherokees began to turn against the blacks.[7]

Most of the blacks near Muldrow were long-time residents. Some, however, had drifted in only a few years before 1891, attracted by the good land. A Mr. Priestly was
one of the largest landowners among the blacks in the
neighborhood, having established a homestead and then,
by shrewd dealing, adding new land. Because of his large

4. *El Reno News,* 4 June 1891, quoted in Hill, "All-Negro Society
in Oklahoma," p. 26.

5. *Washington Post,* 19, 20 September 1891.

6. W. S. Dunn to Coppinger, 20 August 1890; Moses Cade to W. H.
Robert (of Denison, Texas), quoted in *African Repository, 66* (July
1890), 80–81.

7. J. P. Wilson to Coppinger, 26 July 1891; *New York Herald,* 22
February 1892; N. J. Washington, *Negro in Oklahoma,* pp. 27–34.

holdings, Priestly was a leader among the Muldrow blacks. Another leader was the Reverend Prentiss H. Hill, who farmed and preached at nearby Redland. By 1891 Hill had lived in the territory for three years. As a pastor in the A.M.E. church he was under the jurisdiction of Bishop Turner, and having come from Atlanta he was personally acquainted with the bishop and with his African dream.[8]

Letters from Muldrow and Redland inquiring about Liberia had trickled into the Colonization Society office for several years. From nearby Muskogee, several blacks had emigrated and sent back glowing accounts of their good life in Liberia, urging their friends to join them. The people in Hill's congregation excitedly read Bishop Turner's articles in the *Christian Recorder,* and the bishop himself regularly visited the territory, administering the churches and urging the blacks to emigrate. Even though the people were relatively secure on their own land, they became dissatisfied with their condition when they read the glories of Liberia as extolled in the Colonization Society's pamphlets and magazines. Toward the end of 1891, when Bishop Turner's letters from Africa were being published in church newspapers, the excitement for emigration from Muldrow approached that which accompanied the Oklahome land rush.[9]

Priestly, the large landholder, assumed leadership of the excited blacks. With the cooperation of Reverend Hill, he organized the Number One Club of Redland and began recruiting members. While distributing the leaflets and magazines of the Colonization Society, Priestly informed his followers that he was corresponding with the society to arrange transportation to Liberia. The propaganda, written and spoken, portrayed Liberia as a political, if not

8. *New York Herald,* 22 February 1892.

9. Ibid.; R. R. Wright, Jr., *Bishops,* p. 337. Cf. James Green to Coppinger, 28 February 1892.

physical, paradise on earth. The correspondence, Priestly said, promised there would be space on the society's next ship sailing, in March 1892.[10] The Number One Club moved into action early in 1892 and a transportation committee opened negotiations with railways. After lengthy correspondence, the Baltimore and Ohio Railroad agreed to take the club's members from Muldrow to New York for $18 for each adult, children for half fare. With rail transportation arranged and Liberia promised, the blacks around Redland and Muldrow generated tremendous excitement about emigration. Frequent meetings to hear progress reports from Priestly and Hill kept the tension growing. The word spread through the Cherokee nation and beyond. From MacAlister in the Choctaw nation came word that Club Number Two had been formed and would soon join Priestly's group in Africa.[11]

As March approached the revivalist fervor continued and the people prepared to leave. Since many of them owned their farms, it was necessary that they sell them before departing. With the influx of settlers from the East, land values were up, but in their enthusiasm the people from Redland sold for whatever they could get quickly. Farms valued at $1,500 went for $100; others sold for less; and some were entrusted to Priestly to sell. The emigrants behaved like adventists awaiting the end of the world. They sold or packed their few possessions and met at the railroad station in Muldrow, ready to head east toward the promised land. Priestly and Hill joined the twenty-five families camped by the tracks while other blacks watched with excitement and planned to follow this first contingent.[12]

On February 17, in plenty of time to reach New York

10. *New York Herald,* 22 February 1892.
11. Ibid.; J. Green to Coppinger, 28 February 1892.
12. *New York Herald,* 22 February 1892.

before the March sailing, the Number One Club boarded the train and started its journey. The atmosphere of camp-meeting ecstasy still pervaded the 78 adults and 122 children. Their baggage a pathetic collection of bedding, boxes, and bundles, and clothed in tatters—the men wearing soiled sombreros with beadwork decoration, the women in cheap calico gowns, the children without shoes —they headed for the midwinter North.[13] But Priestly, the chief leader of the club, left the party at Fort Smith, just 50 miles from home. He had been taken ill and wanted to return to Muldrow to die—or so he told the others. The evidence indicates, however, that Priestly was a fraud.

During the months preceding the exodus from Redland he had told his followers he was corresponding with the Colonization Society, but there was no such correspondence. Furthermore, according to Priestly the society had promised that the club could sail in March, but other blacks from Redland and Muldrow had written the society frequently and been informed by Coppinger that there was no room for them in 1892. What Priestly hoped to gain from this deception is not difficult to guess. With values rising and Priestly already holding a large tract of land, it is quite possible that he was the buyer or receiver for some of the farms sold by the departing emigrants. With African excitement still running high among the Cherokee blacks, his feigned illness would enable him to return home to acquire even more land.[14]

The emigrants on the train, blissfully ignorant of Priestly's subterfuges, were unaware that the Colonization Society was not expecting them in New York, as Reverend Hill took charge of the party. Despite almost losing some

13. Ibid.
14. Ibid., Cf. Z. Gibson to Coppinger, 21 January 1892; H. Buchanan to Coppinger, 4 February 1892; Coppinger to Buchanan, 8 September 1891.

of his inquisitive people at stops along the way where they detrained to look around, Hill, with the aid of a railway passenger agent, delivered them all safely to New York. The passenger agent, disconcerted by the naïve innocence of his charges, telegraphed ahead to warn the Colonization Society that 200 Cherokee blacks were about to arrive at the port. But the Colonization Society had no office in New York and there was no one to meet the emigrants when they stepped off the train. They wandered about lower Manhattan, cold, wet, and friendless in a strange city, and sheltered for the night at a cheap hotel. The next day they wandered again. Their bedraggled appearance and weeping children attracted first the curious, then the police, and finally the press. Through the good offices of a policeman, a Methodist mission agreed to provide temporary shelter and food; and newspapers spread the pathetic story of the emigrants.[15]

The emigrants at last began to wonder if they had been duped. In the cramped quarters of the mission spirits began to lag on their second day in the city, but Solomon Buckaloo, a venerable member of the group, recharged their faith in emigration to Africa. The *New York Sun* reported his sermon:

"Keep a trustin." I can't give you no bettah advice dan dat, brudders and sisters. . . . We is de Lord's chillen of Israel of de nineteenth centery; dere ain't no doubt at all about dat. . . . If we can't get to Liberia any oder way, de Lord he'll just open up a parf through the 'Lantic ocean jes' as he did for dem oder chillen through the Red Sea. The 'Lantic Ocean is a might big pond, they tells me, and Liberia it lies a heap ob a way oft, but de Lord's equal to the occasion, brudders; don't you go

15. *New York Herald,* 22 February 1892.

and be forgettin' dat. Liberia is so far that there ain't a
man in the party—not even Brother Dolphus Kindle,
and he's de best swimmer we'se got, as could swim
more'n half way dah. It's so long that none of us couldn't
walk it even if the parf through the sea was already
made. We ain't got no mules like the oder chillen had,
but that makes no difference, breddern. De days ob de
miracles ain't done yet, and if we get the road made for
us dere will be street car tracks goin' along wif it, suah
as you live. An' then, breddern, we won't have to wait
very long on de cornah before one of them jingle-bell
cabs ull be comin' along jest as dey do up on de avenue.
The conductor'll say, "All aboard for Liberia," and
we'll get on.[16]

The faith of Buckaloo's listeners was boosted, but unfortunately there was no path through the sea or trolley car
to Liberia. Instead, like Mr. Micawber, they just waited
for something to turn up.

Something did turn up—another group of unexpected
black emigrants.

Arkansas, like Oklahoma, was attracting Negro settlers
to its vacant lands in the 1890s. The parts of the state near
the Mississippi and Arkansas Rivers were rich cotton land
that had been partially settled before the Civil War. As in
other parts of the cotton belt, the owners of Arkansas plantations desperately needed labor and they advertised far
and wide for help. Blacks had drifted into the area during
Reconstruction, and part of the "exodus of 1878" from
Mississippi, Louisiana, and the Carolinas had settled
there.[17]

But the rich cotton land along the rivers was only part

16. *New York Sun*, 23 February 1892.
17. Rayford Logan, *Betrayal of the Negro*, p. 187.

of Arkansas; the rest was poorer land—hilly, rocky, and sparsely settled before the Civil War. After the passage of the Homestead Act in 1862, thousands of Southerners, black and white, arrived in the Arkansas hinterland to establish their claims to land, many of the latter poor people from the upland regions of Georgia, Alabama, Mississippi, and Tennessee.[18] These white settlers, who competed with blacks for the same land or lived on adjacent farms, brought with them their well-developed anti-black prejudices. Racial tension became even more severe than in the other Southern states, for in those states most poor whites lived in areas where there were few blacks. In the older states they opposed the blacks partly because the latter provided greater economic and political power for the large plantation owners. In Arkansas, they still distrusted and disliked blacks. But, despite the prejudice, the combined attraction of available land for homesteading and labor recruiters' soliciting workers for the cotton fields made the black population of the state continue to increase.

The economic ills that plagued blacks in the other Southern states seemed to be worse in Arkansas. High mortgage rates caused many homesteaders to lose their farms. Sharecropping predominated in the lowlands and crop-lien credit shackled sharecroppers and freeholders to the local merchants. "When the year comes around, we's mostly in debt," said one Arkansas black: "We jest makes enough to keep in debt."[19] A sharecropper complained:

We air in veary bad condishion here. . . . We will not know wherther to say we air citisen or a apprentice. we air already Bound men Now. Land Lords has got us Bound To Do Just as they Say or git off of his Land, and

18. Woodward, *Origins of the New South,* p. 108.
19. *New York Herald,* 23 February 1892.

we air Compeled to Do so. . . . and they say that it is not
entend from the begaining for a Dam negro to have.
But, a small peace of Land in the South, an it is only 6
feet by 4 wide 4 ft deep. . . . and no money becose he
has no bisness with money by no means whatever. an ef
He git Corn bread and fat meet and $12.00 twelve dol-
lars per year that is A plenty for ever head of A Negro.[20]

Falling prices, the curse of the single-crop system, also
made life in Arkansas difficult. Low cotton rates plagued
black and white farmers, and farmers' alliances got an
early start in the state. As usual, the black man suffered
most. "We air in sufering conditions and kneed help,"
wrote one man. "I don't want to stay here and make no
more 7 cts. & 4 cts cotton in the U.S. of America and I am
tired of paying 2 & 3 prices for goods and hogged out of
my labor."[21]

Race relations, never good in Arkansas since Reconstruction, took a turn for the worse in the 1890s. Like
other Southern states, Arkansas began passing Jim Crow
segregation laws. The Republican party, moreover, the
blacks' only political friend in the South, became "lily-
white," excluding colored people from its counsels.[22] Violence increased and lynchings became commonplace. The
general conditions of life for the black man were nearly
intolerable. "We don't feel safe here," wrote one black,
"because in the elections last September the whites threatened us with guns against voting. They drove 200 colored

20. F. M. Gilmore to Coppinger, 15 April 1891.
21. E. D. Davis to Coppinger, 14 February 1892. Cf. Woodward,
Origins of the New South, pp. 178–99.
22. Woodward, *Origins of the New South*, pp. 212, 219; John W.
Graves, "Negro Disfranchisement in Arkansas," *Arkansas Historical
Quarterly, 26* (Autumn 1967), 199–225; John W. Graves, "Drawing
the Color Line" (unpublished paper delivered at the 51st Annual Convention of the Association for the Study of Negro Life and History,
Greensboro, N.C., 13–17 October 1967).

from the polls with guns and even shot one man and his horse. The courts fail to take any notice of it."[23] Another complained: "We have a hard time to get along here Works hard and when we make our living ar robed it We are call everything by the White People But still they want our labor."[24]

Migration, not surprisingly, was a frequent topic of conversation for Arkansas blacks. To begin with, many of them were newcomers to Arkansas and were not bound to the state by the sentimental ties of home. They had come seeking independence and a fair deal from life, but when those things eluded them, some concluded that perhaps life could be peaceful only in a black nation. There were people in the state, furthermore, who praised Liberia as the place to go. "I am reading after Bishop Turner," wrote one man from Conway, "an he makes me each all over with gladness to heare of him." Colonization Society propaganda had a wide circulation. Emigrants who had left the area for Liberia in recent years wrote back in praise of Africa.[25]

A number of frauds added to the unrest by trying to capitalize on the widespread emigration sentiment. In the summer of 1890, for example, there were reports from various parts of the state that "Doctor Edward W. Blyden" was in the vicinity, agitating for African emigration and organizing local clubs. He was said to be collecting a dollar from each club member, supposedly to be used to defray the member's expense while he awaited the transport ship in New York. Inquiries poured into the ACS office from people who had been directed by "Blyden" to get further information about Liberia. Secretary Cop-

23. H. C. Cade to Coppinger, 20 November 1890.
24. B. T. Willis to Coppinger, 14 October 1890.
25. R. Barr to Coppinger, 11 March 1892; W. W. Yatt to Coppinger, 22 November 1890.

pinger assured the inquirers that the genuine Blyden was even then in Africa, that the society employed no Arkansas field representative, and that the man they had met was an imposter. Nevertheless, "Blyden" persisted, going so far as to ask the society to endorse his work. Even without such confirmation, he continued to agitate for African emigration, and considered it his sacred duty to dissuade migration-minded blacks from going to Oklahoma.[26]

Like most emigration frauds, "Blyden" was taking advantage of a mass sentiment rather than creating it. Emigration was in the Arkansas air. Economic troubles, crop failures, and low prices underlay the blacks' discontent. A sudden increase in lynchings late in 1891 caused a corresponding increase in emigration from the state. Oklahoma, of course, being adjacent to Arkansas, was a popular goal, but Liberia attracted those who no longer trusted any white Americans. "We wood like to Know Weather We Wood Be traded or bound over in Libery as we are in the U.S.," inquired one Arkansas black. "Are tha any White People over in Libery if there is none ar tha going there . . . [But] if it is a Negro country and We can Be free and speak our own mind & make our own laws then we are redy to come at once."[27] Some could not wait for accommodations to Liberia; they first moved from Arkansas to Oklahoma and from there continued asking the Colonization Society for help. In one month alone, March 1891, the society received fifty-nine requests from Arkansas blacks. Almost every letter claimed to be inquiring on

26. "Edward W. Blyden" (W. W. Meingault) to Coppinger, 12, 13 July, 13, 14 August 1891; Coppinger to "Blyden," 17 August 1891; C. D. Pillow to Coppinger, 26 July 1891; A. W. Diggs to Coppinger, 3 September 1891; J. W. Turner to Coppinger, 3 September 1891; G. W. Lowe to Coppinger, 26 August 1891. Coppinger answered more than thirty inquiries about "Blyden." Many inquirers reported that great numbers of people had joined and paid fees to "Blyden" clubs. Other fraudulent agents also operated in the state from time to time.

27. B. T. Willis to Coppinger, 14 October 1890.

behalf of numerous other blacks. Enrollment blanks with over 300 names accompanied some of the letters. In all parts of the state people had heard of Bishop Turner's dream and the society's operations.[28]

A number of them actually went to Africa, and Colonization Society ships increasingly carried Arkansas people. There were, as usual, some defectors who returned to defame Liberia. James Dargan, for one, tried to dampen the emigration boom. He had left with forty-five other blacks from Morrillton, Arkansas, in February 1891. When the ship landed, he had stepped ashore, and stayed for one hour, and then returned to Morrillton. Letters immediately poured into the society's office asking, first, if Dargan had indeed gone to Liberia, and second, if his morbid description of the place was true. Secretary Coppinger and his agent in Liberia solicited letters from contented settlers who praised their new homes and called Dargan a liar. Abner Downs of Morrillton told the society he was glad to hear that Dargan's stories were untrue for over a hundred blacks in the same area were ready to leave for Liberia. With the stimulation of Bishop Turner's eyewitness reports from Africa, the propaganda of the society, and the letters from successful emigrants, there was altogether too much emigration fire in Arkansas to permit one defector to quench it. The excitement continued to grow and throughout the state blacks banded together in emigration clubs and petitioned the Colonization Society for help.[29]

When it became known that a black family was plan-

28. *Indianapolis Freeman*, 12 March 1892. Cf., for example, the correspondence between W. H. King and Coppinger between 1890 and 1892. King started at Germantown, Arkansas, and moved to MacAlister, Oklahoma.

29. C. T. O. King to Coppinger, 24 March 1891; Coppinger to C. T. O. King, 14, 28 May 1891; A. Downs to Coppinger, 11, 23 May 1891; Coppinger to Downs, 11 June 1891; W. H. King to Coppinger,

ning to go to Africa, persecution by whites intensified. "We are in a deplorable condition," wrote one man. "Our lives are parshally threten for wanting to go to Africa."[30] One emigration club called itself simply the Young Men's Organization to disguise its intentions.[31] Others complained that white postmasters were destroying or returning all correspondence from the Colonization Society in order to discourage would-be emigrants.[32] As usual, they could get little from the sale of their property and stock, and long dry spells hurt cotton production as economic depression spread in the South. Bishop Turner's articles, letters, and sermons were sufficient in these circumstances to lure many Arkansas blacks to the promise of a better land where life was easier, where land was free, where no white men oppressed them. Despite false rumors that an emigration ship had sunk with 5,000 lives lost, the Arkansas excitement came near the boiling point late in 1891.[33]

Abner Downs was the leader of a Morrillton group that was ready to emigrate; the defamatory words of defector Dargan had little effect and many of the blacks in Downs' area were ready to leave immediately. Downs, who had had been writing to the society before the first Morrillton contingent had sailed in February 1891, was notified by Coppinger in November that the society would give passage to forty of Downs' group the following March. Excitement in Morrillton was so great that over 300 people beseiged Downs for places on the ship. Under Coppinger's direction he pared the list to the permitted number. The

8 May 1891; J. Dargan to Coppinger, 11 November 1890; E. W. Blyden to Coppinger, 1 May 1891.

30. *Indianapolis Freeman,* 12 March 1890; G. Johnson to Coppinger, 20 February 1892.

31. W. K. Fortson to Coppinger, 9 July 1890.

32. C. Dothard to Coppinger, 15 February 1892.

33. M. McLain to Coppinger, 21 April 1891.

enthusiastic blacks had to be urged repeatedly between November and March not to leave without express permission from the society. When the sailing date finally approached and the forty blacks from Morrillton were ready to leave, Downs informed Coppinger, without explaining why, that David Rivers would be in charge of the pilgrims, that Downs had decided to come later.[34]

Elsewhere in Arkansas the blacks grew impatient with the Colonization Society. Many had long been corresponding with Coppinger, and many paid small amounts of cash toward their passage and were ready to emigrate. During the winter of 1891–92, Coppinger repeatedly warned them not to come to New York and not to expect passage to Liberia for many months. There were already four families of stranded Arkansas blacks, would-be emigrants, in the city. The twenty-three people had come without permission in October but the ship was too crowded to take them. They had settled down in the port, awaiting the spring transportation belatedly promised by Coppinger.[35]

Back in Arkansas, other blacks were ready to leave without authorization. "Our people is stirred up about goin to Liberia. Some of them is talking of putting themselves up on the Society by going to New York where they expect to ship from," wrote a group leader from Menifee. "We have a great many here has made their applications and forward their moneys, It was received. Now they do not know what to do. Some are waiting the action of the Society and others is talking of resorting to other measures."[36]

Emigration excitement also grew in McCrory, Arkan-

34. Coppinger to A. Downs, 10, 19 November, 4, 11, 18 December 1891; Downs to Coppinger, 22 February 1892.
35. Coppinger to Yates and Porterfield Company, 1 October 1891; typed list of stranded would-be emigrants in ACS letters received in January 1892.
36. W. K. Fortson to Coppinger, 4 January 1892.

sas, where George Washington, a local black, described the situation: "Everyone talked about Africa as the place for us. Yo' see in these old countries everything is crowded up and folks can't make a living. How can a man live with cotton four cents a pound? So we jest thought we'd go to a new country where we could live smart and make more than a dollar a day." The Reverend Judge Thornton, farmer, preacher, and leader of the McCrory emigration club, credited Bishop Turner's writings with stirring up the excitement. At the bishop's suggestion, Thornton wrote to the Colonization Society and avidly read the *African Repository* with its information about Liberia. The club also pooled its pennies to buy a copy of Henry M. Stanley's *In Darkest Africa,* an account of explorations in the Congo country. With so much propaganda at hand, the group could hardly wait for Coppinger to grant them permission to leave home for the ship.[37]

Despite Coppinger's statement that the society could not accommodate them in 1892 and his warning that they should not come to New York, the McCrory club decided the time had come to emigrate. All who could afford to get to New York after selling their belongings gathered to hear Reverend Thornton, who had arranged with a railroad company to get his people to New York for $19.35 each. Many would come as soon as they could get the cash, but thirty-four people were ready to leave immediately. Therefore, according to Thornton, they "jess up and started."[38]

After traveling for several days in railway cars and living on bananas, the McCrory club reached Savannah, where they boarded a coastal steamer for New York. The ship's

37. *New York Herald,* 23 February 1892; *New York Times,* 23 February 1892.

38. Coppinger to C. Williams, 13 October 1891; *New York Times,* 23 February 1892; *New York Herald,* 23 February 1892.

steward took pity on the steerage passengers and provided them food. Although the trip was rough and the people had a difficult time, the voyage was soon over and the colonists stood on the dock in New York on February 22. Thornton expected Coppinger or another society official to meet them, but, like the Oklahoma contingent that had arrived two days before, they had come unannounced and unwanted.[39]

Thornton and the other men in the group stood dejectedly on the pier until someone directed them to the office of Charles F. Geyer, the manager of the Yates and Porterfield Company. Geyer, who coordinated the sailings of ACS emigrants and also served as secretary of the New York Colonization Society, was trying to work out a solution for the Oklahoma people when Thornton appeared. "We've done got here," he reported, and Geyer, to say the least, was dismayed. Counting the 23 holdovers from the October group, the 186 from Oklahoma, the 34 from McCrory, and the expected 40 "authorized" people from Morrillton, almost 300 blacks wanted to sail on the next voyage of the 50-passenger ship. Each group, furthermore, reported that there were others like them preparing to descend upon the society. Geyer telegraphed the secretary of the Colonization Society: "Can you not come tomorrow morning? Passengers here awaiting your decision."[40]

While waiting for the reply from the society, Judge Thornton and his followers returned to spend another night on the ship that had transported them from Savannah. Next day, as they filed ashore to find new accommodations, Thornton carried an old stable lantern on his arm. When asked whether he was a black Diogenes looking for an honest man, he replied that he thought the lamp would be

39. *New York Times,* 23 February 1892; *New York Herald,* 23 February 1892.
40. *New York Times,* 23 February 1892.

necessary in his hoped-for new home. After all, he noted, Africa was the dark continent.[41] Like the Oklahoma group, Thornton's followers from McCrory settled down in New York to wait for something to turn up.

Another factor in the confused emigration picture of February and March 1892 was the American Colonization Society itself; it was faced with a problem of conscience, public relations, and basic policy. First the Oklahoma group and then the Arkansas emigrants had said the society was in some way responsible for their being in New York, and in some way they expected it to transport them to Africa. With the press publicizing the stranded blacks and opponents of emigration attacking the society, the executive committee found it necessary to respond to this sudden publicity. But even before the situation arose, the society had been struck by an internal crisis that nearly paralyzed it. These various troubles brought the society to a major turning point in its long history.

The society's internal crisis had begun in September 1891 when President Latrobe had died. He had presided over the society, setting the tone of its operations and policies since 1853. The heart of those policies had been the emigration of blacks to alleviate the American racial problem and to encourage the Republic of Liberia. Because so many of the society's members had been active almost as long as Latrobe and were committed to the same policies, they looked for a new president from their ranks of long-time members. Because they sensed that the rising interest of American blacks and the opening of Africa heralded great promise for emigration, the members wanted a leader who could generate favorable public opinion in both the black and white communities and attract donations from the new class of wealthy philanthro-

41. Ibid.

pists. The man they chose to follow in the steps of Bushrod Washington, Henry Clay, and Latrobe was Bishop Henry C. Potter.

Bishop Potter was the energetic and influential leader of the Protestant Episcopal church in New York City. In 1889, at a commemoration of the centennial of George Washington's presidential inauguration, Potter had made a surprising speech calling for civic reform, a speech which attracted nationwide attention and was credited with paving the way for the later election of a reform city government in New York. Potter was also noted for planning and starting the Cathedral of Saint John the Divine, despite heavy opposition within and outside his church. A dynamic speaker and a socially progressive man, the bishop was well qualified to take public command of the Colonization Society in its hoped-for new departure of the 1890s. Furthermore, he was a long-time member of the society, having become in 1871 a lifetime director and in 1884 an honorary vice-president. Such a public figure with so long a devotion to the colonization cause, the members thought, would be ideal as the new president.[42]

Potter was elected president at the seventy-fifth annual meeting of the society in January 1892. Although the bishop had been asked to speak at the public services, he had not been told that he was being considered for the presidency, and had declined to speak because he was scheduled to be in Europe during the early months of the year. The society secured another prominent speaker, but

42. For Bishop Potter's interesting career see Dumas Malone, ed., *Dictionary of American Biography*, 15 (New York, 1935), 127–29; G. Hodges, *Henry Codman Potter* (New York, 1913); James Sheerin, *Henry Codman Potter* (New York, 1933); New York People's Institute, *A Memorial to Henry Codman Potter* (New York, 1909). None of these works mentions Potter's connections with colonization, but Booker T. Washington paid tribute to Potter's other activities in behalf of blacks in the last-named volume.

Potter was elected president in absentia and without his knowledge. A committee of three was designated to communicate with him in Europe and to call upon him as soon as he returned to New York.[43]

Meanwhile, Secretary Coppinger continued to run the day-to-day affairs of the society, including the arrangements for the emigrant ship that was to sail in March. But Coppinger, too, was growing old and soon after the election of Potter as president the secretary caught pneumonia. On February 11 he died, shortly after he had authorized the Negroes from Morrillton to proceed to New York in time for the March sailing to Liberia. Unfortunately, Coppinger had always handled the details of planning and embarkation and no one else in the organization knew how to take over. As embarkation time drew near, the scene was set for chaos.[44]

The executive committee tried to coordinate the March sailing from its Washington office. One of its members, Reginald Fendall, was made acting secretary, and a Washington educator, J. Ormond Wilson, was added to the committee. Fendall's first task was to discover which blacks were expected to sail; then he tried to learn how the details of embarkation had been arranged in the past. Urgent letters flowed between Fendall, various applicants for passage, and Yates and Porterfield in New York. No one was certain what would happen but all were determined that a shipload of emigrants would sail on schedule. Fendall notified the authorized group from Morrillton and the holdovers from October that they could sail in March. With the help of Geyer at Yates and Porterfield, he tried to administer the affair as Coppinger had done. Although it was a very difficult situation, Fendall, Geyer, and the

43. *Washington Post,* 18 January 1892; R. Fendall to S. E. Appleton, 5 May 1892.
44. *Washington Post,* 12 February 1892.

executive committee believed they had things under control.[45]

The first indication that all was not well came to the executive committee in Washington on February 22. From New York and Baltimore newspapers, Fendall and the others learned of the 200 destitute blacks from Oklahoma and McCrory who had just arrived in New York and were looking for help from the Colonization Society. In an emergency meeting, the committee decided to send Fendall and another committeeman to New York to investigate. Two thousand dollars was appropriated to help the emigrants get to Africa.[46]

Fendall had two tasks in New York: to help the would-be emigrants and to improve the public relations of the society. Upon investigation, he found that none of the people from Oklahoma or McCrory had received travel orders from Coppinger. Several of them, moreover, had letters explicitly telling them not to come to New York, that there was no room for them on the ship. Fendall was quite relieved, for he had suspected that the ailing Coppinger had authorized 300 people to sail on the ship that could carry no more than fifty.[47]

Satisfied that the Colonization Society was not at fault, Fendall found it easier to face the press. The New York newspapers had been skeptical, if not critical, of the society in their reports of the stranded emigrants. New York black leaders, furthermore, accused the society of trying to deport blacks, of sending them to misery and death in Liberia. Newspaper reporters were somewhat reassured by the appearance of responsible white men who painted the picture in brighter colors. Their editorials absolved the society from blame for the exodus to New York, but the news-

45. ACS Executive Committee Journal entries for February 1892; Yates and Porterfield Company to Fendall, 16, 17, 19 February 1892.
46. Fendall to A. W. Russell, 29 February 1892; ACS Executive Committee Journal, 29 February 1892.
47. Fendall to A. W. Russell, 29 February 1892.

papers were apprehensive when Fendall confirmed the reports that "African fever" was rampant in the South and Southwest. "There are a million," he said, "who want to emigrate." New Yorkers envisioned thousands of destitute refugees joining their charity rolls.[48]

The question, meanwhile, was what to do with the unauthorized emigrants. Should the society try to send them to Liberia, or back to the South, or do nothing? Fendall visited the people from McCrory and found them "very intelligent and of just the sort of stuff to make desirable emigrants." He did not bother to interview the Number One Club of Redland, having heard from several white people who had seen the group that the Oklahoma people were "a most undesirable class of people." The society, nevertheless, decided to try to send both groups to Africa.[49]

The plan of the colonizationists was to hold a large public meeting in New York to raise $18,000 for chartering a steamship to carry the blacks to their promised land. After discussing the matter with Fendall, some of the leading churchmen agreed to plan such a public meeting. Believing that things were once more under control, Fendall returned to Washington to report to the executive committee. In order to better prepare for the coming public meeting, he summoned the Reverend Ezekiel E. Smith, a black North Carolina educator and recent Minister to Liberia. Smith's firsthand knowledge of Liberia would help dispel some of the expected criticism.[50]

In New York, meanwhile, the black refugees still waited for help. The people from McCrory found rooms at a boarding house and the Oklahoma group stayed in its mission-house quarters. After newspapers stories told their plight, charitable people donated warm clothing and

48. *New York Herald,* 24 February 1892; *New York Evening Post,* 23 February 1892; Fendall to A. W. Russell, 29 February 1892.
49. Fendall to A. W. Russell, 29 February 1892.
50. Ibid.

money to help feed them. Some of the boys and young men even found temporary employment. As the days went by, however, some became discouraged and believed they had been defrauded. The picture was not brightened when the acting secretary, Fendall, declared that the society would have to honor its commitments to send the expected party from Morrillton on the March voyage and that the others would have to wait, if they went at all. To make matters worse, public health officials found that the living quarters in the basement of the mission were unsuited for continued occupancy and ordered that the Oklahoma people find other lodgings. Despite the hardships, George Washington—from Redland—continued to smile and tell reporters that, despite all, he was "gaw'n to 'Beria." Judge Thornton from McCrory kept a hopeful grip on his lantern.[51]

Besides the Colonization Society and the press, another group was interested in the fate of the stranded emigrants. Leaders of the Afro-American community in New York and elsewhere were shocked by the whole affair. Most were irrevocably opposed to emigration as a solution to the American racial problem and were bitterly critical of Bishop Turner and the Colonization Society. As soon as the first news stories about the refugees appeared, the New York blacks went into action.

Most active were two men from Bishop Turner's A.M.E. denomination: the Reverend W. B. Derrick, secretary of the church's Foreign Mission Society, and the Reverend Theodore Gould, pastor of the large Bethel A.M.E. church in Manhattan. Together with T. Thomas Fortune, the editor of the black *New York Age* and black affairs reporter for the *New York Sun,* they launched a campaign to remedy the plight of the emigrants. They met with leaders

51. *New York Sun,* 24 February 1892; *New York Times,* 26 February 1892; *New York Herald,* 28 February 1892.

of the Oklahoma contingent to talk them into renouncing Liberia and returning home where they could earn a living. According to Fortune's account in the *Sun,* Prentiss Hill, who had led the exiles to New York, admitted that they had all been mistaken and wanted to go back to the Cherokee nation. Reverend Derrick, meanwhile, sent a telegram to the A.M.E. officials in Arkansas and Oklahoma, ordering them to instruct the ministers throughout the area to tell their people not to start east with the intention of going to Liberia. Contrary to Hill's decision and Derrick's suggestion, however, the rank and file of the Oklahoma group, knowing the problems they had fled, agreed only to stay in New York and look for work. George Washington, moreover, persisted in his dream of a new home. "I'm gwine to 'Beria, foh I don't think I'll enjoy good yelth till I git dere."[52]

The New York blacks also held a public meeting to counter the emigration propaganda and to raise money to aid the exiles. Bishop Turner, the Colonization Society, and Liberia all came under heavy attack. "I wish I could take a bludgeon and smash the head of that American Colonization Society flat, oh so flat," cried Fortune, voicing the almost unanimous sentiment of the assembly. Among the speakers was T. McCants Stewart, who ten years earlier had been inspired by Turner and Blyden to spend two years in Liberia, after which he returned, disillusioned. His testimony was strong but less vitriolic. More than a hundred dollars was raised at the meeting. A similar gathering one week later provided more invective against emigration and more money for the refugees.[53]

The plans of the Colonization Society to hold its own public meeting ran into difficulty. Because one of the men

52. *New York Sun,* 24 February 1892; *New York Tribune,* 27 February 1892.
53. *New York Tribune,* 26 February 1892; *New York Sun,* 24 February 1892; *New York Herald,* 1 March 1892.

most interested in the project had to miss the planning
session, the whole project was postponed. The strong opposition of the local blacks and the reported desires of
some of the exiles to return home undoubtedly dampened
the will of some whites to aid the emigrants to Liberia.
Fendall, furthermore, discovered that the society and its
work were little known in New York. Because the old
leadership had failed to keep touch with the major philanthropists and churchmen, little support could be found
when the crisis came. Despite another hurried trip from
Washington by two venerable and prestigious executive
committeemen, the meeting failed to materialize. Fendall
longer for the presence of the new society president, Bishop
Potter, who would have been able to cope with the situation. But Potter, still in Europe and unaware of his election, was unable to help. The result was that the society
decided to ignore the unauthorized would-be emigrants,
hoping that when Potter returned in April enough money
could be found to send them to Liberia.[54]

In other parts of the United States, however, the story
of the emigration debacle in New York drew editorial
comments for several weeks. If the white press attacked
the Colonization Society for irresponsible propaganda,
the black press, knowing better who was more directly
culpable, attacked Bishop Turner. Fortune's *New York
Age* assailed the bishop openly, accusing him of being the
"agent, the hired man, the oiled advocate of a white man's
corporation, the American Colonization Society, that for
the past fifty years has thrived more or less on the gullibility of simple-minded, irresponsible Negroes."[55]

54. Fendall to A. W. Russell, 29 February 1892; ACS Executive
Committee Journal, 4 March 1892; *New York Herald,* 11 March, 1892.
55. *New York Age,* 5 March 1892, as quoted in the *Indianapolis
Freeman,* 12 March 1892. Although no copies of the *Age* are extant
for these years, the ACS scrapbooks contain clippings from the *Age*.

The nationally circulated *Indianapolis Freeman* re-printed the *Age's* attack and published an open letter to the bishop calling upon him to defend himself against the charges. "As a misdirected, though sincere enthusiast, everything would be overlooked and forgotten," commented the *Freeman*. "But as a bishop of your church, a leader of your people . . . let the impression once become established . . . that you . . . played the role of promoter for a money-making corporation . . . [and] your usefulness as a church savant will end [and] your race will proscribe you." The letter closed with an invitation for the bishop to use the paper's columns to set the record straight.[56]

Turner answered in his usual fashion, blunt and sarcastic, with a renewed assertion that the black man would never find equality in the United States. He denied, of course, the mercenary charge: his love for Africa and his spite for America came from the heart. He also attacked the New York blacks who had so roundly condemned him and the emigration movement. Instead of sending the refugees back into "their hells of existence," the New Yorkers should at least have tried to settle them in the North and get them jobs, Turner said. Again he charged that Northern blacks had no idea of the difficulties in the South. "If I were revengeful, I would flood the North with southern colored people so thick that they could scarcely turn around," the bishop wrote. "And if something is not done for the betterment of their condition, I will do it anyway." As for the people stranded in New York, Turner disclaimed all responsibility. But he added: "I thank God in my heart that they did go there. The nation has been sleeping over the Negro long enough. It is time for it to awake,

56. *Indianapolis Freeman,* 12 March 1892; cf. T. Thomas Fortune, "Will the Afro-American Return to Africa?" *A.M.E. Church Review, 8* (April 1892), 387–91.

and if you force me to put on my war paint, I will awaken it."[57]

On March 10, finally, the emigration ship sailed, loaded to the gunwales with blacks from Morrillton. The furor in the press had died down and the representatives of the Colonization Society had retreated to Washington. The stranded people from Oklahoma and McCrory had scattered throughout the New York area. Some of them wrote pathetic letters to the society pleading for help or for speedy transportation to Africa, neither of which was forthcoming. Some eventually arrived in Liberia at their own expense; others apparently managed to return to Oklahoma. Dr. John Miller, of the New Jersey Colonization Society, tried to raise money to help the McCrory people get to Africa, but he failed. Most of the refugees merged into the black community of New York. So far as the local public was concerned, the incident was forgotten.[58]

The Colonization Society, on the other hand, would never be the same. Although it had once been able to send to Liberia 300 emigrants at a time, it could no longer afford the expense. Although its officers and publicists had continually urged blacks to settle in Africa, the society was totally unprepared for the rapid increase in emigration interest that led to the crisis of 1892. Like an old wineskin full of new wine, the old institution was unable to contain the nationalistic ferment then working among Southern blacks. Although future would-be emigrants would have to look elsewhere for transportation to Liberia, the Colonization Society remained in existence for another twenty years, but like a broken wineskin, it took a different form, which little resembled the society before 1892.

57. H. M. Turner to *Indianapolis Freeman,* 26 March, 2 April 1892.
58. *New York Herald,* 11 March 1892; John Miller to Fendall, 22 March 1892; Fendall to Miller, 26 March 1892.

6

The American Colonization Society, III:
After 1892

The fiasco of the stranded emigrants and the crisis caused by the deaths of President Latrobe and Secretary Coppinger combined to bring the American Colonization Society to a major turning point. Similarly, the sudden change in personnel in the Society's two important offices made a review of policy both possible and necessary. Coppinger, in particular, had administered day-to-day affairs unassisted and his successors needed to decide how to carry on the work. Furthermore, it was not in the nature of the new president, Bishop Potter, to be satisfied with outworn social movements. In Liberia, distress on both the immigration and diplomatic fronts made it necessary for the society to reappraise its policy toward its African offspring. In the face of adverse publicity generated by the stranded blacks in New York, the society stopped sending emigrants while it installed its new officers, investigated the situation in Liberia, and decided upon new policies.

Bishop Potter, abroad at the time of his election and the New York incident, was to play an important part in trying to renovate the society; but when he was finally contacted in Europe for his advice on what to do about the stranded emigrants he disclaimed all responsibility. It seems that after the Colonization Society elected him in absentia, the specially appointed committee failed to notify him of his election. Only when the society came under public criticism did Potter learn of his new post. Because the press had prominently mentioned him as the head of the ACS, Potter had little choice but to accept the office, despite whatever doubts he may have had concerning the present usefulness of the organization.[1]

The executive committee, meanwhile, after canceling plans for an autumn shipment of emigrants, set about selecting a new secretary. Reginald Fendall, a Washington attorney and a member of the committee, agreed to serve temporarily but he insisted that a permanent secretary be named quickly.[2] The person most prominently mentioned for the post was Bishop Turner. Turner's most persistent supporter, Dr. John Miller of the New Jersey Colonization Society, pointed out to the executive committee that Turner's long and vocal advocacy of black emigration qualified him for the job. Miller thought the bishop would be able to persuade better-qualified blacks to go to Africa and generally would put more life into the society. Turner, however, declined the offer. The duties of his bishopric, he said, prohibited his assuming other full-time offices. When other committee members pleaded with him, Turner again declined, on the grounds that "his diseased liver" prohibited his spending much time in Africa, which he believed the new secretary should visit frequently. Unspoken but certainly present in Turner's mind was the criticism then being aimed at him by the *New York Age* and the *Indianapolis Freeman*. In defending himself against these attacks upon him as a mercenary emigrationist, the bishop necessarily declined the job.[3]

The executive committee then turned to its own mem-

1. R. Fendall to S. E. Appleton, 5 May 1892; H. C. Potter, "Address," *Liberia Bulletin,* 2 (February 1893), 11–18; ACS Executive Committee Journal, 16 November 1892.

2. ACS Executive Committee Journal, 15 February 1892.

3. Ibid., 17 March 1892; John Miller to Fendall, 22, 28 March 1892; H. M. Turner to J. Miller, 10 March 1892 (enclosed in Miller to Fendall, 22 March 1892); Fendall to Miller, 26 March 1892.

bers for the new secretary, and to James Ormond Wilson, who had only recently joined the committee. A retired educator, Wilson had long served as Superintendent of Public Schools in the District of Columbia. As a former president of the National Education Association, he brought to the society a great interest in Liberian education. Although he had been actively involved in the society's affairs for less than two months, he was nominated to assume the position held by Coppinger for over twenty-seven years. Wilson's appointment symbolized the shift that would subtly occur in the society's policies after 1892 as education supplanted emigration.[4]

The appointment of the permanent secretary and the redefinition of the society's policies took several months, however, and after the New York fiasco the executive committee had decided to take a close look at its affairs in Africa. Reports had for some time been reaching the society that all was not well in Liberia. Not only did returning emigrants criticize its settlement policy, even responsible Liberian officials wrote to Washington with complaints. Yates and Porterfield, the shipping firm; Benjamin Anderson, the surveyor; Hilary R. W. Johnson, ex-President of Liberia; and Bishop Turner, just returned from his visit to Africa, all complained about the incompetence and/or maliciousness of C. T. O. King, the agent for the society. Secretary Coppinger, however, had ignored the reports, choosing to believe that King did well and that the reported troubles had originated with misfit emigrants. But the executive committee, upon learning of the complaints, resolved to act.[5]

The Reverend Ezekiel E. Smith, who had served credi-

4. *Who Was Who in America, 1* (Chicago, 1943), 1362; Fendall to J. O. Wilson, 15 February 1892; Wilson to F. C. Latrobe, 7 April 1892.
5. ACS Executive Committee Journal, 4, 17 March 1892; Turner to J. Miller, 10 March 1892 (enclosed in Miller to Fendall, 22 March 1892); Wilson to J. Miller, 2 June 1892.

tably as United States Minister to Liberia and more recently as Colonization Society publicist, was summoned to
meet with the committee to discuss the stranded emigrants
in New York. By the time he arrived, the committee had
decided to replace agent King if Smith was willing to assume the task of settling the March emigrants in Liberia;
Smith agreed to serve for six months only. His assignment
was to find the best location for the newcomers, to take
charge of the society's property and affairs in Liberia, and
—especially—to report fully on the general situation,
recommending any necessary changes in emigrant settlement policy. Smith departed immediately for Africa. He
declined to go with the emigrants from Morrillton on the
sailing vessel, choosing rather to avoid black criticism (and
shipboard discomfort) by traveling on a steamship via
Liverpool.[6]

In settling the new immigrants, Smith learned in detail
of the mismanagement by King, who, it developed, never
visited the settlement sites. Sub-agents handled all the local
details and, at least in the Saint Paul's River area, chose
poor land or land they knew was owned by older residents.
Smith met people who had built houses and developed
farms as many as six times, only to be forced away by prior
owners. Despite this confusion over land titles King had
never attempted to set things right, and it was intimated
that he received payments from the older residents for getting the newcomers to clear and plant their land. To remedy
the situation Smith took representatives of the March contingent to various sites to choose their land, and titles were
investigated as thoroughly as possible before the people
were allowed to settle. Smith recommended that the same
procedure be followed for all subsequent settlers.[7]

6. Fendall to E. E. Smith, 26 February 1892; Fendall to G. W.
Samson, 18 March 1892; ACS Executive Committee Journal, 29
February, 4, 8 March 1892; E. E. Smith to Fendall, 5 March 1892.
7. Smith to Fendall, 26 April 1892, 3 May 1892; "Report of Rev.

Another defect in King's administration of land was the manner of surveying. King's method involved establishing just two corners of each long, narrow plot, and untutored settlers had difficulty understanding or determining the full boundaries of their land. Smith insisted that farms for the new party be compact and completely surveyed, a process that required a month's work by a large crew which cut the boundary lines through the dense bush. Complicating the situation, as usual, were the farms of natives who were guaranteed squatters' rights on public land. Benjamin Anderson eventually surveyed 685 acres, only 380 of which were to be occupied by the newcomers and the rest by native farmers. At least the March settlers had clear title and boundaries to their land, thus removing one of the major complaints of earlier emigrants.[8]

Smith also uncovered problems in the system that provided six months' rations for newcomers. He found that the group that had come in December, four months earlier, was nearly destitute. " 'I have not in my house,' says one, 'a mouthful of food of any description. My wife and five children are hungry, dying for something to eat. I am willing, anxious to work for their support. . . . But not a day's work have I been able to get since I've been here.' "[9] Smith fed the settlers from the supplies provided for the March arrivals and suspected that King had sold the food that was due the earlier group.

Joining Smith to investigate the living conditions of the recent settlers, Dr. J. H. Moore, Liberian Secretary of the Interior, reported that, despite their complaints, the newcomers were living well in houses "made of poles and matted, and while not altogether shut up fast, they are

E. E. Smith," *Liberia Bulletin, 1* (November 1892), 8–23.

8. Smith to Fendall, 26 April, 3, 14 May 1892; "Report of Benjamin K. Anderson," *Liberia Bulletin, 1* (November 1892), 25–30.

9. Smith to Fendall, 3 May 1892.

quite ahead of some of the emigrants' homes that have
been here longer." Moore's report concluded that the
settlers were probably as healthy as they had been in the
United States, although their spirits were dampened by
recurrent "ague" due to the "excess of ghastly effluvium
emanating from the earth." The health problem remained
a serious hindrance to successful homesteading in Liberia.
Agent Smith, however, had no new remedies to recommend.[10]

Smith had grievances not only with King but with the
Liberian populace in general. He was convinced that many
of the people made considerable profit from the helpless
and naïve American blacks. He found that, despite the
government's encouragement of immigration and the
eagerness of various towns to have new settlers, many of
the older residents resented the arrival of newcomers and
tried to dissuade them from staying after their money was
spent. Smith met with President Joseph J. Cheeseman and
together they decided to hold a public meeting to convince
the citizens of Monrovia of the urgent necessity that settlers
continue to come and that they be well received. The agent
and the President agreed that immigrants should come in
larger groups and be settled in townships farther in the
interior for their own health, for the benefit of the nation,
and to avoid further exploitation by the Liberians.[11]

One of the charges made by critics, especially by emigrants who returned to the United States, was that Liberia
condoned slavery, and the Colonization Society instructed
its agent to investigate this charge. Smith's ambiguous
report did not disprove the allegations. It was not denied
that there was slavery among some of the indigenous tribes,
although it was much more benign than that practiced in

10. *Liberia Gazette,* 8 September 1892.
11. "Report of Rev. E. E. Smith," pp. 8–23. Cf. George W. Brown,
The Economic History of Liberia (Washington, 1941), pp. 146–58.

the Americas. But even the Americo-Liberians, who themselves had been slaves, practiced a form of "apprenticeship" that bordered on involuntary servitude. Since the founding of the colony, native youngsters had been taken into families as servants and to learn "civilized ways." According to Smith, the parents of such youths, after discovering that the new Liberians would not buy their laborers, lured the youngsters back home in the correct belief that their Liberian masters would pay a "dash," or present, for their return. Some apprentices were legally indentured until age twenty-one, but some masters ignored the legal process and held their servants by force rather than hire farm labor by the day. If such practices constituted slavery, it was a domestic institution; the export of native forced labor had not yet begun. Smith's report, however bland, did little to eliminate criticism of Liberia and less to eliminate slavery.[12]

Agent Smith had been engaged for a six-month term, and upon his return to the United States in October the Colonization Society set about a painfully searching examination of its policies, both African and domestic. The executive committee met, at long last, with President Potter to assess the manifold problems of Liberia, the obligations of the society to its former colony, and the role of emigration in the American racial picture.

Bishop Potter was clear in his belief that although the old methods had been "outlawed by time," there was still an important task for the Colonization Society to perform. The "indiscriminate colonization" of the past had long since outlived its usefulness to either the United States or Africa, he said. The society had lost the confidence and interest of the American public, and the bishop's frank acknowledgment of this fact paved the way for policy

12. "Report of Rev. E. E. Smith," pp. 8–23.

renovation. The task to which the society was called in 1892, he said, was to help Liberia lay new foundations, build a new social order, and assume its proper leadership in awakening Africa. Having founded the nation and helped it through the years, the society had a moral raison d'être so long as Liberia needed aid. No longer would the society view its task as relief of the American racial problem. Henceforth, said Bishop Potter, the society would send not quantity but quality, not poor, ignorant peasants but talented, industrious Afro-Americans who would add to Liberia's stature.[13]

To Secretary Wilson, Treasurer Fendall, and Committeeman Thomas G. Addison went the task of adapting the society's practices to the policy advocated by Potter. Because the charter of the society made colonization its main task, the new leaders could not abandon emigration altogether. Nevertheless, they could choose the emigrants "with less reference to the pressing importunities of the applicants, and more regard to the wants of Liberia; in other words, the work of the Society may wisely be colonization for the sake of African civilization." Wilson, therefore, announced that the funds of the society were too limited to aid peasant emigrants. Furthermore, settlers with usable skills would be located in their new homes with more care and supervision for their own benefit as well as for the good of Liberia. In short, the new policy would control the emigration process more stringently than ever had been contemplated by Secretary Coppinger.[14]

Education was given new stress by the society. The state auxiliary colonization societies had long been supporting Liberia College, a struggling institution with only a hand-

13. ACS Executive Committee Journal, 17 October 1892; Wilson to C. E. Milnor, 21 October 1892; H. C. Potter, "Address," pp. 11–18.
14. "Future Work of the American Colonization Society," *Liberia Bulletin, 1* (November 1892), 4–8.

ful of students and faculty, but elementary and secondary
education were at a minimal level in the republic. Missionaries maintained some schools for natives, and in addition there was a small number of free public schools that
were attended primarily by Americo-Liberians. The new
policy of the society was to help the Liberian government
extend the system of public education rather than start
new private schools. Secretary Wilson, the career educator,
firmly believed that education was the solution to the problems of Liberia and he would see that schools received
money and attention.[15]

During the trouble with the stranded emigrants in New
York the ACS officials were astounded by the public's
ignorance and misinformation about Liberia and the society. Another element of its new departure, therefore, was
a public relations campaign. In order to get the kind of
qualified emigrants they sought and to stimulate donations,
the officers determined to create a new image of Liberia.
The first step in this process was the cessation of the
African Repository, with its news about the society and its
propaganda for emigration as a solution to the American
racial problem. In place of the old quarterly magazine, a
new semiannual *Liberia Bulletin* would contain reliable
information about Liberia, designed to show the attractiveness of that country to educated and enterprising blacks.
The first issue contained the statements of the society's new
policy, agent Smith's report, and excerpts from European
journals testifying to the grand future of Africa. In addition to the *Bulletin,* the society counted on the attractive
and energetic Bishop Potter to redeem the society from
obscurity (or infamy).[16]

More than ever before the new policy recognized the
necessity of commerce between the United States and Li-

15. Ibid.
16. Ibid.

beria. Despite the fact that Yates and Porterfield soon canceled their two annual sailings to Monrovia, the friends of
Liberia insisted that a profit was to be made in dealing with
Africa. Again citing the rapid growth of European shipping to West Africa, the society noted: "Direct steam communication is now the pressing need, and it is believed to
be practical from a commercial point of view. . . . Surely
here is a field for commerce worth the attention of commercial capitalists in the United States." With a lingering
note of prophecy, it concluded that when easy communication was established, more and more intelligent blacks
would leave the United States in the face of increasing oppression.[17]

Finally, the policymakers described the new overall
goal of the society "to be in the line of enabling and stimulating Liberia to depend less and less upon others and more
and more upon herself." Emigration, education, public
relations, and commerce all pointed toward the strengthening of the republic. Thus the society still viewed Liberia
as its child and itself as Liberia's chief contact with the
outside world. On the other hand—from the African side
—although Liberia was still sentimentally bound to the
United States, more and more it was being forced to act
as a sovereign nation. Its immediate neighbors were no
longer African tribes but European colonies. For income
it relied on trade with Europe, and its diplomatic problems originated in Paris, London, and Berlin rather than
in Washington. That the Colonization Society was willing
to stand beside Liberia was commendable, but the society
was less and less able to provide help.[18]

In the years that followed the crises and new departures
of 1892 the society worked conscientiously to strengthen

17. Ibid.
18. Ibid.

Liberia. Liberia's needs were great, however, and the help it needed from the society involved not only securing money and emigrants but working at public relations and diplomacy. The long-range problems of immigration, finances, and education notwithstanding, Liberia's most pressing immediate difficulty lay in the diplomatic realm. Her diplomatic problems, moveover, made her increasingly eager to receive Afro-American immigrants. The zeal with which Britain, Germany, and especially France devoured West African territory after 1876 was phenomenal. The basic spheres of influence and "protection" had been quickly established and by 1891 all that remained was for the European powers to settle the boundaries and other fine points of possession. With the exception of Sierra Leone to the northwest, all the land contingent to Liberia was claimed by France. When it suited her, France even claimed large portions of the Liberian coast by virtue of previous occupancy by French traders.[19] If all the claims had been granted, independent Liberia would surely have vanished from the map. In 1892 the French stepped up their pressure on Monrovia and President Cheeseman appealed to the Colonization Society to intercede with the United States government for aid in dealing with Paris.[20]

The Monrovia government, meanwhile, believing that the shortage of "civilized" Liberians in the hinterland regions stimulated French aggressions, was desperate to attract more American settlers. It asked the ACS whether anything could be done to secure the American government's aid in encouraging emigration. The ACS executive

19. "Why France Wants a Slice of Liberia," *Liberia Bulletin, 3* (November 1893), 78; "French Encroachments," ibid., *4* (February 1894), 6–8; "The Liberian Agreement with France," ibid., *5* (November 1894), 79–82; Johnston, *Liberia, 1:* 282 f.
20. E. W. Blyden to Coppinger, 17 March 1892; Wilson to G. W. Gibson, 2 May 1892.

committee thought, considering the fate of the recent
Butler bill, that chances were slight, especially in an American election year. The Liberian legislature then passed a
bill granting a $6,000 annuity in gold to the Colonization
Society to assist emigration and appointing and immigration agent to facilitate settlement. The purpose of the grant
was to aid the colonization of "our unoccupied Territory,
thereby avoiding international questions and disputes, as
regards our Sovereignty over certain portions of our Coast
as well as interior possessions."[21]

Liberia found 1892 an especially unfortunate year for
a crisis. First, the colonization society was greatly preoccupied with its own policies and personnel and the at-
tendant confusion and disorganization prevented it from
following Liberian affairs closely. The society's agent,
Ezekiel E. Smith, remained in Monrovia for only a few
months and was not primarily concerned with diplomatic
affairs. His replacement did not arrive until mid-1893.
Second, the American Minister to Liberia died in mid-
1892 and the post was left vacant until 1895, leaving the
United States without ambassadorial representation at a
time of trouble in West Africa. Third, after the death of
William Coppinger the Liberian government no longer had
a consul at Washington to present its case to American
officials. The weakened and uncertain society was the sole
communications link between Washington and Monrovia.

With little support from its closest friend, the United
States, and no success in getting help from Britain, Liberia
acceded to French pressure. Through its Paris consul, a
Belgian, the republic signed a treaty establishing new
boundaries with French territory. But because Liberian
government officials believed the consul had given away

21. *Acts, 1891–1892* (Monrovia, 1892), p. 15; Blyden to Coppinger,
17 March 1892; ACS Executive Committee Journal, 1 June 1892;
Blyden to Wilson, 16 June 1892.

too much, they delayed ratifying the treaty, and the Colonization Society decided to pressure Liberia's legislature to prevent ratification. The society hoped it could attract attention to the little nation's problems and generate public opinion that would be strong enough to push the United States into directly helping Liberia.[22]

When the ACS executive committee learned of the proposed treaty it immediately called upon President Grover Cleveland, who expressed interest in maintaining Liberia's independence and territorial integrity but made no promise of aid. The American Secretary of State, W. Q. Gresham, explained to Bishop Potter that, because Liberia's consul had freely signed the treaty, there was little the United States could do. On another tack, the society reminded the State Department that the territory in question had been purchased by the Maryland Colonization Society for the settlement of American blacks and that Liberia had no legal right to alienate the land. This appeal also was made in vain. Meanwhile the Liberian government had commissioned Bishop Turner, just returned from a second visit to Africa, to act as a Liberian consul in the United States. Turner called on Secretary Gresham and received assurances that the United States would continue to press for rejection of the treaty by the Liberian Senate.[23]

Despite verbal pressure from the Colonization Society and the United States State Department, and advice that neither Germany nor Britain was pleased with it, the Liberian Senate ratified the treaty in January 1894. After a year of struggle, the Colonization Society had shown its

22. *Liberia Bulletin, 4* (February 1894), 6–8, and *5* (November 1894), 79–82. G. W. Gibson to Wilson, 19 July 1893.

23. White House to Wilson, 6 May 1893; W. Q. Gresham to H. C. Potter, 24 June 1893; H. M. Turner to B. Sunderland, 16 June 1893; Gresham to B. Y. Payne (Acting U. S. Consul, Monrovia), 9 September 1893 (certified copy, dated 9 February 1901, in ACS letters received for February 1901); *Liberia Bulletin, 4* (February 1894), 6–8.

inability to do anything substantial to protect Liberia from the scramble for African territory.[24]

Despite its inability to help Liberia when help was needed most, the society continued to operate on the premise that the most important facets of its relationship with Liberia were emigration and education. Education was the particular interest of Secretary Wilson, who believed that, in the long run, basic education would do more to raise Liberia in the world than any other factor. Education, he reasoned, could not only make progressive men out of ignorant immigrants from America but could bring the indigenous tribesmen to "civilization" and into Liberian life. As a result Wilson planned to help the common schools as much as the limited financial resources of the society would allow.

The first and most important step in bolstering Liberian education was the appointment of Julius C. Stevens as the society's agent in Monrovia. Stevens, a black man, had been an educator and lawyer in North Carolina. In a time when increasing attention was being paid to the methods of elementary education, he had followed developments closely and had frequently lectured at teachers' institutes throughout the state. Wilson and the executive committee agreed that Stevens would be the ideal man to represent the society's new departure in Liberia.[25] Education rather than settlement of immigrants was to be Stevens's main task. He proved to be a competent educator and administrator. Shortly after his arrival he was granted citizenship and appointed Superintendent of Education for Liberia,

24. Horace Petit to H. C. Potter, 4 October 1893; "Relations of the United States Government to Liberia," *Liberia Bulletin, 4* (February 1894), 8–10; H. W. Grimes to A. M. Burton, 20 January 1894.

25. E. E. Smith to Wilson, 31 January 1893; J. C. Stevens to Wilson, 23, 27 January, 11, 21, 29 March 1893; Wilson to Stevens, 24 January 1893.

and he energetically visited the nation's schools. Through the Colonization Society he made new books available, and he began lecturing on pedagogy and teacher training. His intention was to start a normal institute but the idea was shelved when Stevens later was appointed Liberian Attorney-General.[26]

The society's stress on education certainly did no harm to Liberia, but education was a slow and costly process, and many other problems called for the limited resources of Liberia and the ACS. Liberia, notoriously poor and lacking in income, had to spend money for such things as military expeditions to suppress native revolts and gunboats to ward off smugglers. The society had never been wealthy enough to accomplish its manifold mission, and in the 1890s it was especially impecunious. The tasks of educating the American people to a sense of responsibility for Liberia and collecting donations for its work took much of the society's energy.

The ACS relied primarily on the *Liberia Bulletin* to inform the public about Liberia but, because its circulation was limited, additional methods were sought. Secretary Wilson arranged for several articles to be published in religious and opinion journals, and attempts were made to reconcile the black press, which was critical of the emigration plan and generally considered Liberia a failure. Even the general press was briefed about Liberia and the society's new policies.[27] A boon for the public relations program came in the form of a Congress on Africa held in conjunction with the World's Columbian Exposition in

26. Wilson to Stevens, 15 March 1893; Stevens to Wilson, 9 January, 27 August, 10 October 1894, 30 October, 10 November 1895, 29 December 1896, 6 October, 8 November 1897.

27. Wilson to J. H. T. McPherson, 11 October 1892; Wilson to R. W. Johnson, 27 October 1892; Wilson to H. M. Turner, 28 November 1892.

Chicago during the summer of 1893. Scientists, missionaries, educators, and Africans attended the congress and
presented over a hundred papers on various African topics.
Secretary Wilson, in a well-considered report, "Liberia as
a Factor in the Progress of the Negro Race," admitted
that the "Colonization Society made a serious mistake in
continuing to look upon Liberia as an asylum for an
ignorant, dependent class of Negroes in the United States."
Henceforth, he promised, all possible efforts would be
made to make and keep Liberia not just an idea but an active factor in improving Africa.[28] At the Columbian Exposition, Liberia had an exhibit of flora, fauna, and native
handicrafts, a display that attracted considerable attention
from the public and the press.[29] There is little evidence,
however, that any of this led to tangible aid for Liberia or
support for the society.

The ACS also tried again to raise interest in commercial
shipping between the United States and Liberia, still mystified as to why American merchants were slow to join the
rush for African wealth. Its appeals for government sub-
sidies went unheeded. When a shipping firm started service
between New York and booming South Africa, Secretary
Wilson tried in vain to get the ships to visit Monrovia. At
the annual meeting in 1895, Senator John T. Morgan of
Alabama recommended that the society get a new charter
as a transportation company, sell stock to blacks, and send
black-operated ships to trade with Liberia and the Congo
Free State. The Colonization Society, however, declined
to become a commercial organization or sell stock. The
result was that there was no direct or regular commercial

28. J. Ormond Wilson, "Liberia as a Factor in the Progress of the
Negro Race," *Liberia Bulletin, 3* (November 1893), 2–11; F. P. Noble,
"The Chicago Congress on Africa," *Our Day, 12* (October 1893),
284–91.
29. Correspondence between Wilson and A. B. King in the summer
of 1893.

shipping between the United States and West Africa until well into the twentieth century.[30]

If the new departure of the society after 1892 seemed to be foundering, part of the problem was its timing. During the 1890s race relations continued to deteriorate, and many who might earlier have helped the society either no longer cared about the blacks' welfare or contributed to black educational work in the South. Furthermore, President Grover Cleveland, less inclined than his predecessor to lead the nation on an expansionist course, tried not to become involved in foreign intrigues outside the hemisphere, and his attitude kept the federal government from being more active in the affairs of Liberia and the Congo.

But the most important reason for the society's difficulty was the economic depression that followed the panic of 1893. Nevertheless, President Potter and his associates were persistent in their attempts to raise new money for their cause. Soon after assuming the presidency, Bishop Potter arranged for the employment of Henry T. Buell of New York as general agent of the society, to raise money. He called upon the great philanthropists of the day, but in letter after letter he had to report that "times are not favorable for benevolent investment this month."[31] After a full year on the job, Buell had failed to raise a single dollar for the society. Nowhere could he find any interest in a movement and organization that, as far as the general public knew, had so long been dormant. Unless an entirely new organization could be founded and new ideas employed, there was little hope for income. Despite a few promises

30. H. C. Potter to Wilson, 22 October 1894; Wilson to Potter, 17 January 1895; Wilson to African Section, Liverpool Chamber of Commerce, 21 March 1893; *Washington Post,* 16, 17 January 1895; Norton and Son to Wilson, 1 June 1893.

31. Wilson to D. Bacon, 13 February 1893; H. C. Potter to H. T. Buell, 6 February 1893; C. Geyer to Wilson, 2 May 1893; Buell to Wilson, 27 May, 22 June, 1 July, 22 December 1893.

of money "when the economic situation improves," Buell
was singularly unsuccessful.[32]

Even Bishop Potter failed to arouse support for colonization. Buell arranged for Potter to speak to an open meeting in Boston to inform the public and the Massachusetts
Colonization Society about the new policies and the need
for funds for Liberia. Despite considerable publicity, the
meeting drew only a hundred people, and although the
bishop spoke eloquently for forty-five minutes, his audience was not impressed. After the address several blacks
in the audience stood up and denounced the society and
Liberia. One week later the black leaders in Boston met
to pass a resolution denouncing colonization, and the meeting drew more public notice than Potter's. The bishop's
efforts produced no money for the society and little interest
in Africa.[33] Although Buell continued his efforts until his
death in 1898, he never collected enough money for the
society to justify even his own salary. Shortage of money
and a lack of public enthusiasm after 1892 provided the
background for the society's new departure under Potter
and Wilson.[34]

While investigating conditions in Liberia and deciding
upon new policies, the executive committee postponed all
emigration plans after the fiasco of 1892. When the new
policy of sending only quality emigrants was formulated,
it meant a virtual stop to Colonization Society-sponsored
emigration. Almost immediately after Coppinger's death
the old practices ended and the society began returning

32. Buell to Wilson, 22 December 1893; Wilson to G. W. Gibson, 22
January 1894.
33. *Boston Herald*, 8, 13 February 1894; Buell to Wilson, 8 February
1894; J. C. Braman to Wilson, 9 February 1894; C. H. Adams to Wilson,
14, 16 June 1894.
34. Buell to Wilson, 17 December 1894, 19 January, 3 February
1895; Wilson to E. W. Blyden, 7 July 1897; H. C. Potter to Wilson, 18
January, 20 October 1898.

all contributions made toward individual emigrant passage.[35] Secretary Wilson answered all inquiries to the effect that the society was not at present able to assist emigrants. To the semiliterate blacks who were the most persistent inquirers he refused any comfort, advising them to stay home where friends could look out for them. Of the few people whose letters reflected intelligence and competence, he asked letters of reference, hoping to find about thirty qualified emigrants to send to Liberia in the spring of 1893.[36] Physicians, teachers, pastors, and intelligent farmers were wanted. Problems arose, however. Shipping and caring for the 1892 contingent had cost the society much more than planned and the new officers found their treasury unable to finance even a small group of thirty in 1893.[37]

Another complicating factor was the cancellation by Yates and Porterfield of its Liberia sailings. The Colonization Society had been the merchants' main support, and when the executive committee announced its new policy the merchants diverted their ships to other ports of call. Adult passage to Liberia by sailing vessel had cost about $100. Through correspondence with other companies, Wilson learned that the price of steamship accommodations to Liberia via Europe would be higher, especially because of the expense of waiting between ships at Liverpool or Hamburg. Steamship companies offered to take emigrants directly to Liberia for a guaranteed $15,000 each trip, but such a price was not feasible for the society.[38]

35. *Liberia Bulletin, 1* (November 1892), 4–8.
36. Ida Coppinger to T. Bowman, 26 March 1892; Wilson to H. M. Turner, 31 December 1892.
37. Wilson to J. Miller, 20 January 1893; Wilson to G. L. Patton, 2 December 1892; Wilson to C. McKane, 27 October 1892.
38. Wilson to J. Miller, 20 January 1893; Yates and Porterfield Company to Wilson, 16 September 1892; Elder, Dempster & Co. to Wilson, 22 October 1892; D. Bacon to Wilson, 1 November, 6 December 1892.

Secretary Wilson discovered, furthermore, that the "quality Negroes" he sought for Liberia were unwilling to leave the United States. As Bishop Turner's critics pointed out, the most talented blacks were needed at home and the wealthiest had little desire to leave their American businesses. Wilson sent only four persons via Liverpool steamer in 1893. One was a lady physician, two were missionaries, and the other was J. C. Stevens, the society's agent.[39]

Despite the restrictive emigration policies of the Colonization Society, letters of inquiry and applications continued to arrive at its offices. And as racial oppression increased, Bishop Turner stepped up his propaganda campaign. In the face of continuing evidence that large numbers of blacks in the South wanted to emigrate, the society did not lose hope for eventual large migrations, after Liberia had made more progress as a modern nation. In order to prepare for this expected day and to find better ways of settling emigrants on their arrival in Africa, the society joined the New York Colonization Society in sponsoring the work of Professor Orator F. Cook.

During the 1890s Professor Cook made several visits to Liberia in the interests of the New York Society, one of several groups with money to spend for Liberian education. The New York group, however, had reservations about its beneficiary, Liberia College, believing that the typical graduate produced by the college was of low caliber and full of useless, esoteric information. It was thought that the form of "industrial education" pioneered at Hampton Institute and later at Tuskegee Institute might be more suitable for Liberia. If it was true in the United States that "practical" education was more valid for blacks, the society reasoned that it certainly was true for an undeveloped nation like Liberia. Accordingly, Cook and two

39. *Liberia Bulletin, 4* (February 1894), 3.

assistants were hired to visit Liberia, investigate the college, and start an "industrial department" annex.[40]

During 1892 Cook visited Liberia twice and prepared a report for his backers. He confirmed the stories of weakness in the college, found that there was no room near its Monrovia location for the farm and industrial shop he wanted to start, and discovered a more suitable inland site for the farm. Critical of the way immigrants were settled in lowland areas and left there without instruction about farming, Cook proposed a settlement farm, to be attached to his rural institute, where newcomers could acclimate themselves safely and learn how to grow Liberian crops.[41]

Cook's report, published in October 1892, confirmed many suspicions of the American Colonization Society about the mismanagement of its settlers in Liberia. As a result, part of the society's "new departure" was an endorsement of Cook's projects. With its new stress on education, the society was interested in the "practical" learning he recommended. Because of financial problems, however, Secretary Wilson and his colleagues could not underwrite the professor's next few trips to Africa, but in 1895, when Cook started putting his plans into action, the society agreed to back him with money. It would pay half the expense of surveying the settlement and the farm at Mount Coffee and of building the new access road. In return the society would receive the rights to land bordering on the road and the use of the farm as a receiving center for new settlers.[42]

40. *African Repository, 67* (July 1891), 91–92.
41. *Report of Prof. O. F. Cook to the Board of Managers of the New York State Colonization Society, upon the Present Needs of Liberia* (NewYork, 1892), pp. 9–11 and passim.
42. Ibid.; "Remarks of Prof. O. F. Cook," *Liberia Bulletin, 2* (February 1893), 19–24; Orator F. Cook, *Third Report to the Board of Managers of the New York State Colonization Society* (New York, 1896), pp. 81–100; ACS Executive Committee Journal, 12 November, 5 December

The Mount Coffee project consumed a considerable amount of money and time but eventually came to naught. The road was built, the farm laid out, and a girl's school was started, but Professor Cook, who became president of the ailing Liberia College, was unable to get enough cooperation or money from the United States or Liberia to keep the college operating, Development of the farm and the industrial school were out of the question. By 1899 Cook had resigned and had left Liberia for good. The Colonization Society had spent its money in the hope of improving conditions for newcomers but the net result was a lack of funds for sending emigrants. Like so many other projects in Liberia, Cook's plans in the 1890s consumed good money after bad.[43]

Thus, the most important, though negative, result of the Colonization Society's policies after the crises of 1892 was a cessation of aid to emigration. The policy of selecting only highly qualified applicants, of concentrating on education, of spending money on facilities for future emigrants, and above all the shortage of operating funds, prevented the society from sending more than three or four emigrants to Liberia per year. Thus, during the mid-1890s, when racial and economic crises within the United States made many blacks want to emigrate and when diplomatic crises in Liberia made that republic cry out for more American settlers, the society virtually withdrew from colonization activity. Although its *Liberia Bulletin* continued to provide information and stimulation to dissatis-

1895; O. F. Cook to Wilson, 10, 16 February, 6, 13, 17 March 1893, 30 October, 5 November 1895; Wilson to Cook, 28 November 1895.

43. Gardner W. Allen, *The Trustees of Donations for Education in Liberia* (Boston, 1923), pp. 64–74; Wilson to Cook, 26 January 1897; Wilson to C. T. Geyer, 19 January 1898; Mrs. J. E. D. Sharp to Wilson, 14 December 1899; ACS Executive Committee Journal, 19 March, 2 May, 10 October 1896, 15 May 1897, 12, 24 February 1898; Wilson to G. W. Gibson, 16 November 1909.

fied Afro-Americans well into the twentieth century, and its office served as a clearing house for information about Liberia and independent emigration schemes in the United States, the society could only dream of better times and more money. It did not finally surrender its avowed mission of repatriating blacks until 1910, but after 1892 the task of providing transportation and new homes fell on the blacks themselves.[44]

44. *Liberia Bulletin, 16* (February 1900), 28.

7

Benjamin Gaston and the Congo Company

The American Colonization Society, established and venerable as it may have been, was not the only organization in the emigration movement. The long tradition of attempts by blacks to help themselves get to Africa had not disappeared. Independent movements sprang up frequently during the 1890s—some intended as profit-making schemes, others as cooperative ventures. Even before the decline of the Colonization Society after 1892, an independent emigration scheme was under way. It was fed not only by Bishop Turner's propaganda but by the publicity for the Congo Free State. The United States and Congo National Emigration Company organized strong emigration interest in the South, especially among Georgia blacks. In 1894 it actually transported a colony to Africa.

Without attracting attention, the Congo Company, as it became known, was chartered in 1886 on the initiative of three white men from Baltimore who appeared in Washington with an idea for colonizing blacks in the Congo Free State. Their leader, Martin H. K. Paulsen, claimed to be a representative of the Danish government and used that alleged connection to impress his colored hearers. He talked with black clergymen in Washington and held several open meetings at which he praised the wonders of Africa. In a short time he developed enough interest to incorporate the Congo Company, with a Washington black man as president and white men as secretary and treasurer. To finance the company, Paulsen sold stock to all who would buy. Blacks, eager to share either the profits of the company or the joys of Africa, bought most of the lovely green certificates.[1]

Paulsen, however, was not counting on stock sales for capital. He and his friends had discovered a clause in a long-neglected federal law, dating from 1862, which declared that one-fourth of all the proceeds from the sale of abandoned lands in the rebellious Southern states must revert to the federal government to be used in aiding black emigration from the United States. Federal officials, including Abraham Lincoln, had seriously considered removing all freed slaves from the nation. Colonization experiments in the Caribbean proved disastrous, however, and after 1863 the appropriation for emigration had never been made. W. B. Matchett, the attorney for the Congo Company, asked the comptroller of the Treasury for an opinion as to whether the money, which Matchett estimated to be $500,000, was available to the company. The comptroller replied that it was potentially available but that a congressional act of appropriation would be necessary before the money could be transferred.[2]

This development disillusioned the white entrepreneurs of the scheme. It is probable, in retrospect, that Paulsen, Matchett, and their friends hoped to gain control of a large, profitable subsidy by transporting blacks to Africa. When it appeared that the appropriation would have to run the gamut of a congressional debate, the white men abandoned the company to its black stockholders. The colored owners assumed control, still believing in the possi-

1. *Washington Post,* 21 January 1891; "Prospectus of the United States and Congo National Emigration Steamship Company," in W. B. Matchett to Wilson, 23 January 1893.

2. Matchett to Comptroller M. J. Durham, 29 July 1886, and Durham to Matchett, 3 August 1886, both quoted in the prospectus. U. S. Congress, Act of June 7, 1862, Statutes at Large 12.

bilities of sending people to Africa. They, too, wanted to
make a profit, if possible, but emigration was more important.[3]

After blacks had assumed control of the Congo Company, the Reverend Benjamin Gaston appeared in their
office. Gaston, a Baptist preacher, had emigrated from
Georgia to Liberia in 1866, and twenty years later he
returned to the United States, claiming to have grown
wealthy in Africa. His avowed mission was to persuade
other American blacks to go to Africa. He had informal
authorization from Liberia's President, J. J. Cheeseman,
to encourage emigration. When he reached Washington,
Gaston learned of the Congo Company and offered his
services, including the invitation of the Liberian government. The company accepted the proposition, changing
its promised land from the Congo to Liberia but retaining
the same name. Designated general agent of the company,
Gaston began traveling in the Gulf states, where his intelligent, pious bearing and his elegant African propaganda
laid the groundwork for the company's activity.[4]

For two or three years the Congo Company did little
more than keep Gaston and other agents touring the South.
When, in 1889, Gaston reported a growing African excitement among Southern blacks, officers of the company
decided to pursue the matter of the federal subsidy again.
The company treasurer, William O'Brien, asked Robert
S. Tharin, who worked in the Treasury, to become the
firm's legal adviser. In a flowery speech of acceptance
Tharin promised to devise a plan for getting both money
and emigrants.[5] Tharin renewed the request for federal
aid and arranged to have a bill introduced in Congress

3. *Washington Post,* 21 November 1889, 22 January 1891.
4. *Washington Star,* 21 November 1889, 24 November 1893; *Atlanta Constitution,* 23 August 1891; J. J. Cheeseman to A. B. King, 10
August 1893 (enclosed in A. B. King to Wilson, 16 October 1893).
5. *Washington Post,* 21, 22 January 1891.

that would appropriate the funds the earlier company officers had despaired of getting. The bill, if enacted, would provide $100 for each black adult who wished to emigrate; annual payments to the Congo Company could not exceed a million dollars, and the company would not become eligible for the subsidy until it could show that it controlled a ship that could make monthly voyages carrying emigrants and mail.[6]

To finance the steamship, Tharin decided to do more than just sell stock; he devised a system whereby blacks who purchased tickets for one dollar, plus a postage stamp, could become "preferred passengers" when the steamship started plying the Atlantic. Apparently such passengers were "preferred" only to the extent of being early emigrants and contributing to the capital of the company. To sell tickets, recruit emigrants, and spread the grandiose plans of the company, agents toured the Southern states.[7] Some of the company managers, however, had opposed the ticket scheme, thinking the plan and the circular that publicized it would be misinterpreted by simple farmers, who might infer that their dollar ticket would pay their entire fare to Africa. Indeed, the circular contained a confusing caveat: "Unless a subsidy shall be appropriated by Congress to aid the exodus, we reserve the right, as to other applicants, to raise the price of passage." Despite objections, the company adopted the plan.[8]

Unfortunately for the promoters, the subsidy bill had little chance for passage. It was introduced in the House of Representatives at the same time that Butler's bill appeared in the Senate. Referred to the House Committee on the Judiciary, it was never seen again, but the Congo Com-

6. *African Repository, 66* (April 1890), 52.

7. *Washington Post,* 21, 22 January 1891.

8. "Circular No. 1" of the United States and Congo National Emigration Steamship Company (enclosed in W. B. Matchett to Wilson, 23 January 1893); *Washington Post,* 21, 22 January 1891.

pany still hoped for its success. With considerable zeal its
agents advertised the plans for going to Africa.[9]

One of the agents did his work particularly well if not
too wisely. The Reverend Thomas L. Peak, of Marietta,
Georgia, represented the company in Georgia, Alabama,
and Tennessee. Especially in Georgia, where Bishop Turner had long proclaimed the gospel of race salvation by
emigration, Peak found ready listeners. Speaking from
town to town and from church to church, he distributed
"Circular No. 1" with its offer of "preferred passage" for
a dollar and two cents. Peak spoke in the nationalist terms
used by Turner: Africa was the place where blacks could
enjoy absolute freedom from the rule of white men. He
delivered the word that the Liberian government had
promised land allotments to all bona fide settlers, ten acres
to single men, twenty-five to heads of families. He explained, furthermore, that Congo Company emigrants
would be settled in the interior highlands to avoid the
coastal fevers.[10]

As popular interest in his project grew, Peak began to
embellish the plans of the company with his own dreams.
He interpreted the hoped-for subsidy as a personal gift to
be given each emigrant. He began to paint Liberia as such
a tropical paradise that even the most backward peasant
farmer should have suspected Peak's veracity. When challenged by educated blacks and whites who had at first
ignored the movement, Peak pulled his followers away into
secret meetings and swore them to silence when questioned
by outsiders. When their faith began to lag he told them a
ship had been chartered and would sail from Savannah in
November 1890.[11]

9. *African Repository, 66* (April 1890), 52.
10. *Atlanta Constitution,* 20 January 1891; *Washington Post,* 20
January 1891.
11. *Atlanta Constitution,* 20 January 1891; *Washington Post,* 20 January 1891.

When November came and went, the people who had paid their dollars and many others who wanted to emigrate began to grow restless. Peak postponed the date of his imaginary sailing as long as possible, but just after New Year's, 1891, the people began selling their possessions and preparing to move to Savannah. In hamlets scattered through Georgia and beyond, black families packed their belongings and started moving toward Atlanta where they supposed they would wait for final orders to go to Savannah and Liberia. In Waco, Georgia, for example, Peak had attracted a considerable following. The would-be emigrants elected local leaders who urged them, when January arrived, to pack their belongings and be ready to travel. So eager were they that about 200 people pitched camp at the railroad station to await the final word. Railway men tried in vain to reason with the group and get them to return home. Agents of plantation owners in Mississippi, Louisiana, and Texas tried to woo the emigrants to the West, where labor was desperately needed, but the group hooted down the recruiters. "We have started to Africa where we can have freedom, and we are bound to go." In exasperation, the railway officials put the people on a train and sent them to Atlanta.[12]

After they arrived in Atlanta they sat expectantly in the railway station, presenting a motley picture to passersby. They might have been on a picnic were it not for the cold weather and the serious look in their eyes. When reporters asked who they were and where they were bound, the migrants were uncommunicative. They refused to tell how many were in the group, whether they had tickets for Savannah, and if they had come from Waco. After many hours of sitting in the station, word came that they should go to Haynes Street, where other emigrants for Africa waited. They picked up their bags, bundles, and babies and

12. *Atlanta Constitution,* 20 January 1891.

marched out to vacant houses that had been opened for them.[13] Fifteen hundred people from the hinterland joined over a thousand Atlanta blacks who also were waiting to go to Africa. The newcomers were sheltered in two colored neighborhoods while the entire contingent awaited word that the ship had arrived in Savannah. They held nightly meetings to sing, pray, and listen to speeches.

During mid-January, each day brought more people to the Atlanta rendezvous. Despite criticism from recognized black leaders and amused ridicule from the white press, the migrants refused to believe they had been swindled or duped. Some doubt, nevertheless, existed as to the good faith of Peak and the Congo Company, and a number of would-be emigrants had not paid Peak for tickets but held their money until they arrived in Atlanta. The African Band, as they dubbed themselves, asked one of their number, Orange Davis, a trusted Atlanta grocer, to hold their money and investigate the Congo Company. Davis traveled to Washington, the headquarters of the company, with a reported $1,485 to be paid for additional tickets.[14]

Company officials, including Peak, had been negotiating for a steamship for some time before Davis arrived. In the previous October, Edwin H. Johnson, a Congo Company board member, had called on George W. Moss, the Washington representative of several shipping lines, and asked about the possibility and the cost of chartering a steamship to carry about 1,500 colored people from Savannah to Liberia. Moss communicated with two New York steamship companies, who responded with interest, but Johnson did not return to hear the proposal. Then, in December, Peak and Treasurer O'Brien visited Moss; they explained

13. Ibid., 18 January 1891.
14. Ibid., 17, 20 January 1891.

that Johnson had not been authorized to negotiate for the company but that they were now ready to pursue the matter.[15] Moss, having received no response from Johnson or the Congo Company after investigating shipping arrangements in October, was reluctant to open the negotiations again. Nevertheless, he wrote to the shippers in New York and got a firm bid of $30,000 to carry up to 1,200 passengers to Liberia, which meant that each emigrant would have to pay about $30—considerably more than the dollar apiece the company had collected. Peak and O'Brien urged Moss to inquire of other shippers for a lower rate and explained that they wanted the information in a form that could be presented to Congress to gain their subsidy. Moss agreed to do so but asked for a $500 deposit as evidence of good faith.[16]

When Orange Davis arrived in Washington with ready cash, Peak and O'Brien did not have enough tickets on hand to meet his order. While waiting for the tickets to be printed, they introduced Davis to Moss. According to Moss, Davis deposited $500 with him and gave the balance of the money to the Congo Company officers. With a receipt from Moss, tickets from the company, and hope for a quick sailing, Davis returned home to announce success to his constituents.[17]

In Atlanta, where the emigrants became excited over Davis' return, word that he had the tickets spread far and wide and drew even more blacks to the city. But Atlanta officials grew restless, and soon a grand jury returned indictments against Peak and his assistant, T. F. Fisher. Peak was still in Washington, but Fisher went to jail to await trial for a misdemeanor, doing business (as an emi-

15. *Washington Post,* 21 January 1891.
16. Ibid.
17. Ibid.

gration agent) without a license. Fisher's arrest and Davis'
return only stimulated the emigrants and their nightly
meetings rang with greater excitement about Africa.[18]

By January 17 the press had the story of the Atlanta
gathering and the wire services spread the details to Washington, where the *Post* reported the story as "Colored Men
Shamefully Deluded." Moss, who had been searching for a
cheaper rate for the Congo Company, read the story and
immediately notified the company officers that he would no
longer negotiate the shameful matter. He promised, furthermore, to return the $500 only to Davis and only in
person. Treasurer O'Brien nevertheless asked Moss about
a steamship charter over a period of two or three years, and
hurried to Baltimore to investigate such a lease, or even the
purchase of a ship. Without the necessary money, of
course, he stood little chance of success, for the reputation
of the Congo Company had preceded him to that city.[19]

O'Brien also wrote to Davis, informing him that Moss
wanted to return the deposit to Davis in person. He
reportedly told Davis that only when the money was
turned over to the Congo Company would the ship sail
for Savannah to pick up the emigrants. Davis announced
the message to his constituents, who quickly agreed that
he should retrieve the deposit and pay the company for
more tickets to hurry the ship. On arriving in Washington,
Davis received strong words from Moss, who urged him
to return the money to the contributors rather than give it
to O'Brien. Davis, however, insisted on obeying the instructions of the African Band and bought more tickets.
After all, he told Moss, his people and the Congo Company were working together in the same interest.[20]

18. *Atlanta Constitution,* 20 January 1891.
19. *Washington Post,* 17, 20, 21 January 1891.
20. *Atlanta Constitution,* 31 January 1891; *Washington Post,* 27, 28
January 1891.

Pressure on the Congo Company from the press soon began to tell. Washington and Atlanta newspapers reported the story as though it were a giant swindle, predicting at each new development that all would soon collapse. Company leaders countered with repeated affirmations that they were sincere. Secretary T. J. Clayton wrote letters to several Southern newspapers clarifying the company's policy. He stated that the dollar tickets were to be subsidized by both the sale of stock and government action (of which nothing had been heard for a year). Denying that any agent had authority to set a date for sailing, he maintained that a ship would sail only when $30,000 could be raised. All the money accumulated to date, Clayton insisted, whether from the sale of tickets or stock, was safely banked and would be used only to transport people to Africa. Anyone who was displeased with the operation could return his receipt to the company and receive a full refund.[21]

In Washington, Davis concluded his business quickly. He met with the Congo Company officers to pay them the $500. At this meeting, after the money had changed hands, Davis learned that the company had no prospects for an early sailing—maybe in one month, maybe six. When reporters called at the meeting, Davis was "not available." Instead, company officials accused the press of having blown the story out of proportion. Treasurer O'Brien was convinced that educated blacks and white newspapers had conspired to defeat the Congo Company's plans by prematurely announcing the ship's sailing and thus starting the gathering in Atlanta.[22]

Davis seemed discouraged with the whole affair after his second trip to Washington. He wrote a public letter to the

21. *Atlanta Constitution,* 21 January 1891.
22. *Washington Post,* 20, 27, 28 January 1891; *Atlanta Constitution,* 31 January 1891.

African Band to remind the emigrants that he had bought
the tickets at their insistence. He absolved himself from
any further responsibility for the money. At a meeting of
the band, Davis promised to deliver a ticket, refundable
by the Congo Company, to any individual who was dissatisfied with his promise to get a ship within six months.
He proclaimed that he had absolute assurances about the
sailing and would sue the company if it defaulted. Secretary Clayton wrote again from Washington that the emigrants could get their money back simply by sending in
their receipts or tickets.[23]

While he had been away, the "Exodusters," as the press
called the emigrants, had grown more and more distrustful
of Davis and the company. Davis' second return and his
disclaimer of responsibility made them still more uneasy.
Recruiting agents with orders for 3,000 laborers for Western plantations had kept steady pressure on the transients.
Newspapers and black leaders had tried to win the people
away from the Congo Company by painting it as a confidence ring. According to the press, the meeting that Davis
addressed upon his return almost broke into a riot. Only
by singing "To the land I'm bound, where there's no more
stormy clouds to rise" could the crowd be quieted. After a
prayer, the gathering dispersed, muttering that Davis,
Peak, and the company were crooked. That evening was
the climax of the affair, for little more was reported about
the African Band. Many would-be emigrants yielded to the
appeals of the Western labor agents but others stayed in
Atlanta, still hoping to get to Africa.[24]

The story of the United States and Congo National
Emigration Steamship Company, however, was not yet
finished. During the next six months its officers, including
its general agent, Gaston, who had been laboring in the

23. *Atlanta Constitution,* 31 January 1891.
24. Ibid., 21, 31 January 1891.

Southwest during the furor in Atlanta, tried to arrange for ships to carry their clients to Africa. From time to time in the next few years, occasional news items would mention the company or its personnel. Gaston, especially, would later become well known as the head of his own emigration scheme.[25]

Were the Congo Company and its officers frauds? The press, established black leaders, and eventually the Exodusters thought so, and they had grounds for so thinking. Agent Peak had promised a ship and none had appeared. Davis had exchanged the people's money for tickets that were next to worthless. The whole idea of Africa for a dollar appeared ridiculous to people who were neither involved in the plan nor desperate to get away from their problems in the United States. Attacks by disgruntled individuals furthered the image of the company as a confidence racket.

Other evidence suggests that the Congo Company's plan was honest though not sound and well intentioned if not well managed. The leaders did not hesitate to stand and defend their scheme. They appear to have been serious in seeking ships, both before and after the Atlanta episode threw public attention on them. Their plan to get a federal subsidy was legally proper although politically naïve. When challenged with the discontent in Atlanta, the company publicly offered—on several occasions—to refund ticket money to the purchasers.

On balance it appears that the company was not fraudulent—that it was operated by relatively honest men who saw an opportunity to make a profit while filling a need. The American Colonization Society, Bishop Turner, and some white politicians, moreover, were claiming that thousands of blacks would emigrate if ships were avail-

25. Coppinger to D. Bacon, 15 July 1891.

able. Further, it was logical for blacks to establish a means for what they believed to be their escape from racial persecution. In turn, the inexperience and naïveté of the company's officials led to pathetic blunders that defamed the company and added to the sufferings of several thousand Georgia blacks. Had it not been for the overzealous efforts of one of their agents and the poor timing of their subsidy bill, the story might have ended differently.

Fraudulent or not, the most important facet of the Congo Company and the Atlanta exodus is that they provided an expression, however, unsatisfactory, for the growing discontent of Georgia blacks. Even if no ship existed and no subsidy came forth, the episode showed a desire on the part of some blacks to take action against their fate in 1891. Significantly, the action was directed toward Africa.[26] Ironically, the publicity generated by the debacle seems to have increased emigration fever in Georgia. Bishop Turner, of course, continued his persistent harangue, but Benjamin Gaston also contributed to the ferment.

After the Atlanta fiasco in early 1891 Gaston shifted his operations from the Gulf states to Georgia, where he soon won a following. Rather than preach a general back-to-Africa doctrine, as Turner did, Gaston offered transportation to Liberia. Before he started recruiting in Atlanta, however, Gaston made a quick visit to Liverpool to explain his emigration ideas to one of the largest British shipping firms, Elder, Dempster and Company. According to Gaston, the company, which had extensive trade with Africa, expressed interest in Gaston's emigration scheme and encouraged him to continue. With this support, he moved to Atlanta in the summer of 1891 and began so-

26. *Savannah Tribune,* 31 December 1892; Clarence A. Bacote, "The Negro in Georgia Politics, 1880–1908" (unpublished doctoral dissertation, University of Chicago, 1955), pp. 27–28.

liciting emigrants to sail for Africa as soon as possible, hopefully by September.[27]

By August he had stirred up the local blacks, some of whom had been waiting since the collapse of the African Band in January for a new plan to arise. Although other "steamship agents" had tried to interest the suspicious victims of Peak and O'Brien, only Gaston had been able to rekindle the fever. He explained that he had to raise $15,000 to implement the British offer of transportation. Between 200 and 700 emigrants could go to Africa, he said, but the total of $15,000 first had to be raised. In nightly meetings his eloquence told of the glories of Africa and he proceeded to sign up members for his group. A reported 1,600 to 1,700 people had paid an amount estimated at $1,000 after three weeks of the campaign. The press reported that "African fever has again broken out among the Negroes of Atlanta."[28]

The $15,000, however, did not materialize. The ship promised for September, consequently, was delayed indefinitely. As the "fever" subsided, a number of Atlanta blacks began to doubt Gaston's honesty. The Liberian nevertheless managed to keep his rapport with most of the people who had joined his group. After all, they reasoned, it was not Gaston's fault if they could not raise the $15,000 that was to be used for their benefit, and they decided to wait patiently until the additional money could be found. To keep interest alive, Gaston organized the Liberian Emigration Company in November. A full year passed before the next important development occurred.[29]

During the summer of 1892, legal segregation and il-

---

27. *Atlanta Constitution,* 23 August 1891.
28. Ibid.; Coppinger to C. E. Milnor, 15 August 1891.
29. J. Williams to Coppinger, 24 September 1891; Coppinger to Williams, 26 September 1891; Coppinger to Mrs. J. J. Roberts, 14 October 1891; Coppinger to W. W. Watkins, 19 October 1891; W. B. Matchett to Wilson, 23 January 1893.

legal race violence increased the dismay of Georgia blacks. Lynchings in the United States reached the highest rate ever. The colored people in Atlanta, incensed at new regulations for segregating the streetcars, talked of staging a boycott to secure a change. Assorted indignities led a number of the local black ministers to call for emigration to Liberia, in effect endorsing Bishop Turner's often repeated urging. The increase of insults made this logic more appealing, and Gaston was on the scene with his steamship tickets and his sweet talk.[30]

The extent of emigration interest in Atlanta during late 1892 alarmed a number of middle-class blacks who did not share the African enthusiasm. In December, editors of black newspapers throughout the state met to discuss the condition of the race, and the first and foremost item in their public statement was an attack on emigration.

> The spirit of emigration seems to have taken complete control of certain of our people in different parts of the country. . . . We recommend them to remain where they are; go to work industriously with renewed vigor and increased endeavor to carve a way for themselves and do everything possible to bring forth good results for the race. We further recommend them to cultivate a friendly feeling with their white neighbors.[31]

Accommodation, however, did not suit the mood of Bishop Turner and many other Atlanta blacks, especially the poorer class. Among the dissatisfied, Gaston recruited members for his Liberian Emigration Company. He continued to entice subscribers by telling of the government subsidy he hoped to get. Despite previous failures to obtain the money designated for emigration in the 1862 law,

30. *Washington Star,* 23 November 1892; Bacote, "Negro in Georgia Politics," pp. 27–28 and passim.
31. *Savannah Tribune,* 31 December 1892.

Gaston and his Washington colleague, W. B. Matchett, had again proposed a Senate resolution to get the money. Copies of the resolution were circulated with Gaston's other propaganda. By January 1893 the company claimed to have $5,000 toward the cost of chartering a steamer and "petitions of 10,000 people" who were asking for passage. Matchett and Gaston even tried to ally their group with the American Colonization Society to send a colony to Liberia in 1893. After several letters and a conference, however, the Colonization Society decided against joining forces with Gaston. "Nothing is to be expected from any arrangement with him for the present at least," wrote Secretary Wilson. "I can see clearly a great future in this African business, but the question is a very knotty one just now—all obstacles."[32]

Late in the spring the people who had given Gaston their money began to grow restless. The emigration excitement around Atlanta had calmed down and the prospective emigrants wondered if Gaston was sincere in his proposals. When several contributors threatened legal action against the company to obtain refunds, Gaston apparently silenced them by returning their money. Realizing it would be many months before his $15,000 came in, Gaston decided to send some of the noisiest protesters to Liberia via Liverpool. Seventeen Atlanta blacks, having received their refunds from the company, proceeded to Liberia in June. Gaston supervised their arrangements and wished them godspeed.[33]

Sending small groups to Africa via established shipping companies appealed to Gaston. With the sums collected from all the would-be emigrants, he could transport a few

32. Wilson to D. Bacon, 3 February 1893; *Washington Star*, 3 February 1893; Bacon to Wilson, 23 January 1893; Matchett to Wilson, 23 January 1893.
33. *Washington Post*, 3 May 1893; D. Bacon to Wilson, 19 June 1893.

individuals and relieve the pressure on his company while still living well on the remaining capital. During the summer of 1893 he apparently decided to operate on that basis. Traveling frequently to Washington and New York, he impressed the Atlanta blacks with his importance, but actually he was trying (in vain) to solicit philanthropic aid for his emigration scheme. Meanwhile he lived well on the cash the blacks had entrusted to him.[34] He arranged, eventually, for about thirty of his followers to embark for Africa on an Elder, Dempster ship scheduled to sail in November 1893. Gaston reportedly paid $3,000 to the shipping firm and put another $3,000 on deposit with the shipping company for support of the emigrants in Liberia. When he went to New York to arrange final details, however, Gaston was arrested by the police.[35]

Elihu Belcher, an Atlanta black man, had charged Gaston with fraud and the Atlanta police had telegraphed New York authorities asking them to hold the suspected swindler for extradition. Belcher was one of the many who had paid money to Gaston but had not been selected to sail in the November party. That group of thirty could not sail until Gaston had been cleared by the courts and the passage money released. Two months would elapse before the trial. An officer from Atlanta, meanwhile, escorted Gaston back to Georgia where several other bypassed emigrants had joined Belcher in suing for refunds.[36] Gaston secured two outstanding white attorneys to defend him. Outside the courtroom many of his followers waited to hear the verdict on the several warrants for fraud. When Gaston was found "not guilty," "a shout of glory went up

34. *Washington Post,* 30 October 1893.
35. *Washington Star,* 24 November 1893; Bacon to Wilson, 3 February 1894.
36. *Washington Star,* 24 November, 9 December 1893.

Bishop Henry McNeal Turner. From D. W. Culp, *Twentieth Century Negro Literature* (Toronto, 1902).

Dr. Edward Wilmot Blyden, ca. 1890. Library of Congress Photographic Archives.

Departure of the steamship "Horsa" from Savannah, Georgia, 19 March 1895. From *Harper's Weekly,* 27 April 1895.

Departure of the steamship "Laurada" from Savannah, Georgia, 1 March 1896. From *Illustrated American Magazine*, 21 March 1896.

and the negro women in special were exuberant over the result."[37]

After his acquittal Gaston lost little time in getting the emigrants ready to depart. The ticket money he had paid earlier had been retained by the shipping firm and Gaston's party planned to sail early in March 1894. Traveling by coastal steamer from Savannah, the thirty blacks arrived in New York, eager to start for Africa. Soon they were joined by twelve emigrants who arrived by rail. In the port, Gaston fluttered around his party like a mother hen with her chicks. When a reporter asked why the group was leaving the United States, Gaston replied with pompous eloquence: " 'The Ethiopian shall stretch forth his hand unto God an' shall worship Him under his own vine and fig tree. He shall become as numerous as the stars in de firment, and dis day dey are befo' de throne of God,' he said. The reporter broke his pencil and the old negro carefully went over it again to make sure he had it right. Then he wanted to hear it read." The old gentleman was quite proud of his notoriety for "evasion of fo' thousand dollars"—not many black men could even be suspected of having such an amount. Complaining that the United States was no place for a decent colored gentleman to live, Gaston shepherded his flock, "thirty gentlemen and ladies and twelve adults," onto the ship.[38] Because a number of the Atlanta people who had charged him with fraud were still very upset at his procedures, Gaston decided that he, too, would go to Liberia. Even as the ship departed, word arrived from Washington that some persons there were "anxiously looking for him."[39]

37. *Atlanta Constitution,* 7 February 1894.

38. *New York Times,* 10 March 1894; *Savannah Tribune,* 17 March 1894; D. Bacon to Wilson, 5, 10, 14 March 1894; *Voice of Missions,* April 1894.

39. Wilson to D. Bacon, 8 March 1894.

The subsequent story of Gaston's colony was not unlike
that of many sponsored by the Colonization Society. In
Liverpool, while the party transferred itself and its three
months' rations to an Africa-bound ship, Gaston confidently predicted that another colony would soon follow.
Because he believed that a hundred thousand blacks
wanted to go to Africa, he announced that he would soon
return to the United States to supervise the exodus.[40] From
Africa he reported that the newcomers were eagerly welcomed by the Liberians and were happily settled in their
new homes.[41] A year later, however, Bishop Turner visited
the colony and reported that eleven of the forty-two had
died because they had settled in unhealthy locations. The
last report of Gaston was that he was again under indict-
ment, this time by Liberian authorities, and again charged
with financial irregularities.[42]

The significance of Gaston's emigration schemes, from
his early days with the Congo Company to his final "success" in sending a colony to Liberia, lies not in the schemes
themselves so much as in the popular response. That Gaston was a genteel fraud seems clear. While collecting
emigration money from Georgia blacks and capitalizing
on the African publicity provided by Bishop Turner and
the Colonization Society, he could not resist the tempta-
tion to live high and well. That two groups of emigrants
actually sailed for Liberia under his direction was due
more to their persistence than to Gaston's sincerity. That
such a man could stir up persistent emigration interest in
Atlanta was due more to the general black discontent than
to Gaston's efforts. If he fooled some gullible black peas-

---

40. *African Times*, 2 April 1894; *Sierra Leone Times*, 28 April 1894.
41. *Washington Post*, 8 June 1894.
42. H. M. Turner to *Voice of Missions*, 8 May 1895 (published July
1895).

ants by his rhetoric, he attracted others simply by promising transportation, a means to an end that many of them already endorsed. Rather than wait for the white-dominated ACS to send them to Liberia, they wanted to take control of their own emigration. Gaston capitalized on their pride and desire.

8

Bishop Turner's Emigration Campaign

Benjamin Gaston had shown that Southern blacks were susceptible to African emigration propaganda; and overwhelming interest, rather than apathy, had revealed the weaknesses of the Colonization Society in 1892. Despite Gaston's frauds and the Colonization Society's efforts to dampen the enthusiasm of the black peasants, the society received more and more letters of inquiry and applications for aid in 1892 and 1893. But after the New York fiasco the initiative for propaganda and transportation fell on the blacks themselves. With Bishop Turner leading the way, there was no shortage of agitation on the African question. In response to his rousing praise of Africa, black people made numerous attempts to provide for their own deliverance to the promised land.[1]

Bishop Turner was fully willing to lead the campaign. Just before the Arkansas and Oklahoma emigrants had arrived in New York, the bishop arrived there from Liberia, full of praise for Africa. His first visit to his dream continent had left him more enthusiastic than ever about the prospects for a black nation. He had, to be sure, some criticism of Liberia and the Colonization Society. The society had sent paupers when settlers of means and talent were needed. It had settled them in the malarial lowlands rather than in the healthy hills. It had cast the newcomers adrift rather than helping them learn to farm and live in a new land. The new officers of the ACS listened eagerly to his remarks and incorporated them in their new policies.

1. *Liberia Bulletin*, 2 (February 1893), 5.

The bishop had not changed his basic ideas about emigration. Only an African black nation, he proclaimed, could provide full manhood for the Afro-American.[2]

Having been out of the United States for a time, Turner saw the American racial problem with new vividness. Lynchings had become more frequent, segregation more thorough. Northern efforts to help blacks through federal aid to education and voting laws had collapsed. Even in the North, racism was gaining. As the depression deepened in the rural South, blacks were first to suffer and last to recover. "By virtue of lynchings, murders and outrages perpetrated upon our people and the absolute powerlessness of the President of the United States, the powerlessness of the civil and federal laws," Turner labeled America "the worst, the meanest country" on the face of the earth. The only role for blacks in the United States was as "menials, scullions, servants, subordinates and underlings."[3]

The bishop had no difficulty stirring up emigration excitement in the South. Despite the widespread criticism of Turner, the Colonization Society, and Liberia caused by the stranding of the would-be emigrants in Atlanta in 1891 and New York in 1892, interest in Africa grew, and Arkansas continued to be a center of discontent. Although the white and the black press spread the stories of the New York fiasco and the Congo Company's difficulties far and wide, thousands of Arkansas blacks were ready to leave home for Africa. In Oklahoma, emigration clubs flourished, even as newcomers poured into the territory. Many letters from Tennessee came to the Colonization Society office and a Chattanooga man reported that over 600 peo-

2. *New York Age,* 20 February 1892, in ACS scrapbooks; Wilson to Turner 9 April 1892.

3. *Christian Recorder,* 12 May 1892; *New York Age,* 20 February 1892, in ACS scrapbooks; cf. Woodward, *Jim Crow,* Chapter 3 and passim.

ple from that city alone were ready to depart. In Georgia, emigration sentiment reached a new high. Certainly much of the widespread interest was generated by the violence and economic depression in those states, but Turner's long campaign, punctuated by his glowing letters from West Africa in 1891 and early 1892, was responsible for the direction taken by the black unrest. His name was mentioned by many who wrote to the Colonization Society seeking aid for emigration. After his return from Africa, they waited eagerly to hear more about the promised land. "Bishop Turner is expected to bea here nex week," wrote a Florida man, "an i shal meat him to her him say a wird of Africa."[4]

Turner was fully aware that the major stumbling block in his emigration scheme was transportation. Yates and Porterfield had stopped sending their ships to Liberia after the Colonization Society stopped filling them with emigrants. No other American firm took up the West African trade, and passage via Europe was too expensive for most blacks. Like the Colonization Society, Turner launched a campaign to provide some kind of direct steamship communications with Africa. In May 1892 he persuaded the General Conference of the A.M.E. church to establish a committee to help stimulate shipping routes to Africa. Later in the year the bishop revealed that he was "corresponding with a number of rich men," trying to interest them in African trade. He even tried to get President Grover Cleveland to mention the need for African commerce in his inaugural address. However, Turner had no more success with white merchants than did the Colonization Society.[5]

4. J. H. Glover to Coppinger, 13 February 1892; T. Bowman to Coppinger, 23 March 1892; Bacote, "Negro in Georgia Politics," p. 27.
5. *Voice of Missions,* February 1893 and following issues; Turner to Wilson, 29 December 1892; Turner to B. Sunderland, 29 December 1892.

If white men would not open trade with Africa, black men would attempt the task. As a result of Bishop Turner's agitation and the A.M.E. church's Committee on the African Steamship Line, a new scheme was formed. The Reverend Daniel E. Johnson, of San Antonio, Texas, offered a plan for an all-black stock company to buy and operate steamships. The ships were to be used primarily for commerce but they would, of course, carry emigrants to Africa. Capital was to come from shares sold to blacks all over the nation.[6]

Bishop Turner wrote enthusiastically of Johnson's plan. In a long public letter to Johnson, Turner praised him as a true descendant of Paul Cuffee, the first man to take American blacks to Africa (in 1816). The bishop proceeded to tell how cheaply second-hand ships could be bought in Great Britain, how profitable was the African trade, and how enthusiastically Southern blacks would buy the stock. In a private letter, Turner explained that although he was not himself involved in the organization, it would surely succeed. "Hundreds have written to me to head the enterprise, and if I would do so, thousands would go into it at once," he wrote. "But there will be a steamship between here and Africa in less than five years, purchased by the colored people themselves."[7]

By January 1893 Johnson had refined the plan for his Afro-American Steamship and Mercantile Company. In a prospectus that circulated widely, he included among the purposes of the organization emigration, commerce, responsible positions for capable blacks, teaching Afro-Americans the value of race organization, and joining "our Liberian brethren in their efforts to make such a negro gov-

6. D. E. Johnson to the editor, *Christian Recorder*, 1 September 1892.
7. Turner to Wilson, 25 November 1892; Turner to D. E. Johnson, *Christian Recorder*, 13 October 1892.

ernment on the west coast of Africa as will command the respect of all nations, and thereby make it more tolerable for
the American negro even if he remains under the 'Stars and
Stripes.' " Local clubs could be formed when a hundred
shares had been subscribed. The purpose of the clubs was
to hold interested people together until the company could
be formed "and for mutual encouragement in trying to do
something for ourselves and posterity." To protect against
fraud, the money was to be held in the local clubs until all
the stock was subscribed. With the blessing of Bishop
Turner and the encouragement of the Colonization Society, Johnson launched his campaign.[8]

Press releases carried news of the company's plans
around the nation. Johnson himself traveled about organizing clubs where interest appeared. Because his home
was in San Antonio, many of the clubs were formed in the
Western states, an area not usually considered a seat of
black unrest. But in Denver, for example, there was considerable interest in emigration. Johnson arrived there in
April 1893 to organize the would-be emigrants and attract
public attention. Speaking in black churches, he appealed
to the racial pride and profit motive of his audiences as
well as their desire to go to Africa. "Nothing is impossible
to ten millions of people when they have confidence in
their own efforts," he concluded, to "rapturous applause."
After a week in Denver, Johnson headed east, having
founded two ship clubs in the city.[9]

In Atlanta, Johnson conferred with Bishop Turner and
set out to organize clubs in the South. But there he ran
afoul of the hard facts of life in the 1890s; there simply
was no money. Although people would subscribe for the

8. "Charter and Constitution of the Afro-American Steamship and
Mercantile Co.," in D. E. Johnson to Wilson, 13 February 1892; Wilson
to Johnson, 3 December 1892, 17 February 1893.
9. *Denver Statesman,* 21 January, 15 April 1893, in ACS scrapbooks; *Denver Daily News,* 13 April 1893.

$10 shares, they could not keep up the dollar-a-month payments. By August, only Atlanta, Charleston, and Baltimore, among Southern cities, had clubs. Even the clubs in Ohio, Indiana, Ontario, and the West were not able to pay their subscriptions. Disheartened by the depression, Johnson returned to Texas.[10] For want of money and organizational experience, the Afro-American Steamship Company was dead.

One of Johnson's great problems was the distrust in which such capital-raising schemes were held by black people. Gaston and the Congo Company were two of the more respectable schemes, but many outright frauds had been committed in the name of Africa. Even as Johnson was organizing his clubs, scandals in Arkansas attracted nationwide attention.

In eastern Arkansas, between Little Rock and Memphis, a black preacher named J. P. F. Lightfoot was lynched when his victims discovered that his three-dollar tickets to Africa were worthless. An estimated 3,000 blacks had been duped.[11] Two months later, in another part of Arkansas, two anonymous preachers collected thousands of dollars from their victims, spent $3,000 to charter a train, and sent 410 blacks to Brunswick, Georgia, to meet a nonexistent ship. Unlike Lightfoot, the swindlers lived to spend their profits.[12]

These incidents illustrate not only the gullibility and lack of sophistication of Southern rural blacks but their desire to escape oppression in the United States. Like others before and after them, these swindlers did not generate the

10. *Voice of Missions,* August 1893.

11. *Arkansas Gazette,* 3, 10, 11, 13, 14 December 1892; *New York Sun,* 10 December 1892; *New York Times,* 10, 11, 12 December 1892; *Savannah Tribune,* 17 December 1892; W. C. Love to Wilson, 28 November 1892.

12. *Atlanta Constitution,* 16 February 1893; *New York Times,* 18 February 1893.

desire to emigrate so much as they exploited the interest nurtured by Bishop Turner in the soil of general black discontent. When some slick individual like Lightfoot appeared, or even D. E. Johnson of the honest but stillborn Afro-American Steamship Company, many simple people jumped at the opportunity to follow Turner's recommendations.

Because of Bishop Turner's publicity and the long tradition of Liberian emigration, Africa was most often the goal of blacks who wanted to flee the United States in the 1890s. But from time to time other places were advocated. Brazil was to be the Afro-American's new home, according to Colonel John M. Brown, a black politician from Kansas. Brown had elaborate plans, similar to those of D. E. Johnson's Afro-American Company, but little success in raising money and interest among the blacks.[13] Mexico was suggested by William H. Ellis, a Texas black businessman who had a gift for convincing whites to back his schemes. Since 1889 he had planned a black colony in Mexico to raise cotton and coffee; by 1893, however, despite support from the Mexican legislature and some white entrepreneurs, Ellis had gained little support among blacks.[14] Africa remained the "fatherland," and at Bishop Turner's insistence it was viewed as the promised land.

When the Colonization Society changed its policies and ceased publication of the *African Repository* in 1892, Turner assumed the burden of future mass appeals to American blacks. His actions in 1893 seem, in retrospect, to have been a conscious shouldering of that burden in the form of popularizing and facilitating African emigration. In addition to his efforts to obtain regular shipping routes

13. *Washington Post,* 30 March 1893; *Washington Star,* 1 April, 23 October 1893.
14. *Christian Recorder,* 7 November 1889; *Savannah Tribune,* 19 October 1889; *New York Times,* 6 August 1890, 17 August 1891. Cf. *Southwestern Christian Advocate,* 27 December 1900.

to Africa, the bishop launched his own monthly newspaper, took a second and well-publicized trip to Africa, preached emigration at the Chicago World's Fair, and summoned a national Afro-American convention to consider emigration as a remedy for the American racial turmoil. It was a busy year for the bishop.

The newspaper came first. Because of his zeal for Africa, Turner had, in 1891, been put in charge of the overseas mission work of the A.M.E. church. With the stated purpose of popularizing missionary activity and encouraging donations for converting the heathen, he published in January 1893 the first issue of the monthly *Voice of Missions*. Although it was ostensibly published on behalf of the church, the *Voice of Missions* for the first eight years of its life was very much the personal property and mouthpiece of the bishop. Although the paper contained news about wider church activities, through editorials, letters, and features, it vigorously proposed African emigration for American blacks. By the end of its first year the journal had achieved a reported monthly circulation of over 4,000. Because most of these papers were read by pastors of A.M.E. churches throughout the South, their message reached far more people than the circulation figures might suggest. The monthly proved to be an effective vehicle for Turner's propaganda.[15]

The African bias of the *Voice of Missions* was evident from the start. Writing in the persona of the newspaper itself, Turner editorialized: "I will keep you informed about the improvements made in Africa, such as building railroads . . . and plying steamboats. . . . I will tell you about mines of silver, gold and diamonds that have been . . . and are being discovered, and what the nations of the earth are doing in parceling out the domain of the great

15. *Voice of Missions,* January, February, December 1893 and passim.

continent, regardless of the right or wrong involved in the case." Although no explicit call for emigration appeared in the first issue, there were letters from the Liberian consul at Philadelphia, from missionaries in various parts of Africa, and from recent black emigrants, all telling the advantages of the newly opened continent. In the second issue and thereafter, however, overt emigration propaganda appeared in the editorials, ads, and letters.[16]

In the months and years that followed its beginning, Turner published detailed accounts of emigration schemes, in the *Voice of Missions,* such as that of the Afro-American Steamship Company, and extensive reports of his journeys in Africa. The latest prices for transportation to Liberia accompanied periodic denunciations of the United States' treatment of blacks. In every way, the paper was Turner's personal propaganda sheet, and as such it was the foremost organ in the mid-1890s for spreading the gospel of African emigration.[17]

Whatever restraint he may have used when writing for other journals disappeared in Turner's own paper. He vigorously attacked black leaders who advocated anything less than immediate and full equality for the black man or derided the black nationalism that lay at the heart of the bishop's thinking. He wrote of the opposing press: "We have been denounced and ridiculed a thousand times by a number of these mushroom pimps who know how to scribble a little on paper for the public press." It was "those northern coons" who made the color problem worse by presuming to advise the Southern black man on the race issue, and it was "scullion Negroes" in the South, lacking the ambition or "animal instinct to either fight or run," who drew the bishop's scorn. He could categorize the opposition into either "this young fungus class" or

16. Ibid., January 1893.
17. Ibid. and passim.

"those old fossils who were in the slave pen when [I] was an officer in the army, trying to move heaven and earth to rescue their freedom."[18] Despite the coarseness of Turner's language, his ability and willingness to openly attack both racial oppression and the bland double-talk of white and black spokesmen won him wide readership, quotation, and argument. Even those who disagreed with his emigration plans had to reckon with his undoubtedly wide appeal to lower-class blacks.

Having successfully launched the *Voice of Missions,* Bishop Turner departed in February 1893 for a second well-publicized pilgrimage to West Africa via Europe. The reason for the trip, he wrote, was to answer the appeals of the African people for help in evangelizing the natives and strengthening their churches.[19] Another motive was the bishop's attempt to interest businessmen in the potential of American-African trade. In Britain, he called upon a ship owner who had expressed interest in the project. Then, in an interview that was published in a Liverpool newspaper, Turner stressed the need for shipping. Nothing, however, seemed to come of either the private appointment or the public interview, for no British steamship entered the trade.[20]

A new factor impressed Turner on his second visit to Africa: white men were more in evidence than ever before. On board his ship he met five Americans who were going to Africa to exploit a silver mine one of them had opened.[21] In Liberia, Turner learned of French encroachment on the border.[22] From Sierra Leone, he reported "I can see an increase of whites all along since I last visited Africa." He

18. Ibid., August 1893, March, October 1895.
19. Ibid., February 1893.
20. Turner to Wilson, 29 December 1892; Turner to B. Sunderland, 17 February 1893; interview quoted in *Voice of Missions,* May 1893.
21. Turner to *Christian Recorder,* 23 March 1893.
22. Turner to *Voice of Missions,* 15 April 1893 (published July 1893).

warned that "it means the capture of the only spot upon the face of the globe [where] the black man can ever hope to be in power and demonstrate the ability of self-government."[23] The possibility that white control might destroy his African dream made the bishop plead with blacks and whites alike that Africa be saved for the Africans.

The diplomatic troubles that beset Liberia in 1893 distressed the bishop. Not only did French and British border incursions threaten Liberia's territorial integrity, its very existence as an independent nation was in doubt. There was fear in Monrovia that the nation might be forced to become a protectorate of Britain, and there was fear in England that the Franco-Liberian treaty had already put the republic under French protection. Either development would be tragic to Turner because it would demonstrate that black men could not govern themselves. But the Liberian government believed itself cut off from its traditional source of moral support, the United States. Although Liberia had never had an ambassador to the United States, President Cheeseman asked Turner to serve as his minister at Washington, and Turner, of course, accepted the post. The Colonization Society, however, opposed such an appointment, ostensibly because Turner was neither a citizen of Liberia nor a resident of Washington. Another argument, unspoken but real, held that because Washington had never before accepted a black ambassador it was not likely to do so in the deteriorating state of race relations in 1893. Under Colonization Society pressure, therefore, Monrovia rescinded Turner's appointment and instead made him Liberian consul for the Southern states. When he returned to the United States the bishop called on Secretary of State W. Q. Gresham to plead for verbal if not material support for Liberia against European pressures. Turner's attempt at diplomacy was successful only

23. Ibid., 9 April 1893 (published June 1893).

insofar as the Secretary of State reiterated the American government's view that Liberia should remain independent.[24]

The most important result of the bishop's 1893 trip to Liberia was the generation of more emigration publicity at home. His first visit, in 1891, had provided good propaganda and his second visit did the same. Through weekly letters to the *Christian Recorder* and the *Voice of Missions,* he informed readers of the needs and prospects of Africa. "New blood is certainly needed in Liberia. . . . This is the place to make money by the bushels if you can raise a little to start with."[25] Turner's letters were full of overstated praise for Africa and criticism for American blacks who were letting a great opportunity slip through their fingers. The simple fact that the great advocate of emigration was writing directly from Africa drew enthusiastic responses from many Southern blacks, as was indicated by letters to the press and to the Colonization Society. On his return the bishop reinforced that interest by constantly lecturing and writing about Africa. Even the Southern white press carried a wire service feature that told Turner's life story, included a picture of the bishop, and called him the "Black Moses." As a propaganda junket, the trip was a success.[26]

Never one to let public occasions pass without raising the emigration question, Turner took full advantage of the

24. *Voice of Missions,* July 1893; Wilson to Turner, 13 June 1893; Wilson to J. J. Cheeseman, 19 June 1893; G. W. Gibson (Secretary of State of Liberia) to W. Q. Gresham, 21 April 1893 (in Liberia Notes to U. S. Department of State, 9 July 1862 to 16 February 1898, U. S. Archives); Turner to B. Sunderland, 16 June 1893; G. W. Gibson to Wilson, 19 July 1893; Gresham to B. Y. Payne, 9 September 1893 (U. S. State Department No. 43; certified copy, dated 9 February 1901, in ACS letters received for 1901).

25. Turner to *Voice of Missions,* 15 April 1893 (published July 1893).

26. *Liberia Bulletin, 4* (February 1894), 1–2. Turner's letters from Africa appeared in the *Voice of Missions* from April through July 1893 and in the *Christian Recorder* on 23 March, 20 April, 11 May, and 8 and 15 June 1893. Cf. *Arkansas Gazette,* 1 October 1893.

Columbian Exposition at Chicago. After his return from
Africa and his diplomatic efforts in Washington, the bishop
appeared in Chicago for a number of meetings that were
held in conjunction with the exposition. As usual, he spoke
out against lynching and violence. To his surprise and obvious pleasure, other black speakers supported Turner's
protests and emigration ideas. Even the aging abolitionist
hero Frederick Douglass, a resolute integrationist, was
friendly.[27] At the small exhibit sponsored by the Liberian
government the bishop took pride in the native crafts and
the nature objects, although he would rather have seen
more industrial displays to attract Afro-American settlers.[28]

Turner's best opportunity for emigration publicity at
Chicago came during the week-long Congress on Africa.
Speeches and papers about Africa from over a hundred
explorers, travelers, missionaries, scientists, and sociolo-
gists were delivered, and Turner participated in a discussion of "The African in America." In a speech on the
achievements of the black man in the United States and
elsewhere, the bishop announced that the first man, Adam,
had been black. The statement shocked whites, pleased
blacks, and won Turner a story in the *Chicago Tribune*
with a portrait and a summary of his emigration views.[29]
Later the same week the topic of discussion was "What do
American Negroes Owe to Their Kin Beyond the Sea?"
Turner once again spoke eloquently for emigration and

27. *Voice of Missions,* May, October 1893; *Chicago Tribune,* 26
August 1893. See also Elliott Rudwick and August Meier, "Black Men
in the White City: Negroes in the Columbian Exposition, 1893," *Phylon,*
26 (Winter 1965), 354–61; Arna Bontemps and Jack Conroy, *They Seek
a City* (Garden City, 1945), p. 167.

28. *Voice of Missions,* October 1893; *Liberia Bulletin, 3* (November
1893), 66–69.

29. *Chicago Tribune,* 16 August 1893; Frederick P. Noble, "The
Chicago Congress on Africa," *Our Day, 12* (October 1893), 279–300;
Voice of Missions, October 1893.

was supported by some who had spent years in Africa. In light of the increasing racial violence in the United States, a number of blacks in attendance agreed with the bishop.[30]

The Chicago exposition served Turner well as a platform for African propaganda. The Congress on Africa, in particular, was well attended by Negroes, albeit most of them from the North and not sympathetic to emigration. They nevertheless spent a week with their attention focused on the people and prospects of Africa, hearing authentic information from people who were neutral about emigration. But Turner did not convince many to leave the United States. As the secretary of the congress commented, "Had his audience been southern negroes, he could have carried his point; but these negroes belong to the best classes . . . and show no signs of race duty."[31]

Despite the lack of general endorsement of his ideas by blacks at Chicago, Turner was not discouraged. Some outright opponents of emigration had changed their position to advocate emigration by the qualified few who could help build Africa. Turner believed that education about Africa's land and people could not do otherwise than make it more appealing to intelligent blacks. In general he was pleased with the publicity, for publicity was his major task in 1893. The launching of the *Voice of Missions* and his trip to Africa supplemented the Chicago appearances, but his most determined effort was yet to come.

Encouraging responses to his public relations campaign combined with the reaction to increased racial violence to convince Bishop Turner that in 1893 the time was ripe for a major effort to get emigration off dead center. Influential black leaders and white men who sympathized with the plight of black men must be convinced of the

30. Noble, "Congress on Africa," p. 291.
31. Ibid., p. 286; *A.M.E. Zion Quarterly Review, 4* (October 1893), p. 120.

validity of emigration if money was ever to be available for transportation. To mobilize all possible support, Turner issued the following call for a national convention of Afro-Americans.

I do not believe that there is any manhood future in this country for the Negro, and that his future existence, to say nothing of his future happiness, will depend upon his nationalization. . . . Knowing that thousands and tens of thousands see our present condition and our future about as I do; and after waiting for four years or more for some of our colored statesmen or leaders to call a national convention, or to propose some plan of speaking to the nation or to the world, or to project some measure that will remedy our condition, or will even suggest a remedy, and finding no one among the anti-emigration party or anti-Negro nationalization party, disposed to do so, and believing that further silence is not only a disgrace, but a crime, I have . . . resolved to issue a call . . . for a national convention to be held in the city of Cincinnati, where a spacious edifice is at our disposal, to meet sometime in November, for the friends of African repatriation or Negro nationalization elsewhere, to assemble and adopt such measures for our future actions as may commend themselves to our better judgement. The call of the contemplated convention will have no application to party politics or to the stay-here portion of our race. They can project their own plans, resolve upon their own action, or do nothing as they are doing now. We will not interfere with them and they need not interfere with us unless they desire. But the Negro cannot remain here in his present condition and be a man . . . for at the present rate his extermination is only a question of time.[32]

32. *Voice of Missions,* August 1893.

The response to the call gratified the bishop. He announced that over "three hundred responsible Negroes" had endorsed the summons and that delegates from all over the nation would attend.[33] Although journalists and other prominent men were not enthusiastic about emigration, the black press was sympathetic to the call insofar as it was a protest against injustice and violence. The most widely read black newspaper in the nation, the *Indianapolis Freeman,* predicted that the "Turner convention" would be a great and important gathering that had not been called a moment too soon. "A certain amount of tolerance will be accorded Bishop Turner's views, more out of courtesy than anything else," the *Freeman* predicted. "Aside from this unpleasant shadow, it is possible to turn the occasion into one of real practical benefit to the race, and we do sincerely hope, that after the immigration [*sic*] idea has received its death blow, and quickly, that the time . . . will be utilized thoroughly and well."[34]

The *Freeman* conducted a poll among black leaders to ascertain their thoughts on the convention and on Turner's emigration ideas and it published thirty-nine replies just before the convention met. Of the people responding, only two favored emigration as a solution to the race problem and twenty-two categorically rejected emigration to Africa or elsewhere. The remaining fifteen, who included some of the most highly respected black leaders, opposed any kind of mass exodus but agreed that qualified individuals should voluntarily go to Africa. Ida B. Wells, the spirited young lady who by her articles and talks raised international protests against lynching in America, wrote: "I do most emphatically favor emigration to Africa for all those who wish and are able to go." P. B. S. Pinchback con-

33. Ibid., October 1893.

34. *Indianapolis Freeman,* 11, 18 November 1893; *Christian Recorder,* 16 November 1893; *Savannah Tribune,* 21 October 1893.

curred. John M. Langston said: "While I am not opposed
to any man's going to Africa—I have no confidence in . . .
colored Americans going to Africa en masse." Bishop
Alexander Walters agreed. Frederick Douglass concisely
summarized the views of this group: "Every friend of the
race will rejoice that Bishop Turner has bravely called
this convention. . . . Nevertheless I do not believe in any
wholesale plan of colonization to Africa. Emigration? Yes.
Exodus? No." Although Turner could be gratified with
the qualified approval of emigration to Africa, the *Freeman's* poll did not bode well for the bishop's plans to use
the convention as a springboard for a great emigration
scheme.[35] Even before the meetings began he asserted that
they were primarily for protest, not emigration.[36]

About 800 delegates joined a throng of local blacks to
hear Bishop Turner's opening address. It was a genuinely
eloquent appeal for black men to take their fate in their
own hands in one way or another. He called for a thorough,
impartial investigation of the widespread charge that black
men were vicious rapists. If the charges were true, he said,
blacks themselves must undertake to "organize against the
wretched in our own ranks." But he maintained that the
charges certainly were not true in every case of lynching.
Violence was a way of reasserting slavery by American
whites who in 1893 had no disposition to grant black men
genuine freedom, manhood, or citizenship. "If this country
is to be our home," said Turner, "the Negro must be a self-
controlling, automatic factor of the body politic or collective life of the nation. In other words, we must be full-
fledged men." Physical resistance to white oppression
would be literal madness, he believed, because the military
strength of white society was too great. "When a race war

35. *Indianapolis Freeman*, 25 November 1893. Cf. August Meier,
Negro Thought, pp. 66–67, 82.
36. *Cincinnati Commercial Gazette*, 28 November 1893.

is spoken of it comes from some white quarter. The black man never thinks about it, much less speaks about it." The only solution, Turner believed, was to leave the United States. "But some of you may think I am over gloomy, too despondent, that I have reached the plane of despair. . . . I confess that I have seen so much . . . of American prejudice that I have no hope in the future success in our present circumstances." No amount of education or talk could elevate either a man or a race, according to the bishop. "Underlying all school culture must exist the consciousness that I am somebody, that I am a man as much as anybody else, that I have rights, that I am the creature of law and order, that I am entitled to respect, that every avenue to distinction is mine. For where this consciousness does not form the substream of any people," he concluded, "ultimate degradation will be the result." He called for radical action to alleviate the situation and he suggested asking Congress for millions of dollars to help the blacks establish their own nation.[37]

The audience received the bishop's words enthusiastically. The response was especially fervent when Turner remarked that, despite his efforts in the Civil War, he "thanked God that he had never shed blood for a country that would not own him." Several minutes of wild cheering and demonstrations ensued. When, at the end of his speech, Bishop Turner proposed emigration as a solution for race problems, another loud response followed. Shouts of "Africa!" were met with shouts of "Mexico!" and "Canada!" Despite the enthusiasm of the local audience, most of the convention's voting delegates opposed emigration. In sessions to come, this opposition carried the day.[38]

Committees were established to report recommendations to the convention at large, and the Committee on Emigra-

37. *Voice of Missions,* December 1893.
38. *Cincinnati Enquirer,* 29 November 1893; *Cincinnati Commercial Gazette,* 29 November 1893.

tion produced the first and most controversial report. It was chaired by W. H. Councill, the president of Alabama State Normal Institute and a believer in emigration to Africa. Also on the committee were W. H. Ellis, the advocate of Mexican emigration, Bishop Turner's son, John T. Turner, and several others.[39] Its report stated: "We fail to find in any part of the United States, outside the colored man himself, any considerable influence which encourages African genius and progress. . . . The oppressed of all ages have had recourse to revolution or emigration. . . . To adopt the former is to court utter extermination. The latter may bring relief. . . . We recommend the colored people of the United States to turn their attention to the civilization of Africa as the only hope of the Negro race as a race."[40]

An uproar followed the reading of the report and many sought the floor to denounce the idea of emigration. C. H. J. Taylor, who had attacked Blyden's ideas in 1889, refused to acknowledge that Africa was any better than the United States. Ellis pointed out that Mexico was not only closer but more civilized than Africa. Others assailed the thought of leaving the nation to which all the world was flocking in the 1890s. Bishop Turner, sensing that the report would be rejected by the convention, attacked the paper for being too mild. According to the bishop, who gave a long and impassioned defense of emigration, the committee should have been more radical and should have petitioned Congress for a billion dollars to help establish a new nation. To avoid a showdown vote, which would surely have gone against him, Turner had the report sent back to the committee for revision.[41]

On the following day, the last day of the convention, a

39. *Denver Statesman,* 9 December 1893, in ACS scrapbooks.
40. *Cincinnati Enquirer,* 1 December 1893.
41. Ibid., *Cincinnati Commercial Gazette,* 1 December 1893; *Voice of Missions,* January 1894.

large audience of townspeople joined the delegates to hear the discussions on emigration. They were disappointed, however, for the convention chairman, Turner, managed to postpone the emigration report several times until there was no time left to consider it. Instead, it was passed along to an executive committee for final discussion. The resolution that finally disposed of the emigration report was a bland compromise urging the executive committee to study the conditions of blacks in each part of the nation with a view toward recommending migration from the sections that were most oppressive. The motion was passed unanimously, and Turner avoided open defeat at the hands of emigration's opponents.[42]

Despite the bishop's powerful personality and his bold, accurate descriptions of the race problem, the most important name at the convention was not Turner, but Albion W. Tourgee. Tourgee was perhaps the strongest white advocate of civil rights for the blacks. At that time he was trying to keep alive his own interracial organization, the National Citizen's Rights Association, which was losing public support and disintegrating from lack of organizational leadership.[43] In November 1893 he had written a long irenic letter to Bishop Turner in which he explained why he opposed emigration. Public opinion, he believed, could force the nation to realize and repent of the injustices done to the blacks. All that was needed was a new and powerful journal to publicize the idea of equality and integration, Tourgee said. With injustice remedied and violence stopped, he said, there would be no need for emigration.[44]

42. *Cincinnati Enquirer,* 2 December 1893; *Cincinnati Commercial Gazette,* 2 December 1893; *Voice of Missions,* January 1894.

43. Otto H. Olsen, *Carpetbagger's Crusade: The Life of Albion Winegar Tourgee* (Baltimore, 1965), pp. 319–24, Chapter 24 and passim.

44. A. W. Tourgee to H. M. Turner, in *Christian Recorder,* 16 November 1893.

On the second day of Turner's convention, a long letter from Tourgee was read to the delegates in which he documented the many charges of injustice to blacks in the South and discussed the proposed solutions. Three were commonly debated: submission, rebellion, and emigration. Rejecting all three, Tourgee argued that the American public still had a vital sense of justice and that white people would respond if only the black people would stand up and appeal to the whites' sense of outrage at oppression. Relief would then be at hand, he said, for "we have reached that time in the world's history when public opinion is not only the law but the real law." At the close of the letter, a storm of applause rocked the hall, and the anti-emigration faction cheered loudest.[45]

The delegates polarized around Turner and Tourgee. Although by parliamentary maneuvering the bishop could avoid outright defeat on the emigration issue, the various actions of the convention showed that the integrationists had won the day. The delegates decided to establish a National Equal Rights Council with Turner as "chancellor." The council was to work with Tourgee's National Citizen's Rights Association by mobilizing blacks to protest more efficiently against injustice. Local chapters were to organize for "protection of our lives and liberty." In approving such an organization, it was clear that Bishop Turner had capitulated to convention pressures. As he himself wrote: "All of you anti-emigrationists and anti-Africans and anti-go-anywheres now fall in line. . . . There is no African emigration in this, so you need not be afraid of it."[46] The other acts of the convention were protests and petitions that were sent to Congress, state governors, and the American people, calling attention to injustices and

45. A. W. Tourgee letter to the Turner convention, quoted in full in the *Cincinnati Commercial Gazette,* 30 November 1893.
46. *Voice of Missions,* February 1894.

asking for a change. On such protests both convention factions could unite.

Not only from Bishop Turner's viewpoint but also in the larger perspective, the Turner convention was a failure. The editor of the *Denver Statesman* summed up the results.

The colored national convention had its say at Cincinnati last week. It legislated upon numberless propositions, resolutions, and communications, but outlined no particular, practical action for the people. We do not believe that the work of the convention came up to the expectations of Bishop Turner, the prime mover. . . . The STATESMAN is unable to tell what there was about [it] that deserves to be considered encouraging. . . . A colored national convention . . . is full of life and bristling with pithy eloquence from start to finish. But there is more pith than anything else. The real hard substance is wanting. The Cincinnati convention was no exception. It was airy, eloquent and useless. All the radical propositions bearing upon the future welfare of the race were talked to death. A majority of the delegates seem to have gone to the convention for the sole purpose of thwarting the ideas of its author. The Afro-American went to down the would-be African, and so far as the convention is concerned, he did it. But he did nothing else. Neither did anybody. The determination to establish a permanent organization, with gilt edge officers, was so much time lost. . . . The national convention apparently attracted no more outside attention than a big local gathering. It accomplished little more than a big local gathering might have accomplished. It was passive when it should have been radical. It was cowardly when it should have been heroic.[47]

47. *Denver Statesman,* 9 December 1893, in ACS scrapbooks.

Lasting results of the convention were nonexistent. Like Tourgee's collapsing Citizen's Rights Association, the Equal Rights Council attracted little attention and was essentially stillborn. The protests of grievances were lost on an American public where, indeed, public opinion was the real law—opinion that was content to let the violent prejudices of the South set the real law for the nation. Lynching did not abate. Indeed, a radical solution was needed to solve a radical problem, but emigration was the only one proposed. Thus ended the last of the great black conventions of the nineteenth century, and the world little knew what they said and did there.[48]

The significance of the Turner convention was the fact that it was a major attempt by a Southern black man to fill the void in race leadership and ideology. The years that preceded the convention had witnessed a precipitous drop in blacks' status and most black spokesmen had nothing new to offer their suffering people. It would be two more years before Booker T. Washington pronounced the Atlanta Compromise. In this time of great difficulty and lack of direction, Bishop Turner was as well known and respected as any other Afro-American, save perhaps Frederick Douglass. The Cincinnati convention attempted to unite American blacks behind a philosophy of vigorous protest and nationalism. The delegates, however, were drawn from that middle class of blacks, mostly Northern, who optimistically believed Tourgee's predictions about justice and good will. Black nationalism might have won more support if Turner had not wedded it to emigration. Jealousy of other would-be black leaders further condemned Turner and the convention to failure, just as jealousy would continue to plague black spokesmen. Only the strong support of powerful white men would later enable Booker T. Washington to gain preeminence among blacks.

48. Meier, *Negro Thought,* p. 71.

Turner did not have such support and the void in black leadership and ideology went unfilled for the time being.

Bishop Turner went back to Atlanta still convinced about emigration. "What under heaven [he wrote] would [I] want with a national convention of over seven hundred delegates to endorse African emigration, when at least two million of colored people here in the South are ready to start to Africa at any moment, if we had a line of steamers running to and fro."[49]

To some extent Turner was correct. Even though his major effort at publicizing African emigration had failed to convince Northern or middle-class blacks, the idea of going to Africa seemed to be as popular as ever among the black peasants of the South. They, of course, were not the people Liberia needed to strengthen herself, nor the people the Colonization Society would send, nor even the people Bishop Turner thought should go. Nevertheless, after his strenuous year of publicizing Africa, Turner had only attracted more of those on the bottom rail. For the most part Africa would continue to appeal, in the years to come, only to the lower classes, who were eager to go wherever they could to escape from their problems. Even as the Turner convention ended, the party of emigrants was preparing to leave Georgia under Benjamin Gaston. African fever was still very much alive in the South.

Transportation, as always, was the major stumbling block for blacks who wished to emigrate. Africa was too far away and ship tickets were too expensive for the many who wanted to go there. That many *did* want to emigrate was demonstrated by the success with which W. H. Ellis soon recruited people to settle on his development in Mexico. Even though many returned to the United States later, several thousand blacks went to Mexico during 1894

49. *Voice of Missions,* January 1894.

and 1895.[50] Blacks were willing to leave the United States, especially for places that were romanticized and over-praised by agents or enthusiasts, if only a cheap way could be found. Bishop Turner, after failing to interest Northern blacks in his schemes, again turned to the South for support of a steamship line to Africa. In 1894, at long last, he succeeded.

50. *Washington Star,* 8, 20 March 1895; *Washington Post,* 18 March, 25 July 1895; *Birmingham Age-Herald,* 10 March 1895; Alfred W. Reynolds, "The Alabama Negro Colony in Mexico, 1894–1896," *Alabama Review,* 5 (October 1952), 243–68, and 6 (January 1953), 31–58.

9

The International Migration Society, I

"We take pleasure in announcing to the public generally, and to the Afro-American especially, that we have lately organized a company, and incorporated under the laws of Alabama, for the purpose of establishing a steamship line between the United States and Africa direct, and to do a general migration business."[1] So read the prospectus of the International Migration Society, which was organized January 1894 in response to Bishop Turner's agitation. During the years that followed, the Migration Society held center stage in the drama of black repatriation.

In Birmingham, four white men took the tantalizing bait with which Turner had so long fished in the troubled waters of American race relations. His confidence that Southern blacks would pay to emigrate and his prophecy of great gain from American-African commerce persuaded the group to enter the emigration business, not for charity but for profit. Little is known of the background of the organizers but the president was J. L. Daniels. Other officers were Jeremiah R. McMullen, the corresponding secretary; Edwin B. Cottingham, financial secretary; and Daniel J. Flummer, treasurer. An "advisory board" consisted of Bishop Turner and several other prominent blacks, including Bishop Alexander Walters and the Reverend A. J. Warner, both of the A.M.E. Zion church, but only Turner

1. International Migration Society circular in unclassified packet of printed material in ACS Papers.

and Warner actively participated in the Migration Society's operations. Despite his preference for blacks, the problems of economics and business organization had forced Turner to rely upon white men for transportation.[2]

The new organization lost little time in getting its emigration program under way. Three aspects of the operation had to be launched more or less simultaneously. First, the officials devised a plan for getting prospective emigrants enrolled and paying for their transportation. Next they began a widespread publicity campaign. Then they started a shipping scheme.

The Migration Society's plan of operation relied partially on the experience of the older Colonization Society and Bishop Turner. The Colonization Society had both transported emigrants to Liberia and supported them for six months after arrival. The Migration Society agreed that more than transportation was needed, but decided to support its emigrants for only three months. The bishop had found that, although many blacks were willing to leave for Africa, they had little ready cash. The Migration Society, therefore, based its plan on a dollar-a-month payment of the passage fee.[3]

The would-be emigrant agreed, after paying a one-dollar membership fee, to pay one or more dollars monthly until forty dollars had accumulated, for which the society agreed to furnish him steamship passage and provisions. Included was a clause providing that any would-be emigrant who defaulted on his contract would forfeit all previously paid money to the Society. Given the money problems of the depression and the possibility that migration enthusiasm might wane over a forty-month payment period, the Society would likely accumulate a considerable amount in

2. Ibid.; *New Orleans Times-Democrat,* 4 August 1900; *Washington Star,* 22 January 1894.
3. Cottingham to Wilson, 27 January 1894.

forfeitures. In the final analysis, most of the society's income came from forfeited payments.[4]

Once the plan was made the society began a broad campaign to bring the good news to Southern blacks. It used standard methods of publicity with considerable skill. First, the officers sought endorsement from the men and organizations associated with African emigration. Then they launched a campaign, using printed circulars, newspaper advertisements, and press releases. To drive home the message and enroll the emigrants, a wide network of local black agents was employed.

Within a week after its incorporation the society had published a circular that was mailed to prominent men with a request for endorsement. Bishop Turner, of course, needed no persuading. With glowing headlines in his *Voice of Missions* and with personal appeals from pulpit and platform, he praised the society profusely. The bishop's support was undoubtedly the key to any success the society might achieve.[5] When other blacks questioned his acclaim for this profit-making white-man's plan, he replied that he saw nothing wrong in profits from good works. It would be better, he acknowledged, if blacks could do the job and earn the profits, but they had neither the capital nor the organizational ability.[6]

The new society also sought support from the old American Colonization Society. In light of its experiences with weak or fraudulent migration societies, the Colonization Society had little confidence in the new group. Privately, Secretary Wilson believed the scheme "altogether impractical." "But we have not sufficient information . . . to justify us in denouncing it as a fraud or in publishing our opinions

4. Passage contract of the IMS in unclassified packet of printed material in ACS Papers.
5. *Voice of Missions,* March 1894; *Birmingham Age-Herald,* 29 August 1894.
6. *Voice of Missions,* July 1895.

that it will turn out a failure." Wilson politely refused to endorse the new project.[7]

The Migration Society was more successful in getting support from Africa. Liberia was still under pressure from France and therefore welcomed any hope of new immigrants. The annual appropriations for the republic's immigration agent and his work were promised to the Migration Society and other governmental aid was to come later.[8] Letters of support from prominent Liberians and recent emigrants helped the society in its propaganda campaign.[9]

The society relied heavily on the printed word for its publicity. In addition to the original prospectus, first published as a one-page circular, the society started a series of bulletins and pamphlets. They echoed Bishop Turner's thinking about the race problem in the United States and the glories of Africa. The pamphlets amplified on these themes, also drawing heavily on articles first published in the Colonization Society's *Liberia Bulletin* for information about Africa. Monthly flyers kept the members of the new society informed on the progress of new colonies as they continued the propaganda barrage.[10] Through letters and news releases the society kept its plans in the public press. Small black newspapers, in particular, were con-

7. Cottingham to Wilson, 27 January 1894; Wilson to Cottingham, 1 February 1894; Wilson to R. B. Davidson, 31 August 1894; Wilson to C. E. Milnor, 20 October 1894.

8. *Acts, 1891–1892,* p. 15; *Acts, 1894–1895,* p. 10; and *Acts, 1896–1897,* p. 17.

9. Majola Agbebi to H. M. Turner, 5 May 1894, in *Voice of Missions,* July 1894.

10. No file of these bulletins has been discovered; their existence and contents were reported in a series of detailed articles in the *New Orleans Times-Democrat,* 4 August 1900. Some of the pamphlets are available, however, and they include a short prospectus and a longer pamphlet titled *Prospectus of the International Migration Society* (Birmingham, 1894), W. K. Roberts, *An African Canaan for American Negroes* (Birmingham, 1897), and Daniel J. Flummer, *The Negro and Liberia* (Birmingham, 1897).

tinually informed of its actions. The major colored papers in the North, of course, opposed all emigration schemes and refused to cooperate with the society. One of the journals that supported the society was the *Voice of Missions,* in which editor Turner gave full coverage to each new turn of policy or action by the society, as well as his own propaganda.[11]

Because few black newspapers of the period have been preserved, it is impossible to know how many supported emigration and the society. The *Denver Statesman,* from which some clippings remain, was probably representative of a number of small Southern and Western papers. Its editor had supported Turner at the Cincinnati convention and the black community of Denver had eagerly enrolled in the abortive "ship clubs" of D. E. Johnson. The *Statesman* was cautious about full endorsement of the new scheme, but it published various letters and reports from the Birmingham headquarters which painted a glowing picture of Africa. The editor announced in May 1894 that he had become the Western agent for the society and would assist any who wished to enroll for emigration. If only a few other newspapers emulated the *Statesman,* the Migration Society did not lack broad coverage in print.[12]

Once endorsements had been received and printed propaganda circulated, the society turned to local conventions to arouse emigration interest. The drive started in Birmingham. A. J. Warner, a prominent local black churchman, and a member of the society's advisory board, issued the call.[13] According to one account, "the attendance was large and enthusiastic. Bishop Turner was on hand and orated on the beauties of Africa. The desire to emigrate

---

11. *Voice of Missions,* March 1894 and thereafter.
12. *Denver Statesman,* 24 February, 24 March, 12 May, 9 June, 21 July, 4, 25 August, 1 September, 6 October 1894, in ACS scrapbooks.
13. *Washington Star,* 27 February 1894.

reached a fever heat."[14] The editor of the *New Orleans Crusader,* one of the small black newspapers that carried the society's message, commented: "Heretofore we had not favored emigration to Africa, but migration of the colored people in the States, West and North; but today, if there are any who want to go to the Dark Continent, we shall offer no objection. The Negro can lose nothing by migration or emigration."[15] The success of the Birmingham meeting led the society to call other conventions.[16] With the increase in lynchings and the decrease in cotton prices, Southern black farmers were ready to listen.

To channel the excitement, the society appointed black "special agents" throughout the South. According to its headquarters, 138 such local representatives worked in sixteen states. A New Orleans agent reported that he received the first dollar paid in by new members plus 5 percent of later payments. In addition to circulating the literature of the society, he published his own material and held frequent meetings to stir up interest. He also appointed numerous subagents who carried the emigration gospel to outlying towns. Among the agents were some long-time emigrationists who carried on regular correspondence with the older Colonization Society. The success or failure of the back-to-Africa campaign in any area depended heavily on the industry and ability of the local agent. From what followed in the next years, it appears that most agents had good success in recruiting members but little luck in getting them to pay installments.[17]

14. (New Orleans) *Crusader,* quoted in *Denver Statesman,* 7 April, 1894, in ACS scrapbooks.
15. Ibid.; cf. "Scipio Americanus" in *Savannah Tribune,* 24 March 1894.
16. Cf. *Savannah Tribune,* 16 June 1894; *New York World,* 17 September 1894.
17. Agent William Royal as interviewed by the *New Orleans Times-Democrat,* 4 August 1900. Numerous letters in the ACS Papers mention IMS agents and their activities.

Needless to say, opposition arose wherever thoughtful blacks heard of the scheme, and Northern and urban leaders had changed little since the Turner convention in Cincinnati. Journalists like T. Thomas Fortune expressed more and more anger as the prospects of a successful emigration movement grew. Nevertheless, economic conditions were so bad in the entire nation that, according to one report, more whites returned to Europe than immigrated to the United States.[18] And many blacks, outcasts in their own country, were also ready to leave. Such conditions prompted the *Christian Recorder* to register a more tolerant view of black emigration. "It cannot be said that any new arguments have been presented to support the project of the [Migration] Society; but there can be no doubt," said a *Recorder* editorial, "that the new propaganda has been directed with great practical intelligence and earnestness. . . . Every right-thinking and right-feeling man will follow with interest the fortunes of the brave men and women who are about to make this experiment."[19] Thus encouraged, the society proceeded with its work.

Within a few months after its founding in January 1894, the International Migration Society had made an auspicious start. Its plan of operation was formed and endorsements had been secured. Conventions, circulars, and newspapers carried the propaganda through the South. Agents collected money for passage. It remained to be seen, however, whether the society could make good its claims. The next crucial step was the organization of its shipping line.

At the start, the society had intended to charter steamships to take emigrants and freight to Africa. Operating through shipping agents in Philadelphia, the society in

18. *New York Times,* 21 July 1894. Cf. *Denver Statesman,* 24 March 1894, in ACS scrapbooks.
19. *Christian Recorder,* 15 November 1894.

June 1894 claimed to have secured a German vessel to call at various Atlantic coast ports to collect 820 Liberia-bound blacks.[20] No ship materialized, however, and the announcement of a July sailing may have been intended merely as a come-on for would-be emigrants. For making authentic shipping arrangements, the society decided in the summer of 1894 to operate through another company that would handle ships and traffic. From Birmingham came word that the African Steamship Company had contracted with the Migration Society to ship 5,000 emigrants each year to Liberia.[21] The company, however, was not an old established firm; it was created as a subsidiary of the Migration Society. The senior officer of the company was J. R. McMullen, vice president of the society. The other officers were Philadelphia businessmen. After a period of planning and propaganda, the company was incorporated in New Jersey in August 1894. Its operations were clearly dependent upon the Migration Society's success in recruiting emigrants.[22]

The company's prospectus, nevertheless, stressed the potential value of freight and trading. Glowing reports of both actual and potential commerce with Liberia lured investors. The republic was portrayed as a source of great natural wealth and an eager market for American manufactured goods. Once the company's regular steamships began operation, they would monopolize most of that trade. The prospectus did not mention the fact that Yates and Porterfield had found the African trade too poor to continue nor that the best estimate of the United States government put Liberian-American trade at only $44,000

20. *Washington Star,* 26 June 1894; Wilson to C. E. Milnor, 28 June 1894.

21. *Boston Evening Transcript,* 30 August 1894; *Denver Statesman,* 8 September 1894, in ACS scrapbooks.

22. Thomas Pentlarge to Pennsylvania Colonization Society, 19 September 1894 (forwarded to the ACS). *Philadelphia Ledger,* 29 August 1894, in ACS scrapbooks.

in 1894. Instead, the company estimated that trade with Africa would be at least $400,000 in the first year alone. This optimism strongly echoed Bishop Turner's enthusiastic claims.[23]

A "sideline" of the company would be trade with Cuba. The prospectus barely mentioned the island, but Thomas Pentlarge, comptroller of the company, stated that the company's first shipping venture was the chartering of a freighter for Cuban commerce. The mid-1890s, of course, were years of gun-running to Cuban rebels who were struggling against their Spanish masters. Later events would heighten the suspicions that the African Steamship Company was running guns, probably more profitable but more risky than trading with Africa. Such developments offer some clues to the character of the otherwise unknown leaders of the company.[24]

Capital for the company was to come from two sources. Stock was offered for sale, although Pentlarge claimed that he did not want to spread the base too widely because the profits promised to be so high, about 33 percent. In September 1894 he asserted that "a foreign banking institution" had guaranteed $50,000 and a Southern concern $25,000. Nevertheless, advertisements were placed in the Migration Society bulletins offering stock at $50 per share.[25] The second source of capital, according to the prospectus, was a $10,000 annual subsidy from the government of Liberia. Liberian records show no evidence of such a grant.[26]

23. Prospectus enclosed in T. Pentlarge to Pennsylvania Colonization Society, 19 September 1894; *Commercial Relations of the United States with Foreign Countries, 1894 and 1895* (Washington, 1896), p. 22.
24. Pentlarge to Pennsylvania Colonization Society, 19 September 1894. The captains of two ships later hired by the Migration Society were subsequently convicted for gun-running.
25. Ibid.; *New Orleans Times-Democrat,* 4 August 1900.
26. Prospectus in Pentlarge to Pennsylvania Colonization Society, 19 September 1894. Published volumes of the legislative acts of Liberia

Although the company claimed that its business would be based primarily on freight, it promised that "passengers of every kind will receive due attention." The Migration Society contracted with the company for passage for 5,000 colonists per year. According to the prospectus, the shipping firm expected some 2,000 tourists to visit Africa annually, in addition to the emigrants. All in all, it was a glowing picture of forthcoming profits. But in the midst of a severe worldwide depression, it was too glowing to be credible.[27]

With its plan, organization, and shipping company established, the Migration Society was prepared to go into operation. Paid-up passage contracts, however, came in slowly. The lack of cash among the blacks and the annual cycle of Southern cotton farming made the summer and fall of 1894 a difficult time to lure impoverished farmers away. The first scheduled ship, which was supposed to sail from Philadelphia on July 6, never appeared. Nor did its 820 colonists.[28]

The steamship company next promised that its first ship would leave in early October. "Any being desirous of going on this first trip must make application and pay their money not later than September 20, and must pay the same in full in order to go with the first vessel. The Steamship Company," President McMullen announced, "has enough freight to pay all the expenses of the first trip, and absolutely and positively refuses to wait any longer to receive passengers."[29] Again the response was too small to

give no evidence of this subsidy. Nevertheless, Liberia had earlier offered $6,000 annually to the American Colonization Society for aid to emigration and this money might have been transferred to the African Steamship Company for helping get desperately needed immigrants.

27. Ibid.; *Philadelphia Times,* 2 October 1894.

28. *Washington Star,* 26 June 1894; Wilson to C. E. Milnor, 28 June 1894.

29. J. R. McMullen to *Denver Statesman,* 8 September 1894, in ACS scrapbooks.

warrant sending the ship. The November issue of the Migration Society's bulletin reportedly said that during the ten months the society had been in existence "just ten people have paid the full amount of their passage money. . . . About 800 have paid nothing but their membership fees, and then ceased to pay installments. A very large percentage have continued to pay their installments in an irregular manner."[30] Freight, similarly, was not forthcoming.

By November 1894 it appeared that the entire venture —Migration Society, steamship company, and all—would sink in the financial quicksand of the depression. If the society was honest in its plans to aid emigrant blacks, some new spark of enthusiasm had to be kindled. To prove their sincerity and thus increase the confidence of the blacks, the officers decided to send the few paid-up members to Liberia via Europe and summoned to their Birmingham headquarters the fourteen who had paid their passage. Eight people came from Arkansas, four from Denver, one from Alabama, and a missionary from Toronto. The man from Alabama had second thoughts, but the remaining thirteen, amid much publicity, boarded a train for New York and then sailed to Liverpool and Liberia. Thus the "first colony" of the Migration Society made its exodus, but in a style somewhat less grand than the promoters envisioned. Although it was about one percent of the grandiose prediction, it was at least a beginning.[31]

The society's publicity made the most of this first "success." President McMullen, who had succeeded Daniels, wrote to his agents scattered throughout the country: "We look for the greatest good to ensue, not only to this Society and your race, but also the Republic of Liberia, from these

30. Quoted in *New Orleans Times-Democrat,* 4 August 1900.
31. *New York Times,* 15 November 1894; *Denver Statesman,* 17 November 1894, in ACS scrapbooks; *Voice of Missions,* December 1894.

people who are representative people and who will create a good impression, and if they are properly received in Liberia and send back favorable reports, thousands of people and hundreds of thousands of dollars will go to Liberia for investment."[32] The press and Bishop Turner's *Voice of Missions* carried extensive reports of the colony's departure, but nothing was reported about the fate of the thirteen once they arrived in Africa. Apparently they were reasonably satisfied with their Liberian accommodations for none returned or sent back complaints.

Reaction to the publicity developed slowly—too slowly, apparently, for some of the backers of the project. During the winter McMullen, resigned as president of both the society and the steamship company; he was replaced by Secretary Daniel Flummer. Even Bishop Turner was disheartened. The great "exodus to Africa," he said, was "a total disappointment" because of the fall in cotton prices to five cents per pound.[33]

Opposition to the Migration Society's scheme continued among educated blacks, especially in the North, and one man in particular had what he considered solid grounds for criticizing any Liberian emigration plan. Charles S. Smith, the Secretary of the A.M.E. Sunday School Union, had visited West Africa in the autumn of 1894, while the society was struggling to get its first group to Africa. Smith traveled by ship for three months along the coast as far south as Angola. His purpose, he said, was to "ascertain whether that continent holds any special inducements to young, intelligent and industrious Americans of African descent to emigrate there."[34] His "explorations," however,

32. Quoted in *Denver Statesman*, 17 November 1894, in ACS scrapbooks.

33. *Voice of Missions*, January 1895; the *Washington Post* of 10 March 1895 mentioned Flummer as president of the society.

34. Charles S. Smith, *Glimpses of Africa* (Nashville, 1895), pp. 22, 23, 131.

consisted of watching harbor activities and recording weather phenomena from the deck of his ship, a German freighter. He went ashore at Monrovia for only ten days, and visited Freetown, Sierra Leone, for five days, but in neither place ventured beyond the sound of the ship's whistle. Nevertheless, he managed to antagonize the Africans with his harsh judgments and tactless words about Liberia.[35] On his return to the United States in early 1895, Smith openly opposed the Migration Society because it painted such a seductive picture of Africa. "I am not disposed, in the least, to disparage the interests of Liberia," he wrote. "But I am certainly opposed to schemes taking advantage of the name of that republic to swindle and defraud innocent and ignorant colored people."[36] In the weeks to come Smith would prove a painful thorn in the flesh of Bishop Turner and the Migration Society.

The American Colonization Society, meanwhile, officially declared that, in the opinion of its officers, "the plans proposed are likely to prove abortive from inexperience and want of sufficient financial backing of the promoters."[37] Despite opposition by Northern blacks in general and Smith in particular, and despite the financial panic, the Migration Society continued to publicize Africa and recruit emigrants. Once winter had come, the crops were gathered, and their farm contracts were completed, black farmers were more ready to listen and join. The publicity created by the departure of the thirteen people for Liberia in November was not completely vitiated by opposition attacks. At that time the society had noted with candor that less than a thousand had joined its ranks and that

35. *New York Age,* 22 November 1894, 17, 31 January 1895; *Lagos Weekly Record,* 23 March, 20 April 1895; *Voice of Missions,* May 1895. All in ACS scrapbooks.

36. C. S. Smith to Wilson, 6 March 1895.

37. Minutes of the ACS Board of Directors (1869–1912) entry for 15 January 1895.

most of them had lapsed in their payments. In January, however, the society reported that 7,000 were on its rolls. If the later figure was reported with as much honesty as the former, there was indeed a significant rise of emigration interest among rural blacks. During the same months, furthermore, the scheme for settling blacks in Mexico attracted considerable numbers from the Gulf states.[38]

Another indication of the success of the society's propaganda was the rise of frauds that were designed to capitalize on the emigration sentiment. From various places around the country came reports of swindlers who sold "tickets to Africa" for a dollar.[39] To later copies of its prospectus the Migration Society added warnings against confidence men who might use the society's name.[40] In Hancock County, Georgia, a black man impersonated Benjamin Gaston for several months after the real Gaston had sailed back to Liberia. Taking advantage of the excitement created by the Migration Society and by Gaston's success, the imposter managed to collect a dollar apiece from an estimated 3,000 black farmers. So many had left their jobs at a critical time that plantation owners despaired of making a crop. But the victims of the swindle finally discovered the fraud, and in the ensuing violence "Gaston" was killed.[41] Another "Gaston" materialized shortly thereafter in Washington County, Georgia, and a suspicious black asked Secretary Wilson of the Colonization Society about the man, who had collected several hundred dollars from his victims. "A good many colored folks," he wrote, "are camping along the line of the railroads waiting for tickets and suffer-

38. *Voice of Missions,* January 1895; *New Orleans Times-Democrat,* 4 August 1900; *Atlanta Constitution,* 6, 9 March 1895.
39. W. W. Marmaduke (Washington, Ind.) to Wilson, 14 November 1894; *Savannah Morning News,* 6 February 1895.
40. *Prospectus of the International Migration Society* (Birmingham, 1894), stamped on inside back cover of the copy in the Library of Congress.
41. *Washington Star,* 4, 6, 7 September 1894; *Atlanta Journal,* 4, 5, 6 September 1894.

ing."[42] The winter of 1894–95 had seen a sudden upturn of emigration excitement among Southern rural blacks.

The Migration Society, as well as the fake African agents, benefited from the new interest. After being in near despair in November, society officials announced impending success. "As a result of our efforts people have organized themselves into clubs in almost every precinct in the South," the society's bulletin said. "Applications for membership have been increasing. . . . Membership now amounts to many thousands."[43] A short time later the society announced that "Colony Number Two" would sail from Savannah on March 9 and that a special train would leave Memphis and pick up passengers along the way. If the promise sounded suspiciously familiar, Bishop Turner was cautiously excited. This might indeed be the beginning of his long-dreamed-of exodus.[44]

C. S. Smith, however, just back from Africa and displeased with what he had seen there, was skeptical. He launched his attack in an open letter to Turner. While in Monrovia he had discussed American emigration with Liberian officials, including President Cheeseman, and—contrary to claims of the Migration Society—Smith reported that Liberia wanted capitalists as immigrants, not paupers, that the government would not be responsible for the reception and care of newcomers, and that the only inducement the nation offered was land. "I look upon the so-called 'International Migration Society' as an organized swindle," he wrote. "They are holding out hopes and promises in regard to [Liberia] which can never be fulfilled or realized."[45]

Smith claimed, furthermore, that he had investigated

42. Eldridge Irwin to Wilson, 18 February 1895; Wilson to Irwin, 20 February 1895; Wilson to G. L. Boatwright, 6 July 1894; Wilson to J. H. Davis, 30 October 1894.

43. Quoted in *New Orleans Times-Democrat*, 4 August 1900.

44. *Voice of Missions*, March 1895.

45. C. S. Smith to Turner, in *Christian Recorder*, 28 February 1895.

and had found no evidence that the society was able or was planning to send a ship to Africa in March. The thirteen blacks in "Colony Number One," he said, all suffered from the fever and lacked proper shelter and care. "In my opinion," he wrote, "our people might just as well rush into the jaws of death as go to Liberia poor and penniless and dependent."[46] Smith vowed "to awaken sentiment sufficiently strong to crush out the black schemers and scoundrels who are preying upon the ignorance and innocence of their people."[47]

As the announced day of sailing approached, activity increased, and the Migration Society issued a press release that proclaimed about 200 blacks would leave Memphis by train for Savannah and the ship to Africa. On reading this, Bishop Turner grew ecstatic, but C. S. Smith traveled to Atlanta to try to dissuade the would-be emigrants. Citizens of Savannah, meanwhile, grew apprehensive at the prospect of black paupers descending upon their city.[48]

First came reports that two carloads of blacks had left Pine Bluff, Arkansas, for Liberia. Then the Memphis newspapers told how poor and illiterate colored people from Arkansas, Mississippi, Louisiana, and Texas had converged on the local railway depot. "Farmers were in the majority, but there were any number of carpenters, blacksmiths, shoemakers and men of nearly all trades." The travelers slept on the benches and floors of the crowded waiting rooms. Poverty was visible everywhere, although a few migrants had money. When questioned about their journey, the transients echoed Bishop Turner's ideas, saying they were "tired of a country where the white man is king and the Negro the servant." If their venture proved a failure, they reasoned, they could not be worse off than they

46. Ibid.
47. C. S. Smith to Wilson, 6 March 1895.
48. *Atlanta Constitution,* 6 March 1895.

were at present. T. D. Howard, the recently appointed treasurer of the Migration Society, was in charge of the train of emigrants. He made sure that the newspapermen learned the whole story of the society and its plans for it was evident that success was its best publicity.[49]

The migrating group caused considerable excitement among Memphis blacks. As the travelers congregated in the depot awaiting departure, word spread rapidly through the city, and within a few hours "fully 1500" blacks were gathered around the depot to see and to question their more adventurous brethren. One newspaperman predicted that many local blacks would soon follow this group to Africa. "[Those] who saw the departure will no doubt become imbued with the restless spirit which dominates the black race, and in a short while there will no doubt be a Memphis colony rehabilitating the site of old Memphis on the banks of the Nile."[50]

The exodus train also attracted attention elsewhere. An *Atlanta Constitution* editorial opined that the "map of Africa, . . . showing colonies with flourishing cities and railroad lines, shows that life is not only possible there but pleasant."[51] The train arrived in Atlanta at dawn the day after it left Memphis, its three emigrant cars carrying bold banners announcing that its 200 passengers were on their way to Liberia. Again, local blacks who had heard much about Africa from Bishop Turner and who even then had an independent scheme for getting there, gathered around the train with excitement.[52] C. S. Smith arrived in Atlanta that night to debate the merits of Africa with another prominent black educator, W. H. Councill of Alabama.[53]

49. *Memphis Evening Scimitar,* 7 (?) March 1895, in ACS scrapbooks. *Memphis Commercial Appeal,* 7 March 1895.
50. *Memphis Commercial Appeal,* 7 March 1895.
51. *Atlanta Constitution,* 7 March 1895.
52. *Atlanta Journal,* 8 March 1895.
53. *Memphis Commercial Appeal,* 7 March 1895.

In Savannah, the approach of the train caused concern among the town's officials, who found no evidence that the Migration Society had made preparations either to house or transport the blacks. Expressing hope that the emigrants would not be stranded in their city, the local newspaper concluded that "Savannah could very easily spare a few hundred of her idle colored population and nobody desires to have their number increased at this time."[54]

When the train arrived in Savannah, late on March 8, no ship was waiting nor were quarters provided for the emigrants. Treasurer Howard, who had accompanied the train from Memphis, had little information to give reporters; he seemed as mystified as they. Nevertheless, he was fully confident that the ship would appear in due course; emigration was "a big thing," he told newsmen. There were 4,700 active members of the society, and more were joining daily—according to the Birmingham headquarters. But singing praises of the movement would not care for the new arrivals, and Howard found an empty warehouse for housing them until the ship could take them away. Citizens of Savannah were less sure about the ship. "We will not become a dumping ground," said an editorial that accused the society of bad management, or perhaps worse.[55]

A dispatch from Philadelphia, meanwhile, reported progress in obtaining an emigrant ship. D. J. Flummer, the new president of the society, told the press that he had chartered a vessel that would soon ferry the emigrants from Savannah to Monrovia. The society, it developed, had contracted with its ally, the African Steamship Company, to provide a ship at Savannah on March 9, as announced in the society's literature. The steamship company, however, despite a $1,510 deposit made by the

54. *Savannah Morning News,* 8 March 1895.
55. Ibid., 9 March 1895.

society, was unable to produce the craft and the company collapsed under this pressure. Its achievements amounted to nothing more than advertising its stock and perhaps taking a consignment of cargo to Cuba. Flummer, without help from the defunct company, and having already announced the date of departure from Savannah, proceeded on his own to charter a Danish ship, the "Horsa." Despite the delay of several days in securing and fitting out the vessel, Flummer promised that the migrants in Savannah would certainly leave for Africa within a week.[56]

The "Horsa" was a small ship, 210 feet long and 26 feet at the beam, and displaced only 728 gross tons. She had been in the Caribbean fruit trade, and her skipper, Captain Wiborg, would later be charged with running guns into Cuba.[57] To adapt the undersize steamer for passengers by building wooden bunks in the holds and cooking shacks and comfort facilities on deck would take several days' work in Philadelphia. But her skipper promised to make up for lost time by a fast crossing to Liberia.[58]

The would-be emigrants settled into their makeshift quarters in Savannah. They had an implicit, serene faith in Howard and the Migration Society and, as usual, attracted considerable attention, not only among the local blacks but among whites as well. Reporters for the white newspapers, who kept a steady watch over the group, discovered that half the group came from Arkansas and that Mississippi, Alabama, Tennessee, and Texas were represented in that order, while some came from other Southern states. Between thirty and forty of the pilgrims were small children. All the migrants predicted that more blacks would soon follow them, and there were constant rumors

56. Ibid., 8, 11 March 1895; *Atlanta Constitution,* 10 March 1895; *Washington Post,* 10 March 1895.

57. *Savannah Morning News,* 19 March 1895, 1 January 1896.

58. *Washington Times,* 14 March 1895; C. T. Geyer to Wilson, 11 March 1895.

that additional Georgia blacks would join the contingent in Savannah.[59]

The press pestered Treasurer Howard with embarrassing questions about the Migration Society, and he answered the obvious query candidly. The society, after it learned that the ship would not be ready on time, had decided to run the Memphis train on schedule because the emigrants would have been confused if the society altered its announced plans. It was better, the officials reasoned, to support the group in Savannah for a few days than risk losing them altogether. The stay in the port city would cost the society almost $75 daily for room and board. "We are not in this business for our health, but expect to make some money out of it," Howard said. "This is our first party and it was to be expected that there would be some hitches. . . . We will not make any profit this trip; in fact we shall lose something by it. . . . We expect to make another trip about ninety days from now when we will probably carry six hundred emigrants."[60]

When word finally came on March 14 that the "Horsa" was leaving Philadelphia for Savannah and it seemed that the 200 emigrants would actually leave for Africa, the opposition spoke out. Opponents of emigration had, of course, continually attacked the Migration Society and its premise, but emigration movements had come and gone without achieving significant results, and the advocates of integration and accommodation had not been unduly alarmed. When the train trip from Memphis had begun, a few newspaper editorials took notice of it and either ridiculed the blacks for thinking they could do better elsewhere or criticized the Migration Society as a fraud. As

59. *Savannah Morning News,* 9, 10 March 1895.
60. Ibid., 10 March 1895; *Memphis Evening Scimitar,* 12 March 1895, in ACS scrapbooks.

the days dragged on in Savannah, the white newspaper of that city also criticized the emigrants. "There is nothing to prevent them from accumulating property or of rising to a higher moral and intellectual plane [in the United States]. It is their own misfortune that they cannot see that this is so."[61] The local black weekly at first said nothing about the visitors. Many in the local black community undoubtedly opposed emigration but they did little to embarrass the emigrants or the society. But the announcement of the "Horsa's" imminent arrival brought to Savannah the sworn enemy of the project, C. S. Smith.[62]

Smith first attempted to dissuade the emigrants from leaving and then to keep the ship from sailing. When he arrived in Savannah he told the press about his recent visit to Africa and his observations about the economy and the unhealthy climate of West Africa, repeating his contention that only capitalists should settle there. Further, the emigration movement was a fraud, he claimed. "I saw a party of Negroes in Florida camped out beside the railroad track waiting for a free train to Africa. In Northern Louisiana recently a party of a hundred sold all, having been promised transportation to Africa for a dollar." Smith concluded that "there is absolutely no reason for any civilized person to emigrate to Liberia."[63]

But his words to the reporters did not faze the emigrants, and when he tried to speak to them directly he was rebuffed. Treasurer Howard countered with a charge that Smith was being paid for his obstructive effort by men who were eager to attract "Ohio farmers to the South, and who do not like the negro emigration movement as tending to give this section a black eye." In answer to Smith's accusa-

61. *Savannah Morning News,* 13 March 1895.
62. *Savannah Tribune,* 9 March 1895.
63. *Savannah Morning News,* 16 March 1895.

tion that the migrants were already sick and should not be packed into close quarters, Howard produced a doctor's evaluation that the people were healthy enough.[64]

Scoring little success with the emigrants and the society, Smith concentrated his energies in trying to stop the ship from sailing. From what he had read about the "Horsa," he was convinced that it was unseaworthy and did not meet the federal standards for emigrant accommodations. He decided to call the situation to the attention of customs officers, and request them to inspect the ship and find her unsuitable. Smith confidently predicted that the "Horsa" would be found too small to handle 200 people, that rations would be short, and that adequate ventilation and medical care would be lacking. When the long-awaited vessel finally steamed up the channel to its pier on Sunday, March 17, Howard assured the public that all was well. Confident, he joined the call for the ship's inspection.[65]

The inspection took an additional day. Crowds of Savannah citizens, both black and white, visited the dock to see the "Horsa" while the local customs officers scrutinized her facilities. "[They] found her in excellent condition, with a few minor exceptions. In fact she has better accommodations than most immigrant ships that dock in northern ports," the press reported. On the basis of cubic feet of space below decks, the authorities ruled that she could handle 220 passengers, twenty more than she had been booked for. Smith, of course, did not moderate his attack, even though the officials refused him permission to board the ship. He hired a proxy to visit the craft and used the man's reports to challenge the official report. Among other deficiencies, he found that the topside cook houses and water closets were so poorly built that the first heavy sea would wash them away. "The inspectors may be willing

64. Ibid., 17 March 1895.
65. Ibid.

to pass the vessel on the grounds that anything is good enough for a nigger," Smith concluded, "and that is the only way in which she can be passed." When the local officials refused to heed his challenge, Smith prepared an appeal to the Secretary of the Treasury and the press.[66]

Meanwhile, preparations continued for the departure of the emigrants. Three Birmingham white men, including the Migration Society's secretary, Cottingham, arrived in Savannah and announced that they intended to travel on the "Horsa" to Liberia. They planned to investigate business opportunities after overseeing the settling of the newcomers there. Supplies were loaded and the emigrants' baggage was stowed aboard. All was in readiness for the day of farewell.[67]

Because of the newspaper publicity created by the emigration and the long delay in Savannah, there was great general interest in the departure. As the emigrants left their warehouse quarters for the last time and trekked to the dock, townspeople left their shops and offices to watch the embarkation. Reporters from several Northern newspapers and a number of photographers were said to be present. Churchmen came to pray with the voyagers. Several thousand people, according to the press, jammed the piers as the "Horsa" waited for the noon tide. According to the local black newspaper, which was not emigrationist in sentiment, the people of Savannah, black and white, sympathized with the emigrants.[68]

A festive air prevailed on the wharf. Preachers preached and the Migration Society officers beamed. The local agent

66. Ibid., 19 March 1895. Cf. C. S. Smith to Wilson, 23, 28 March 1895; Wilson to Smith, 25 March 1895; open letter from C. S. Smith to the Secretary of the Treasury, J. G. Carlisle, 27 March 1895 (copy in ACS correspondence file); C. S. Smith to *Christian Recorder,* 11 April 1895; Smith to *New York Age,* 11 April 1895, ACS scrapbooks.
67. *Savannah Morning News,* 19 March 1895.
68. Ibid., 20 March 1895; *Savannah Tribune,* 23 March 1895.

for the society darted among the onlookers and solicited members for the next "colony." A lusty singing of hymns attracted more people to the waterfront. When a quartet of emigrants sang about the promised land, a voice from the pier shouted in response: "Tell the people on the other side we're coming too." As the "Horsa" cast off, a great cheer went up from the people on the wharf and the emigrants echoed the shout. As they steamed down the river and out to sea they continued to sing, as though they were entering heaven.[69]

The crowd on the pier dissolved slowly, discussing what it had seen. Treasurer Howard reveled in relief that the ship had finally sailed. The editor of the local white newspaper predicted that the joy of the emigrants would fade as soon as they hit the open sea.[70] While many blacks mused over the siren call of Africa, at least thirty-five joined the Migration Society on the spot. C. S. Smith, fuming and furious, wrote out his accusations that the ship was overloaded, that insufficient supplies had been taken, that the white officials who had promised to travel on the "Horsa" had really left the ship with the pilot boat.[71] But the sailing of the "Horsa" was a triumph for the society and vindication against the charges of fraud. Despite the economic depression, despite the opposition of upper-class blacks, despite the attacks of Smith, a ship loaded with people had left for Africa. Migration Society officials spoke confidently of the coming exodus.

69. *Savannah Morning News,* 20 March 1895.
70. Ibid.
71. Ibid.; C. S. Smith to Wilson, 28 March 1895; Smith to J. G. Carlisle, 27 March 1895, in ACS Papers.

10

The International Migration Society, II

The departure of the "Horsa" on March 19, 1895, though an important publicity boost to emigration also excited anti-emigrationists to new activity. The opposition was particularly strong just after the ship sailed, but later, when first reports of success in Liberia began to arrive in the South, the International Migration Society was in a better position to proceed with its mission. As soon as the ship pulled away from the pier, C. S. Smith had directed new fury at the project. He had been publicly humiliated by his failure to prevent the "Horsa" from sailing, and in response he pressed his attacks against the Society. In an open letter to the Secretary of the Treasury, Smith enumerated his complaints about the "Horsa." Treasury officials, however, were no more impressed by Smith's letter than by his dockside complaints.[1]

Next, Smith tried to discredit the Migration Society in the eyes of blacks. Attempting to dispel their illusions, he pointed out that the society was operated not by black men but by whites. "The Society is organized solely for the purpose of making money out of the transportation of the emigrants to Africa without any regard to the interests of those whom they may succeed in persuading to go," Smith charged.[2] Because his own honesty had been questioned

1. C. S. Smith to J. G. Carlisle, 27 March 1895 (copy in ACS Papers).
2. Smith to *Christian Recorder,* 11 April 1895.

by Migration Society officials, he protested that "my fight now is against organized greed and selfishness."[3] Because his veracity and judgment had been challenged by offended Africans in Lagos, Sierra Leone, and Liberia, he proposed in vain that the Afro-American press choose a commission to visit West Africa and report the truth.[4]

Instead, editor T. Thomas Fortune of the *New York Age* chose to seek the opinions of prominent Southern blacks on the emigration question. The replies he received varied in their estimates of how many blacks would, if possible, go to Africa; they ran from "not one thousand of the race in Texas" to "about 20 or 25 per cent"—"the shiftless, floating, good-for-nothing class" of blacks in Oklahoma. An educator from Arkansas, whence came most of the "Horsa's" passengers, acknowledged that "a considerable percentage of the Afro-American population would go to Africa," but it would be only the poorest people. Again it was made clear that educated and middle-class blacks still opposed African emigration.[5]

As the "Horsa" steamed across the Atlantic, white newspapers commented extensively on the ship and its supporters. Although a few editorials in the *Charleston News and Courier,* the *Minneapolis Times,* and the *Memphis Commercial Appeal* endorsed the scheme, most editors viewed it as foolish or fraudulent, misguided or tragic. They agreed with the *Washington Post* which said "Of course, there will always be found in the South communities pervaded by a spirit of unrest and discontent, from which recruits for the emigrant ships may be obtainable. . . . The overwhelming majority of Negroes in the South

---

3. Smith to Wilson, 28 March 1895.
4. Smith to *New York Age,* 11 April 1895, in ACS scrapbooks.
5. *New York Age,* 18, 25 April 1895, in ACS scrapbooks. Cf. *New York Sun,* 14 April 1895.

want to stay where they are, and there will never be much diversion of them beyond the seas."[6]

All the controversy, of course, was irrelevant to the "Horsa's" passengers as they departed American shores. A ship which passed near them on the high seas reported the emigrants on deck and singing, "I'm Bound for the Happy Land."[7] Despite the dire predictions of C. S. Smith, the voyage was not a miserable affair. Although they were crowded together, the passengers stayed healthy—only one person, an infant, died. Some of the older folk were not well, but after eighteen days at sea all 197 were eager to set foot on land again. On Sunday, April 7, the squat little ship anchored off the Monrovia bar. The passengers were understandably excited on seeing their new homeland, but after several hours of waiting at anchor they realized that something was wrong.[8]

The port officials were taken completely by surprise; the cablegram that the Migration Society supposedly sent to Monrovia to announce the coming of the party never arrived. The society did not have an agent in Liberia, and no preparations had been made to receive the "Horsa." Moreover, it was Sunday, and the lighters that unloaded incoming ships were not working. No one from the shore, consequently, visited the vessel for several hours, until the master of the port rowed out to the anchorage to learn about the unexpected ship with the Danish flag. When he returned to shore and announced that almost 200 penniless immigrants were about to descend on Monrovia, town officials and citizens scurried about trying to arrange makeshift accommodations. Julius C. Stevens, the African agent for the American Colonization Society, volunteered the

6. *Washington Post,* 20 April 1895. *Public Opinion, 18* (11 April 1895), 370–71.

7. *Savannah Tribune,* 30 March 1895.

8. Among various accounts of the voyage, the best is in J. C. Stevens to Wilson, 10 November 1895.

empty half of his warehouse for storage of the immigrants' baggage. The Liberian Immigration Agent, Robert T. Sherman, after consultation with President Cheeseman and others, found vacant buildings for housing some of the people. Private citizens of the town planned to take in the remainder.[9]

The next morning Stevens and Sherman went out to the "Horsa" and began debarking the passengers and by nightfall every immigrant and his baggage was safely on shore. The only thing missing was the three months' provisions the Migration Society had contracted to divide among the newcomers. When the African Steamship Company collapsed at the time its ship was to meet the emigrants in Savannah, the society had been forced to charter the "Horsa," a much smaller craft than expected. After the passengers and their baggage had been put aboard, there was room for only a small portion of the promised provisions. Even though enough food had been purchased and placed on the wharf in Savannah, the "Horsa's" officers had refused to overload the ship. Consequently the newcomers were thrust upon the charity of the Liberians.[10]

The immigrants remained in their temporary quarters at Monrovia for three weeks, dining at the tables of local citizens, before they were taken to their new homesteads. All the preparations that had preceded the groups sent out earlier by the Colonization Society now had to be rushed. The government's gunboat, furthermore, which was to ferry the new settlers to their homesites during intervals in its customs-enforcement duties, was unable to move because it had no coal for its boilers. During the enforced delay, representatives of the new colonists visited the out-

9. Ibid.; Stevens to Wilson, 1 May, 6 June 1895; W. H. Heard to Wilson, 30 July, 18 September 1895; Cottingham to Wilson, 31 October 1895.

10. Stevens to Wilson, 10 November 1895; Cottingham to Wilson, 31 October 1895.

lying settlements near Monrovia and decided to settle in three groups, at Royesville, Brewerville, and Johnsonville.[11]

The Liberian government had on past occasions made brave offers of assistance to immigrants but now it was called upon to produce. To encourage immigration, it had appointed an immigration agent and it was this man, Sherman, who prevailed upon the local people to help the newcomers. The little food that had been given the settlers by the Migration Society was soon depleted and Sherman purchased enough rations to keep the people happy. When the gunboat finally became operative, it took the three groups to their new homes. But because the rainy season was upon them, the settlers lodged for a time in the houses of older residents while surveyors proceeded to lay out their farms. Within a few weeks, when the first attacks of fever had passed, the immigrants began clearing their land and planting crops. The Liberians had risen to the occasion and had done well by their unexpected colony.[12]

The immigrants had scarcely left Monrovia when Bishop Turner arrived in Liberia. He had sailed via Europe for Africa a week before the "Horsa" had departed Savannah. As usual, his official task was the administration of church affairs but again he used this third trip to publicize the glories of Africa in the American press. He visited the Savannah immigrants who had settled near Johnsonville and reported that they expressed themselves well pleased. "They were looking at the possibilities of the future."[13]

Accompanying the bishop was another A.M.E. church pastor, William H. Heard. Heard, a protégé of Turner since Reconstruction days, had just been appointed United

11. Stevens to Wilson, 10 November 1895.
12. Ibid.; Heard to Wilson, 18 September 1895.
13. Turner to *Voice of Missions,* 8 May 1895 (published July 1895); *New York Age,* 7 March 1895, in ACS scrapbooks.

States Minister Resident and Consul General to Liberia by President Grover Cleveland, a commission that resulted from several years of political maneuvering by Turner and his friends, Senator John T. Morgan and Secretary of the Interior Hoke Smith. In his new post, in addition to representing his government, Heard would serve as an A.M.E. missionary. Furthermore, as a convinced emigrationist, his reports and letters from Africa would help the Migration Society in its propaganda efforts. For all practical purposes, Heard became the society's agent in Liberia.[14]

Despite the happy scenes reported by Turner and Heard it was predictable that some of the "Horsa's" passengers would be disillusioned with Liberia and return to the United States. After six weeks in Liberia, three Arkansas farmers grew so discouraged with Africa that they worked their way back to Philadelphia. When they arrived late in July, the newspapers were eager for their accounts of the voyage and the settlements, and the returnees told of being deluded by glowing propaganda into sailing for the "promised land." That they had left their wives and children in Arkansas, however, indicated that they were prepared to find less than Migration Society agents had promised. They told of poor food on board ship and the deaths of many passengers on their arrival in Africa. According to the returnees, the society's secretary, E. B. Cottingham, who traveled with the colonists, returned to the United States on the "Horsa" and left the newcomers without food, shelter, land, or instructions on how to survive. The three men had refused to go to the farm settlements, choosing instead to work for wages in Monrovia. But there were no

14. William H. Heard, *From Slavery to the Bishopric* (Philadelphia, 1924), pp. 57 ff.; W. H. Heard, *The Bright Side of African Life* (Philadelphia, 1898), passim; *New York Age,* 25 January 1890, 30 May 1895, in ACS scrapbooks; *Voice of Missions,* July 1895; Turner to President Grover Cleveland, 1, 8 March, 1 July 1893, in State Department Applications and Recommendations for Office, 1893–97, U. S. Archives.

wages in Monrovia other than the "quart of rice and a yard of cloth" for which the natives did a day's work. They told of colonists who had been reduced to eating dead animals and snakes. As a result, the trio's disillusionment turned to despair. Theirs was the old refrain of returnees who told exaggerated tales of Liberia in order to justify their defection and win sympathy at home.[15]

The three Arkansas farmers' story differed from that of Bishop Turner and Minister Heard, of course, and it attracted widespread attention and generated criticism of the Migration Society. Returnees were an old story to the American Colonization Society, and Secretary Wilson wrote that it was his belief the "Horsa" group had done better than the average colony and that the returnees were "worthless drifters who would not do well in *any* country."[16] Migration Society officers, however, could not afford to dismiss the charges so lightly, for the press reports were hurting recruitment for the next ship. Consequently the society's bulletins and Bishop Turner's newspaper were preoccupied for some time explaining what had happened.[17] The best defense, of course, was a strong offense, and the society made the most of Minister Heard's letters and the encouraging reports from those most recent settlers who were satisfied with Liberia. The adverse publicity may have slowed the society's operations but certainly it did not stop the undercurrent of Afro-American unrest. Consequently, the emigration movement continued to recruit new members in the South.

Savannah blacks were particularly excited about African emigration, but prior to the departure of the "Horsa" there had been little talk about leaving. Even though one

15. *Philadelphia Inquirer,* 30 July 1895; *Washington Post,* 31 July 1895.
16. Wilson to W. M. Hall, 22 August 1895; Wilson to H. T. Buell, 5 August, 13 November 1895.
17. *New Orleans Times-Democrat,* 4 August 1900.

black physician, Cornelius McKane, had lived in Liberia
and planned to return, he spoke little about his goal. But
when the emigrants for the "Horsa" arrived and spent ten
days in Savannah spreading Liberian propaganda among
the local people, excitement began to grow. After the ship
sailed it was reported that Migration Society agents had
enrolled thirty-five new members right on the wharf. The
local black newspaper judged that C. S. Smith's opposition
had actually lent strength to the movement among Savannah blacks. "The emigrants have received the sympathy of the Savannah people as a whole, and have made
an impression on colored people here that will probably
prompt a great many in this section to follow them."[18] Dr.
McKane, writing under his pen name, "Scipio Americanus," now spoke out for emigration. He noted a "madden-
ing enthusiasm on the part of a number of our people to
migrate, notwithstanding the learned articles and logical
discourses" which opposed the move. Although he urged
caution and preparation (he himself had been preparing
since 1886), he concluded: "African migration is a good
thing viewed from any aspect."[19]

If Dr. McKane, an educated man, was willing to emigrate, many of the simple people around Savannah were
more zealous for the cause. The day after the "Horsa" had
sailed, Migration Society Treasurer T. D. Howard decided
to open an emigration office in the city. In looking for a
local agent he met one J. W. Masters, a tall, handsome
black man with "a slouch hat and a Prince Albert coat."
Masters claimed to have lived in Liberia for two and a half
years and Howard promptly hired him to be agent. Mas-

18. *Savannah Tribune*, 23 March 1895; *Savannah Morning News*,
20 March 1895.
19. *Savannah Tribune*, 6 April 1895. For McKane's background see
New York Press, 27 November 1892; *Savannah Tribune*, 3 December 1892; and the extensive correspondence between McKane and the
ACS.

ters' recruiting efforts were successful and in six weeks he had collected money from a hundred people and expected to enroll another hundred and twenty-five to make up a Savannah colony for Liberia. Early in May 1895 he called a public meeting of all those enrolled or interested in the society's plan, at which Masters read favorable reports from the "Horsa" emigrants and Dr. McKane read similar letters from his friends in Liberia. The audience, according to the white press, was made up not of paupers but substantial citizens, and a number of them owned real estate they entrusted to Masters to sell for them. African fever had indeed struck in Savannah.[20]

Within a week, however, Masters had absconded. Daniel Flummer, the president of the Migration Society, had read reports of Masters' giant meeting and became suspicious; the society did not accept real estate in payment. But Flummer arrived in Savannah as Masters was departing with the income from property he had sold for a fraction of its value. The victims of the swindle were enraged and the local press indignantly called for the society to make good the loss. Flummer calmed the critics by explaining that Masters had regularly paid the headquarters all the money that had been given him for transportation and that it was safe—any who wanted refunds would be satisfied. Masters had stolen only the proceeds of the land sales, about $3,000. Thus prompt action by the society restored confidence in its organization even though some had lost their homes. Masters was never caught but this did not dampen the African excitement in the vicinity. Dr. McKane, who was soon to emigrate under the auspices of the New York Colonization Society, wrote that "Negroes of southeast Georgia, Alabama and other sections of the South are bent on leaving for Liberia."[21]

20. *Savannah Morning News,* 5 May 1895.
21. McKane to Wilson, 11 May 1895; *Savannah Morning News,* 11–15, 17, 18, 21, 26 May 1895.

On the basis of reports from its various agents, the Migration Society planned to send another shipload of migrants to Africa in September. Especially from Arkansas came evidence of large numbers of blacks planning to leave. "There are three thousand people in this and adjoining counties who want to go to Liberia," wrote a pastor, "but they are unable to pay any part of the expense."[22] From Florida came word that the "Liberian movement has assumed considerable proportions."[23] A man from Memphis reported eighty heads of family ready to depart if money could be found.[24] Despite the fact that the American Colonization Society had not sent an emigrant group for three years, letters of inquiry and application continued to arrive at the rate of twenty-five each month, most of them claiming to speak for many people. The Migration Society, with its network of agents and its publicity machine in full operation, reported signing up thousands who expected to find homes in Africa.

Problems were continually present. Money, or the lack of it, kept most of the interested blacks from paying their passage in the summer of 1895. The depression still made ready cash scarce, and the sharecrop and crop-lien systems kept most blacks in poverty. Those who owned property or livestock could not find buyers and farmers could not harvest their crops during the summer months. As a result the Migration Society was forced once more to postpone the next voyage; no ship would sail in September.[25]

Steady opposition from middle-class blacks also took its toll. The Migration Society's agent in Memphis, J. N.

22. J. G. Davis to Pennsylvania Colonization Society, 10 June 1895, in ACS Papers; *Voice of Missions,* July 1895.
23. *The Evangelist,* 25 July 1895, in ACS scrapbooks.
24. J. N. Daniels to Wilson, 14 March 1895.
25. Cottingham to Wilson, 31 October 1895; *Savannah Morning News,* 23 January 1896.

Daniels, after hearing from emigration opponents that the "Horsa's" passengers had landed without provisions, decided to quit the Society, "though they have seven or eight dollars of mine."[26] Because interest in emigration was widespread, however, leading black churchmen considered it necessary to speak out against it. Leaders of the A.M.E. Zion church, in a report titled "The State of the Country," announced that "the proposed exodus to Africa as a mass finds little sympathy with us."[27] Bishops in Turner's own denomination declared: "We do not endorse nor encourage the efforts of individuals nor associations to distract the people from their moorings—poor though they are." Turner rejoined that over 2,500 blacks had been lynched in the past ten years and only 361 blacks had emigrated to Africa. "Some of us, who endorse a reasonable emigration," he wrote, "are ready to compare notes on the point of benevolence and rendering relief to the suffering."[28]

Unexpected opposition came from another source. Professor Edward W. Blyden, fresh from representing Liberia in treaty negotiations with Britain and France, arrived in the United States to study and lecture. Because he had done much to launch the emigration movement five years earlier, the Afro-American public was surprised to hear him say that repatriation must wait. "There are lessons to be learned in the house of bondage, both by the negroes and their former masters, before a large exodus to Africa would be anything but a peril and a stumbling block to the cause of genuine African progress."[29] Amplifying these sentiments, Blyden also wrote: "No greater evil could

---

26. J. N. Daniels to Wilson, 19 June 1895.
27. *A.M.E. Zion Quarterly Review,* 5 (July 1895), 137.
28. *Voice of Missions,* August 1895.
29. *Baltimore Sun,* 23 July 1895.

befall Africa or the negro at the present than an exodus of
negroes from the United States."[30] Opponents of emigration pounced on these statements and flung them at Bishop
Turner. "I am glad of [Blyden's] thrust into the ribs of that
turbulent, screeching and screaming creature," wrote Alexander Crummell, once a Liberian missionary but now a
staid Episcopal priest in Washington.[31]

Never one to run away from a fight, Turner first explained that Blyden must have thought the present generation of American blacks was too lacking in "common
sense, race patriotism [and] respect for black [man-
hood]" to be able to build up Africa. As for his critics, the
bishop was not deterred by "the billingsgate of this young,
fungus class, and some of these old fossils." Such language
was not calculated to win over his critics but it served to
titillate and encourage Turner's followers.[32]

During the summer of 1895 Afro-Americans had many
leaders and listened to many voices, and Bishop Turner
was one of the most active and vociferous spokesmen who
sought a following. Frederick Douglass, who died early in
1895, had worked for the integration of blacks into the
mainstream of American life. Turner, of course, advocated
nationalism, while others urged the accommodation of
black people to their lowly status in order to avoid friction.
In the difficult years of the early 1890s no one philosophy
gained clear ascendancy, although accommodation was
the easiest approach to the race problem for the simple
people who did not want trouble. By the end of September
1895, however, the leadership and ideological vacuum had
been filled. In his "Atlanta Compromise" address Booker
T. Washington, the head of Tuskegee Institute, urged

30. E. W. Blyden, "The African Problem," *North American Review,
161* (September 1895), 337.
31. Alexander Crummell to J. E. Bruce, 26 November 1895, in J. E.
Bruce Papers, Schomburg Collection, New York Public Library.
32. *Voice of Missions,* October 1895.

blacks to accommodate themselves to their inferior social status. He told them to work hard and become wealthy and thereby gain the respect of white men. To the loud applause of whites, followed by their economic and political support, Washington set the tone for Southern race relations for many years to come. Obviously, African emigration was not part of the pattern.[33]

Bishop Turner objected. "We only wish," he wrote, "that [Washington] had deemed it impolitic to say: 'The wisest among my race understand that the agitation of questions of social equality is the extremist folly.' " Predicting that those remarks would be quoted by whites to prove that blacks were satisfied with degradation, Turner also predicted that Washington would "have to live a long time to undo the harm he has done our race."[34]

Despite the opposition to emigration by middle-class Afro-Americans, by black bishops, and by the newly powerful Professor Washington, many southern blacks were still susceptible to the enticements of Africa, the promised land. During the late autumn of 1895, as the depression continued and cotton prices fell still lower, enrollment in the Migration Society began to rise. By January 1896 enough people had paid their passage money to warrant the society's officers chartering another ship. From Philadelphia came word that a 1,200-ton steamship, the "Laurada," would sail from Savannah with a full complement of emigrants for Liberia. A circular advertising the departure proclaimed that the Society's "agents in Liberia and the Liberian government" were prepared to receive the settlers. President Flummer himself planned to accompany the ship to make "permanent arrangements in

33. Meier, *Negro Thought*, pp. 100–18; Louis R. Harlan, "Booker T. Washington and the White Man's Burden," *American Historical Review, 71* (January 1966), 441–67.
34. *Voice of Missions*, October 1895.

Liberia for the reception and better settlement of our future colonists." For the convenience of the proposed "Laurada" passengers, another special train would travel from Memphis to Savannah collecting passengers for the departure planned for February 27.[35]

The "Laurada" was already in the current headlines; its skipper was being held in Charleston on charges of carrying illegal guerilla soldiers to Cuba. Although he later received the benefit of the jury's doubt, the press alleged he was acquitted "because he was helping a people fight for their political liberty." The ship's owners were probably happy to find for their ship a legally less risky task such as taking emigrants to Africa.[36] Shortly after this, the "Horsa," which had carried emigrants the year before, was charged with gun-running. After conviction of her Danish owners and crew, she was sold to American interests in Philadelphia.[37]

The "Laurada," like the smaller "Horsa," had to be fitted with makeshift passenger accommodations. The American Colonization Society, watching the entire operation of the Migration Society with distant but sympathetic concern, made certain that government officials inspected the ship to forestall the crowding that occurred on the "Horsa's" voyage.[38]

To avoid other problems which had arisen on the earlier journey, Migration Society Treasurer T. D. Howard visited Savannah a month before the sailing date to make arrangements for housing the expected blacks during their few days' layover in the port. While there Howard placed orders

35. *Washington Post,* 12 January 1896; "Special Bulletin #3," dated 14 January 1896 and published in *Voice of Missions,* February 1896; D. J. Flummer to Wilson, 17 January 1896; Wilson to Flummer, 20 January 1896.

36. *Savannah Morning News,* 22, 25 January, 1 March 1896.

37. Ibid., 1 January, 16, 26 February 1896.

38. C. E. Milnor to Wilson, 15 February 1896; Wilson to Milnor, 9 April 1896.

for several thousand dollars worth of provisions for the emigrants. Criticism of its earlier failure to provide sufficient provisions had damaged the reputation and slowed the work of the society, and its officers seemed determined to meet the complaints and honor their contracts. The local newspaper, viewing the proceedings with favor, pronounced the society honest and sincere.[39]

Others were not so sure about the Society or about Liberia. Just as C. S. Smith had come to Savannah to harass the departing "Horsa," so a year later there was opposition to the sailing of the "Laurada." The chief critic was Dr. Cornelius McKane, the same man who for several years had prepared to go to Africa as a physician. In the summer of 1895 he and his wife had indeed sailed to Liberia and with the help of the local residents had established a small hospital and medical training school. Then McKane tried to secure legislation which would prevent non-professional physicians from practicing so-called "bush medicine," but Liberian officials balked at this step because there were so few doctors in the nation. To prohibit amateurs from applying folk remedies might seriously impair the health of the people. In disgust the McKanes packed up their belongings, closed their hospital, and returned to Savannah —all within a few months' time.[40]

When he heard that a new emigrant colony was soon to depart, McKane, as fresh from Africa as C. S. Smith had been, launched a series of lectures in the black churches. Professing only good will to Liberia, he told the blunt facts about the republic: Immigrants received their promised

39. *Savannah Morning News,* 23 January, 29 February, 1 March 1896.
40. The McKane story is somewhat blurred by conflicting reports. The account given here seems to be the most plausible and is based primarily on a letter from J. C. Stevens to Wilson, 5 August 1896. See also the extensive correspondence between Wilson and McKane before and after McKane's visit to Africa.

twenty-five acres, but had no houses until they built their own. Each immigrant fell sick and death visited each family. A poor government and its poor citizens could not help newcomers substantially. During the five years it takes his coffee crop to mature the farmer will have to subsist on native foods. "There is vexation and lamentation awaiting the emigrant," McKane reiterated. "He will be hustled ashore like cattle and told to do or die, and that while sick and heartbroken." As for the people who had sailed on the "Horsa," McKane reported that a third of them were dead and most of the others were sick when he left Monrovia in December. He ventured that no one who sailed on the "Horsa" would hesitate if it were possible to return to the United States.[41]

Whatever its effect on Savannah blacks, McKane's warning came too late to stop the parade of emigrating blacks who began to converge on the city. Similarly, reports of fake emigration schemes from such places as Denison, Texas, and Albany, Georgia, rather than dampening enthusiasm, only testified to its wide geographical spread.[42] From Memphis the chartered train arrived carrying about 240 people, over half from Arkansas, the rest from Alabama, Mississippi, Tennessee, and Oklahoma. They were joined by others from Florida, South Carolina, Illinois, and Delaware. Four people came from New York where they had lived since being stranded in March 1892. With their farm equipment and hound dogs, some 311 people awaited the arrival of the ship.[43]

On the appointed day the "Laurada" failed to appear. While awaiting the ship, Migration Society officials busied themselves with defenses against their ubiquitous critics.

41. *Savannah Morning News,* 20–25 February 1896.
42. Ibid., 9 January, 26 February 1896.
43. Ibid., 26 February, 1 March 1896; Roberts, *African Canaan,* p. 18.

President Flummer pointed out that political reverses had soured McKane on Liberia and that his attacks were based on pure jealousy. The emigrants, meanwhile, either rested patiently in their boarding houses or tried to purchase equipment for Liberia. The people of Savannah waited somewhat apprehensively to see whether the ship would materialize. Newspapermen who questioned the emigrants about their backgrounds and motives for going to Africa discovered a consensus: it was just too hard to make a living in the South, and crop failures, low cotton prices, and the shortage of money persuaded the blacks to act upon the emigration propaganda.[44]

When the "Laurada" finally appeared she was immediately impounded by customs officials; her long-overdue arrival made the government agents suspect that she had rendezvoused at sea with a gun-runner and transferred an illicit cargo for Cuba. But at last her skipper convinced the officers that bad weather and helping a distressed ship off Cape Hatteras were to blame for the delay.[45] After another half-day's delay the ship approached the wharf, where a crowd of eager people stood watching. Suddenly, as she was turning in close quarters, the "Laurada" lurched forward and struck the pier with her bow. The damage was slight and no one was hurt but the subsequent repairs caused yet another day of waiting by the harassed captain, the hard-pressed Migration Society officials, the patient emigrants, and fascinated Savannah citizens.[46]

As the ship lay alongside the wharf loading supplies and having her bow repaired, she was the center of interest for the Friday afternoon crowds. According to newspaper accounts, thousands visited the dockside. Blacks grumbled when they discovered that only white people could tour

44. *Savannah Morning News,* 26, 27 February 1896.
45. Ibid., 28, 29 February 1896.
46. Ibid., 29 February 1896.

the ship, but blacks by the hundred crowded onto the pier and adjacent wharfs to watch the carloads of supplies being loaded aboard the ship. The emigrants who visited the dock out of curiosity found themselves drafted into longshoreman gangs to help load the vessel. Customs officials inspected the passenger quarters and found them adequate. If Dr. McKane or other critics appeared, their warnings were eclipsed by the conspicuous presence of Bishop Turner, and crowds of blacks flocked around him as he told of the great possibilities of life in Liberia. When he found departing emigrants who had no money to help establish themselves in Africa, the bishop tried to persuade them to remain at home, but to no avail; their minds were set on going. Ten Savannah blacks, furthermore, paid their passage money on the spot and rushed home to pack for the departure.[47] The next day was spent loading the ship. Then at sundown, 321 emigrants filed aboard to find their living spaces and stow their baggage. President Flummer and three other white men, including a journalist, also prepared to sail. The ship's repairs were complete and all that remained was the final farewell ceremony on Sunday morning.[48]

The services were glorious. According to the local press, black people began gathering at the waterfront at daybreak. By seven o'clock 5,000 had arrived and more kept coming, crowding around the ship while the emigrants finished their breakfast. Friends of the emigrants went aboard to bid them goodby as the festivities began on the crowded decks. The Reverend A. J. Warner of Birmingham, a popular and witty speaker, told of the Migration Society's great triumph despite its problems and critics. Another speaker praised Africa as the true home of every black man. Then Bishop Turner spoke, and for well over

47. Ibid., 29 February, 1 March 1896; *Voice of Missions,* April 1896.
48. *Savannah Morning News,* 1 March 1896.

an hour he enthralled his black and white audience with the glories of Africa, the future of Liberia, and the promise of the transatlantic trade. Shouts of "Amen," "Hallelujah," and "God bless Liberia" punctuated his remarks. Many Savannah blacks again caught "emigration fever" and proclaimed they would join the very next colony. As Turner finished speaking, agents of the society enrolled more members among the audience. President Flummer and other society officials spoke after Turner; and the crowd, both ashore and afloat, sang "I am going home to part no more." The finale was the baying of the thirty hounds that the emigrants insisted on taking to Africa. At eleven o'clock the visitors went ashore, and everyone agreed that the services had been glorious.[49]

When the speaking and singing and praying and shouting had ended, everyone expected to see the "Laurada" cast off and steam toward Africa, but still another delay arose as port officials discovered that the ship lacked one of the required engineers. While one of the mates hurried by rail to Charleston to recruit a man, the captain argued with the port officers and at length persuaded them to allow the "Laurada" to move down river and anchor below the city until the engineer arrived. Such a move would keep the emigrants from straying, disperse the large crowds, and prevent the crew from deserting. Early on Monday morning, March 2, 1896, the "Laurada" finally headed toward Africa.[50]

Even before the ship had left the wharf there was grumbling about the minuscule shipboard rations, complaints that increased as the voyage progressed. "None of us had more than half enough to eat," said one. "We received no tea or coffee and were given hot water instead." Moreover, because of adverse winds the trip took three full weeks.

49. Ibid., 1–3 March 1896.
50. Ibid., 2–4 March 1896.

Two infants and an elderly man had died and been buried
at sea, but two newborn babies helped raised the passengers' spirits. Despite the grumbling, most of the emigrants
were still eager for Liberia. When the African coast first
appeared they lined the rails, "straining their eyes to make
out what manner of land it was." When Monrovia, with
its white houses and church steeples came into view, the
newcomers were almost delirious with joy.[51]

But again the gaiety soon disappeared, and permanently.
Two hectic days were needed to put the emigrants ashore
and into their temporary quarters in Monrovia. Then they
were told that for political reasons, they could not stay in
one settlement but must find land in different townships, as
the earlier groups had done. Even after several weeks some
of the emigrants had not chosen their land. When the provisions were unloaded from the ship and given to the
settlers, more grumbling occurred. According to one emigrant's account, President Flummer, who stayed in Liberia
several weeks, issued rations to only 200 people and sold
the remainder for his own benefit.[52]

Soon after the newcomers moved to their farms the rains
began, and with the rain came fever. Sometimes isolated
from other settlers, usually without medical care, always
suffering, the immigrants began to weaken and die. By
August, according to one report, the number of dead
totaled one hundred. If the number was exaggerated, a
few more weeks would rectify it, for the rain-and-fever
season would continue through November.[53]

By midsummer a reverse exodus had begun, and within

51. Roberts, *African Canaan,* p. 20; *Washington Post,* 19 October
1896.
52. *Washington Post,* 19 October 1896; B. Y. Payne to U. S. Department of State, 30 March 1896, in Dispatches of U. S. Consuls in Monrovia, U. S. Archives; J. C. Stevens to Wilson, 10 April 1896.
53. *Washington Post,* 19 October 1896; *Washington Star,* 26 November 1896; *Christian Standard,* 24 October 1896, in ACS scrapbooks.

a few months the majority of "Laurada's" passengers were either dead or had left Liberia. The first evidence of disaster arrived in New York in August with Mrs. Lizzie Green. She and her family had sailed on the "Horsa" in 1895, but after her husband died and she could not find work to support her nine children, she had packed her bags and recrossed the Atlantic with her brood. She told of misery and death among the "Laurada" people.[54]

In late September, six members of Colony Number Three returned to the United States and swore vengeance on the Migration Society. They went home to Forrest City, Arkansas, promising to do all in their power to stop further emigration.[55] Soon others began arriving in American ports with tales of horror. One man alleged that promises of gold and diamond mines in the Migration Society's propaganda had lured him away from his prosperous farm in South Carolina. In South Africa there was gold, and in Sierra Leone there were diamonds, but all he found in Liberia was starvation and fever.[56] Other returnees soon followed and they verified the stories of general misery. American newspapermen interviewed many of them and published their accounts in sensational detail. The net effect of the reports was that the "Laurada's" passengers —those who were still alive—would all return to the United States if they could afford the passage.[57]

But most, of course, had little or no money. Some had only enough money to get to Sierra Leone, 200 miles up

54. *New York Age,* 20 August 1896, in ACS scrapbooks; *New York Sun,* 30 August 1896.

55. *New York World,* 28 September 1896; *Boston Daily Globe,* 28 September 1896; *Voice of Missions,* November 1896.

56. *Washington Post,* 19, 22 October 1896.

57. *Christian Standard,* 24 October 1896; *Boston Daily Globe,* 22 June 1897; *New York Times,* 22 June 1897; *Washington Star,* 26 November 1897; *Philadelphia Times,* 14 February 1898; *New York Age,* 12 May 1898. All in ACS scrapbooks. *New Orleans Times-Democrat,* 4 August 1900.

the coast from Monrovia. A few may have joined the diamond rush, but most likely they went to Sierra Leone hoping to find employment or charity to help them get back to the United States.[58] By the time they reached Liverpool the refugees were certainly penniless. They approached the American consul in that city only to learn that he had no funds to return them to the United States. Occasionally, however, the Society for the Relief of Foreigners in Distress would help blacks get to New York. Some apparently remained in Britain. In any event, the consul reported "a continual stream of American colored emigrants who have been returning disappointed from Liberia."[59]

Some of the "Laurada" passengers survived in Liberia. The American Colonization Society had followed the story with considerable interest, and secretary Wilson, when questioned about the returnees, explained that through July 1897 the percentage of emigrants who came back to the United States was smaller than in the groups that had been sent by the Colonization Society. Wilson nevertheless wrote to his agent in Liberia: "Can't you send me a letter from someone who stayed and does *not* desire to return?"[60]

The agent, J. C. Stevens, replied with accounts of several farmers who had settled near Johnsonville and thrived. An elderly lady, after her husband died, had built her house singlehandedly and had laid out a prospering farm. From

58. *Sierra Leone Times,* 25 September 1897, in ACS scrapbooks; *New York Age,* 12 May 1898, in ACS scrapbooks; *New York Times,* 22 June 1897; George Reddick to U. S. State Department, 16 December 1903, forwarded to the Colonization Society 27 January 1904.

59. *Liverpool Daily Post,* 26 June 1899 (clipping enclosed in Consul James Boyle to D. J. Hill, U. S. State Department, and forwarded to Colonization Society). Cf. *Washington Star,* 29 September, 26 November 1897.

60. Wilson to C. E. Milnor, 2 July 1897; Wilson to J. C. Stevens, 18 August 1897.

another successful farmer he solicited a letter saying that he and his family were satisfied. "The white people say the Negroes went to Africa to find money growing on trees. After landing I see plenty of men that have money growing on [coffee] trees and I expect to wait until I have some money growing on trees." He claimed that far from being given short rations by the Migration Society, he had enough flour and meal to sell because he had conserved his provisions by supplementing them with native foods. His land was bountiful and he had most of it set out in coffee trees. By hard work and prudent use of his resources, he had made a good start. Urging his friends to join him in Liberia, he said that he "would not come back if some one would pay my way and give me $500."[61]

Several families stayed in Liberia and prospered;[62] others stayed but suffered. A group of about twenty "Laurada" emigrants petitioned President William McKinley for aid in their destitution: "Please send some food. Not a hundred dollars or a thousand dollars, just food." Protesting that they wanted to stay in Liberia but were slowly starving, the petitioners blamed the Migration Society for short rations, the "hard times," and the high price of supplies in Monrovia.[63] Six months later Stevens reported that many of the petitioners had since departed for Sierra Leone while the rest remained in need in Monrovia. The Liberian government, having spent several thousand dollars in settling the "Laurada" people on their farms and incensed by the critical remarks of the returnees, was too hard-pressed to help the stragglers. The government

61. Charles Hayes to G. Battle, 4 October 1897 (enclosed in J. C. Stevens to Wilson, 14 October 1897).
62. J. C. Stevens to Wilson, 23 May 1898.
63. J. M. Woodson et al. to President William McKinley, 13 September 1897, and W. H. Heard to Secretary of State John Sherman, 23 December 1897 (Dispatches from U. S. Ministers at Monrovia, U. S. Archives).

had never been wealthy, and a severe drop in coffee prices had cut its revenues to almost nothing. Nor could private citizens help in Liberia.[64]

By 1900, few of the 321 emigrants who crossed the Atlantic on the "Laurada" remained in Liberia. Death had claimed many; disappointment and hunger drove others away. In the large view, although a handful of emigrants prospered, the "Laurada" project was a tragic failure.

Among emigration advocates in the United States, however, the mood was not one of failure but of happy success after the "Laurada" sailed in March 1896. Bishop Turner, of course, had been elated. "We predict grand results for the major part of the emigrants who went over on the steamship." They were, furthermore, "the pioneers of a great and grand future . . . and will live in the esteem of God and man when those who pronounce them fools will be lost in oblivion."[65]

President Flummer of the Migration Society, who traveled aboard the "Laurada," remained in Liberia for a month. After supervising the landing and the distribution of the people and supplies, he visited various settlements around Monrovia to study conditions. Flummer and his three white companions also established the Liberian Land Development Company, a subsidiary of the Migration Society, while they were in Monrovia. The company was to handle the society's affairs in Africa by acquiring land, promoting immigration, starting local industries, and teaching practical skills to both newcomers and old settlers. The initial appearance of success for the "Laurada" and "Horsa" people obviously had stirred Flummer and his associates to envision a giant operation.[66]

64. J. C. Stevens to Wilson, 18 April 1898.
65. *Voice of Missions,* April 1896.
66. B. Y. Payne to U. S. State Department, 30 March 1896 (in Dispatches of U. S. Consuls at Monrovia, U. S. Archives); *Acts, 1896–1897,* pp. 22 ff.

William K. Roberts, the journalist who accompanied Flummer, busied himself observing the country and the people. When the party returned to the United States Roberts produced a booklet, *An African Canaan for the American Negro*—a propaganda piece that was given large circulation by the Migration Society. His account of the voyage of the "Laurada" and the conditions in Liberia were reasonably accurate but overly optimistic.[67] With this new propaganda and its grandiose plans, the society was ready to capitalize on the emigration excitement the "Laurada's" departure had generated in March.

In addition to the interest stirred up by news of the "Laurada's" sailing, by Bishop Turner's regular propaganda, and by the work of its local agents, the society gained a potentially helpful boost from the American Colonization Society when Wilson, the ACS secretary, began referring all people who inquired about emigration to the Migration Society. Reports from ACS representative Stevens in Liberia had convinced Wilson that Flummer's organization was acting responsibly, although it had problems because of inexperience. Furthermore, the self-supporting aspect of the Birmingham society's operation appealed to the impecunious society in Washington. Wilson naïvely assured inquirers that "a better class of emigrants are paying their own way through the [Migration Society] than those sent out by [our] Society for the last thirty years. The latter were largely of the pauper class and most of them wholly illiterate."[68]

The Colonization Society also aided the Migration Society in another way. The ACS's semiannual *Liberia Bulletin* was available to all who asked for it, and the Migration Society's propaganda sheets frequently contained

---

67. Roberts, *African Canaan,* passim.
68. Wilson to C. E. Milnor, 15 October 1896; Wilson to Cottingham, 2 April 1897.

information or whole articles that had been lifted from the
Liberia Bulletin, describing the wealth of Africa, news of
prominent Liberians, and discussions of the American race
problem. The *Liberia Bulletin* also helped the Migration
Society counter the charges of the returnees who slandered
Liberia. Commenting on these defectors in its annual report, the ACS said that emigrants had been returning to
the United States since the founding of Liberia in 1822.
The only difference was that now the "Argus-eyed Associated Press" spread woeful stories of the returnees
throughout the land. "These exaggerated, and to some extent false, reports serve their authors in successfully appealing to the charitable for assistance, which is usually
the first business in which the returned Liberian emigrant
engages on his arrival in this country."[69]

Despite the direct and indirect help of the Colonization
Society and the early excitement generated by the sailing
of two emigrant ships to Africa, the Migration Society
faced serious obstacles. The complaints and criticism of
the returning emigrants hurt the society's campaign, and
many of its news releases and circulars were devoted to
defending itself against the attacks. Nevertheless, enough
emigrants had returned to their homes in the South to provide firsthand information that countered the glorious pictures of wealth and independence painted by Flummer and
Bishop Turner. The press, especially the black newspapers
that had always opposed emigration, made the most of the
African tales of despair.[70] More general influences also
worked against the emigration movement. The depression,
which had lingered throughout the nation but longer and
more damagingly in the South, was attended by further
panic and plunged even deeper in 1897. Cotton prices

69. *Liberia Bulletin, 10* (February 1897), 5.
70. *New Orleans Times-Democrat,* 4 August 1900; *New York Sun,*
30 August 1896.

again dropped and money became more scarce. While the nation at large debated whether to change from gold to silver, penniless Southern blacks could do little toward paying their way to Africa.[71]

Threats of war with Spain further distracted the nation and the blacks. As insurgents in Cuba waged sporadic warfare against their Spanish masters, the American public became emotionally caught up in the struggle. Profit and principle tied Americans to the rebels. The press made the most of every incident and a new breed of war correspondents painted vivid word pictures of the struggle. Gun-running ship captains were received in the United States more as heroes than as criminals. Because blacks as well as whites were committed to the growing tension with Spain, Bishop Turner envisioned a decline in emigration sentiment; involvement in a patriotic struggle would increase rather than decrease the blacks' ties to the United States. Turner, bitter as ever over the black man's suppression in America, warned that once they realized that most of the Cuban rebels were blacks, the American people would back down on their commitment to liberty. "We hope no Negro in this country will allow himself to be beguiled with [patriotic] sophistry," wrote the bishop. "If the United States gets into war with Spain, we shall stump the country against the black man taking up a gun."[72]

There was little Turner and the Migration Society could do to counteract the effects of the war threat but they were not totally helpless against the money shortage. Just after Flummer returned from Liberia, the society announced that its emigration rates had been drastically cut: $32 would now pay an adult's passage to Africa. Difficulties caused by the shipping and the distribution of three months' provisions in Liberia, as well as the lack of cash among

71. Cf. *Voice of Missions,* February, March 1897.
72. Ibid., April 1896.

blacks, made the change expedient. New emigrants would no longer get rations but must provide them for themselves—an irresponsible change, especially in view of the Liberian government's inability to help the penniless newcomers who might be lured by the low passage price. Bishop Turner, however, concurred in the new arrangement, noting that immigrants to the United States received no official aid on their arrival.[73]

President Flummer and his chief co-worker, E. B. Cottingham, continued to expand their plans. In each of the four counties of Liberia they appointed agents to prepare land and housing for new settlers. The agent for Sinoe County was R. A. Wright, a member of the Liberian legislature, through whose efforts the society was granted 500 acres in each county on which to build hospitals, schools, supply depots, and temporary housing for incoming settlers to use while they adjusted to the climate. In the United States, the propaganda campaign continued but the response was weaker.[74]

The lower migration fare and the elaborate organization in Liberia could not prevail against the criticism of the returned emigrants, the patriotic pull of a war threat, and the deadening effects of a prolonged depression. There was not even enough response in 1896 to enable the society to make the usual promise that "a ship would soon leave for Africa." In response to queries from the Colonization Society, Flummer reported in early 1897 that he was "quite sure that we will not be ready to sail . . . earlier than next fall."[75] In March, the anniversary month of the "Horsa" and "Laurada" sailings, Bishop Turner sadly noted that the next ship would be indefinitely postponed. "The prevailing

73. Ibid., May 1896.
74. R. A. Wright to Wilson, 3 July, 12 October 1897; *Acts, 1897–1898,* p. 26; Flummer, *Negro and Liberia,* passim.
75. Flummer to Wilson, 12 January 1897.

low price of cotton for the last year, together with the un-settled state of affairs in politics and the Cuban war scare has well nigh demoralized all business."[76] By April Flummer thought conditions looked better, and in October he announced that "Colony Number Four" would sail from Savannah in December 1897. But the colony was never formed and its ship never sailed.[77]

Late in 1897 Flummer issued a propaganda booklet, *The Negro and Liberia,* which contained most of the old and familiar information but concluded with an explanation and a new plea: "In order to get any considerable number to go at any one time, it became necessary to place the fare at such a low figure that the plans were not self-sustaining." To survive, the society would need aid from the government or philanthropists, or both.[78] Bishop Turner praised the society's efforts in behalf of blacks and urged not only "the rich people of the entire world" to donate to the cause but impoverished blacks to give their pennies to help Flummer and Cottingham continue publicizing Africa. "Those who are not able to pay their own passage but who wish the Society to secure assistance for them," the bishop suggested, "should . . . send their names and the small donations asked for."[79]

The Migration Society had clearly declined since 1896. According to Flummer, its failure to send ships regularly had made the blacks lose interest. "Then the war came along [in 1898] and the Negroes became frightened," he said in retrospect. "That virtually put an end to our project."[80] But propaganda leaflets continued to circulate and local centers of interest arose and disappeared. In March

76. *Voice of Missions,* March 1897.
77. Ibid., October 1897; Wilson to Cottingham, 2 April 1897; Flummer to Wilson, 5 April 1897.
78. Flummer, *Negro and Liberia,* p. 28.
79. *Voice of Missions,* February 1898.
80. *New Orleans Times-Democrat,* 4 August 1900.

1899, for example, reports from Texas said that emigration interest was high and that the Migration Society had promised a ship at Galveston if 300 adult passengers would come forth.[81] That summer the society bravely announced that regular sailings for Liberia would start in the fall. Bishop Turner, alarmed at the marked deterioration of race relations in the wake of the Spanish-American War, wrote that "never before was the [emigration] sentiment so strong and interest so intense."[82] But Turner and Flummer were making a desperate effort to keep the spark aglow. The last issue of the society's monthly flyer appeared in December 1899. Shortly thereafter Flummer's co-worker, Cottingham, died and so did the International Migration Society.[83]

Bishop Turner, the mainspring of black emigration for so many years, did not let the decline of the Migration Society demoralize him. From platforms and in newspapers he continued to portray the American situation in terms of despair and to call for increased race pride among the blacks. In one address he proclaimed that "God is a Negro." No man who does not consider himself made in the image of God will ever amount to anything, reasoned the bishop. "Hence, the indispensable necessity of establishing a Negro nationality, where black men can be taught to respect themselves."[84]

Turner's own zeal for Africa was heightened by his visit to South Africa in 1898. There he consolidated a new branch of the A.M.E. church composed of native Christians who had rebelled against the race prejudice in the Wesleyan missions; they had formed their own "Ethiopian

81. W. Bowman to H. M. Turner, *Voice of Missions*, March, May 1899; Bowman to Wilson, 24 April 1899. Cf. *Birmingham Age-Herald*, 10 February 1898.
82. *Voice of Missions*, June 1899.
83. *New Orleans Times-Democrat*, 4 August 1900.
84. *Voice of Missions*, November 1895.

Church" and later had united with the A.M.E. church by correspondence.[85] In a region torn by growing tension between Briton and Boer, the bishop traveled for five weeks organizing churches, ordaining new pastors, meeting government officials and, above all, being seen and heard by the black Africans. "The Africans and colored people went wild by the thousands," he reported.[86] Other authorities, confirming this reception, agreed that directly or indirectly Turner stirred up a nationalist spirit within the hearts of the Africans, a spirit which spread rapidly throughout southern Africa. A South African government panel later reported that "this close connection between Ethiopians and the Negroes of the Southern States is viewed with grave misgivings by many South Africans, who fear that, by stimulating the spirit of racial jealousy and exclusiveness, it may have a sinister influence on the future of South Africa."[87] When he returned from his journey, Turner was reinvigorated in his African dream and he rejoined the emigration movement with new force.

In the years of decline for the Migration Society, various small emigration movements continued to sprout throughout the South and individual Afro-Americans ventured on

85. Josephus R. Coan, "The Expansion of Missions of the African Methodist Episcopal Church in South Africa, 1896–1908" (unpublished doctoral dissertation, Hartford Seminary, 1961), passim. Coan deals with the ecclesiastical side of Turner's visit.

86. *Voice of Missions,* November 1898.

87. South African Native Races Committee, *The South African Natives: Their Progress and Present Condition* (New York, 1909), pp. 192–205. Other works mention Turner in connection with the birth of African nationalism. Cf. George A. Shepperson and Thomas Price, *The Independent African: John Chilembwe and the Origins, Setting and Significance of the Nyasaland Native Rising of 1915* (Edinburgh, 1958), pp. 73, 93–109; Daniel Thwaite, *The Seething African Pot: A Study of Black Nationalism, 1882–1935* (London, 1936), pp. 35–39; Bengt G. M. Sundkler, *Bantu Prophets in South Africa* (London, 1961), pp. 41, 65. Turner's letters were first published in *Christian Recorder* and *Voice of Missions* and were then collected in *A.M.E. Church Review, 15* (July 1899), 809–13.

their own to Africa. But the only movement that produced any results arose in the Indian Territory, long a seedbed of black discontent. Letters from these would-be emigrants had trickled steadily into the Colonization Society's headquarters, and the Migration Society's agents had found success there. When the Birmingham group failed to send a ship to Liberia in 1897, Samuel Chapman, of Muldrow in the Cherokee country, pushed a scheme to buy a ship with black money, fill it with emigrants, and sail it to Africa.[88]

Chapman's Liberian Emigration Clubs seem not to have flourished, however, and certainly they bought no ships, but they spread the word of Liberia through the territory. In March 1899 twenty-seven black families from Kingfisher County grew restless waiting for Chapman or the Migration Society to send them to Africa. Like the other Oklahomans in 1892, they sold their belongings, hired a train, and set out for New York, where they expected to receive free transportation to Liberia. After sitting in the Jersey City depot for a week and living in two cramped passenger cars, the 104 people were finally discovered by the New York newsmen and their pathetic plight moved local citizens to help them find quarters and jobs in New Jersey. Only three families eventually reached Liberia, and that at their own expense.[89] This episode, added to the evidence of individual blacks who went to Liberia in the late 1890s, indicates that although no large organization could raise enough money to operate, there was still Afro-American interest in emigration.

88. *Muldrow Register,* 8 April 1897, in ACS scrapbooks; S. Chapman to Wilson, 3 June, 27 August, 8 November 1897; Wilson to Chapman, 7 June, 11 November 1897; Samuel Chapman, *Constitution of the Liberian Emigration Clubs; Destiny of the Black Man* (Muldrow, Okla., 1897); Samuel Chapman, *Destiny of the Black Man* (Muldrow, 1897).

89. *New York Age,* 23 March 1899, 6 April 1899, in ACS scrapbooks; *Voice of Missions,* April 1899; O. L. W. Smith to U. S. State Department, 31 May 1899 (Dispatches from U. S. Consuls in Monrovia, U. S. Archives).

Such interest encouraged Bishop Turner to turn once more to the federal government for financial assistance. In mid-1899 he persuaded the A.M.E. elders of Georgia and Alabama to call upon Congress to provide 100 million dollars to aid black emigration. The bishop urged his followers throughout the South to sign a petition that would be a mile long. Whether or not he had any hope of getting a federal grant, Turner was not giving up the fight to get Afro-Americans to Africa. During the 1890s racial persecution had taken more drastic form as lynch law was reinforced by disfranchisement and Jim Crow legislation. At the end of the decade Turner found himself appealing for help to the same reluctant federal government that had declined to endorse the Butler bill in 1890. Although the organized emigration movement appeared to have died at the end of the century, Turner was determined that it should continue.[90]

90. *Birmingham Age-Herald*, 4 August 1899; *Voice of Missions*, November 1899. *Indianapolis Freeman*, 21 October 1899.

11

Into the Twentieth Century

The coming of the new century brought renewed activity by emigrationists, especially Daniel Flummer and Bishop Turner. There still was much reason for discontent among Afro-Americans as racism, violence, and segregation intensified the bitter pattern of black subordination. Southern whites made it clear that they intended to keep the black man "in his place"—a place physically, socially, economically, and politically removed from whites. Jim Crow laws rapidly separated the races by residence and in public accommodations while various forms of disfranchisement precluded any possibility that colored people could solve their problems through political processes. Furthermore, most Northern whites who—for whatever reasons—had previously tried to help the blacks had clearly abandoned the struggle by 1900. The Supreme Court, the Congress, and the federal administration, either by direct action or by inaction, had endorsed the Southern "solution" to racial difficulties. Violence, in the form of lynching and rioting, spread even to the North. For Bishop Turner, hypersensitive to every racial insult, the situation called for renewed efforts to get Afro-Americans out of the "abominable United States."[1]

Although black affairs had reached a new low, other

1. For a general discussion of race relations at the turn of the century see Rayford Logan, *The Betrayal of the Negro,* Chapters 16–19. Cf. Woodward, *Origins of the New South,* Chapters 12, 13, and Woodward, *Jim Crow,* Chapter 3.

factors also made Turner's task of mobilizing an emigration movement more difficult than ever. The economic
condition of the entire nation, impaired by the panics of
the 1890s, had improved perceptibly. Most black people
found it was easier to bear the abuses and outrages of the
South if they could earn enough to feed their families.[2]
Furthermore, the vacuum of leadership had been more
than filled by Booker T. Washington. The professor from
Tuskegee had risen to national prominence by virtue of
his great ability to interest white philanthropists in black
education. His rapport with powerful northern whites led
to his political influence in the Republican party. Money
and political authority gave Washington more absolute
power within the Afro-American community than any
man, including Frederick Douglass, had ever wielded before. Much of Washington's influence stemmed from his
attitude toward the racial problem: accommodation was
his basic plan for blacks. He urged them to work for economic self-sufficiency and moral rectitude, qualities which
would combine to lift blacks into the mainstream of American life. Work rather than civil rights or protest would
provide the key to the future. Industrial education for
manual trades rather than academic training for erudition,
according to Washington, was more suitable for Afro-
Americans. He counseled patience and optimism in the
face of segregation, disfranchisement, and violence.[3]

Washington opened the new century with a direct attack
on emigration, a counsel of restlessness and despair as
preached by Bishop Turner. In Macon, Georgia, on January 1, 1900, Washington revealed that "for every negro
that is sent to Liberia, a negro baby is born in the cotton

2. Woodward, *Origins of the New South,* Chapter 15.
3. Meier, *Negro Thought,* Chapter 7 and passim; August Meier
and Elliott Rudwick, *From Plantation to Ghetto* (New York, 1966), p.
181.

belt, so that scheme is a failure. As we came to this country at the urgent solicitation and expense of the white man," he said, "we would be ungrateful to run away and leave him now."[4]

" 'Stay here,' says Booker T. Washington, while Bishop Turner says, 'We must go to Africa.' Which shall we obey?" asked a black editor from Arkansas.[5] By the end of 1903 the answer, if not clear before, would become obvious when Turner's final emigration effort would collapse and the "stay-at-home" policy advocated by Washington and most other prominent blacks would prevail. But when the century opened, even though Washington's ideas dominated race leadership, the emigrationists were not yet finished.

The first six months of 1900 found Bishop Turner's effectiveness much reduced. Late in the previous year he had suffered a stroke that partially paralyzed him and impaired his speaking ability. But enforced rest and more time for reconsideration did not change the sixty-five-year-old bishop's views about the race problem. "[Turner] though sick, believes that African emigration . . . is the hope of the Negro," reported the *Voice of Missions*. "He admits that lynching is not so prevalent as formerly, but control for the colored man is still a hopeless state of affairs." Meanwhile his public efforts to stimulate emigration were limited to pleading for a "mile-long petition" asking Congress for aid to blacks who wanted to return to Africa. When a Brooklyn black man suggested that 100,000 Afro-Americans unite in a mass march on Washington, D.C., to press Congress for emigration aid, Turner rejected the idea because it would expose too many black people to white violence.[6]

4. *Washington Post,* 2 January 1900.
5. *Helena Reporter,* 1 February 1900, in ACS scrapbooks.
6. *Voice of Missions,* January, March, December 1900.

Violence nevertheless brought the emigration movement back to the public's attention in July 1900. In 1899 Robert Charles had become a New Orleans subagent for the International Migration Society, having come from Mississippi, where he was alleged to have murdered several people.[7] In the anonymity of New Orleans he worked at various manual jobs, saying little about his background but impressing those about him with both his surliness and his intelligence. Then William Royal, the local agent for the Migration Society, appointed Charles a subagent to spread emigration propaganda and enlist members for Liberia, and collect a commission on the emigrants' payments. In addition, he sold subscriptions to Bishop Turner's paper and handled large quantities of the *Voice of Missions* each month. When he encountered blacks who did not want to emigrate, he asked contributions for the aid of those who wanted to go to Africa. According to his acquaintances, Charles bragged that he could make five dollars a day in the emigration business.[8]

In order to better convince black people to join the Migration Society, Charles read the propaganda religiously, and eventually could recite verbatim Bishop Turner's attacks on white America. In one *Voice of Missions* editorial the bishop had urged that "Negroes Get Guns" for self-defense. Furthermore, the shrill tone of Turner's descriptions of American race relations could be interpreted as a call for revolt. Charles chose that interpretation and, to keep his converts from lapsing in their payments, continually preached what the white press called "this propaganda of hatred."[9]

According to his acquaintances, Charles' hatred of white men rapidly overshadowed his emigrationism. Some of his

7. *New Orleans Times-Democrat,* 26 July, 10 August 1900; *New Orleans Picayune,* 26 July 1900.

8. *New Orleans Times-Democrat,* 29 July, 4 August 1900.

9. Ibid.; *Voice of Missions,* March, May 1897.

friends, after the Migration Society collapsed late in 1899, dissociated themselves from him as fanticism took hold of Charles. He harangued blacks to arm themselves with rifles and ammunition. When a particularly grim lynching took place in Georgia, Charles became infuriated and announced that the time had come for every black man to defend himself. New Orleans blacks reported that Charles had "talked vaguely about an uprising and hinted that some kind of organization was being formed." As the summer of 1900 progressed, his anti-white bitterness deepened, fed by Bishop Turner's strong words.[10]

On a hot July night Charles and another man sat on a dark doorstep in a residential section of New Orleans, presumably discussing their grievances against white people. Neighbors protested to police that the two men did not live there and might be up to no good. When three officers arrived and told the two men to move on, Charles slowly rose as if to leave, then suddenly drew a pistol and fired at the patrolmen. The shots were returned but Charles and his companion fled, leaving one of the officers seriously wounded. Later the same night a police captain and three of his men traced Charles to a small house on an alley. In desperation, Charles fired several rifle shots, killing the captain and one of his men. While two other officers took cover, Charles escaped.[11]

The next day, as word of the crime spread through the city, many incensed whites joined the search for Charles. Quick police action prevented a crowd from lynching one of Charles' friends, but the mob wanted vengeance and began beating black people who ventured an opinion of the affair. Soon New Orleans witnessed a genuine race riot as a throng of whites surged through the black quarter,

10. *New Orleans Times-Democrat*, 29, 30 July 1900.
11. Ibid., 25 July 1900; *New Orleans Picayune*, 25 July 1900.

searching for Charles and beating and shooting any blacks who appeared on the streets. Several blacks were killed and many hurt before auxiliary police and state militia dispersed the mob.[12]

Charles, meanwhile, had fled to a nearby town, but after the violence subsided he returned to the city. Told where the renegade was hiding, a large company of police and troops surrounded the house; from an upper-story window Charles began firing and soon three more policemen and a young boy were dead. As a last resort, the troops set fire to the house, driving Charles into the open. A militia man, spotting him running from the building, shot and killed the man who had slain six whites. After the crowd killed another man who ran from the burning house, they mutilated Charles' body beyond recognition. Finally the police scattered the mob and ended the New Orleans riot of 1900. Six whites and eight blacks lay dead; many others had been injured when whites burned black schools and homes.[13]

Police and reporters found much evidence among Charles' belongings to tie him to the emigration movement. A trunk contained copies of Flummer's *Liberia and the Negro,* one of the pamphlets that had been used to recruit members for the defunct International Migration Society, and the authorities also found great bundles of the *Voice of Missions.* Journalists said the newspaper was "edited by Bishop Turner, and [was] the official organ of all haters of the white race. Its editorials are anarchistic to the extreme, and urge upon the negro that the sooner he realizes that he is as good as the white man the better it will be for him." The police also found other "scandalously

12. *New Orleans Times-Democrat,* 25, 26 July 1900; *New Orleans Picayune,* 25, 26 July 1900.
13. *New Orleans Times-Democrat* and *New Orleans Picayune,* 27, 28, 29 July 1900.

incendiary literature," guns, ammunition, and a bottle of cocaine, "the modern negro's requisite."[14] "Without a doubt," concluded the *New Orleans Times-Democrat,* "it was from these booklets that Charles originally derived his fiendish animosity against the white race in general."[15] The police investigated and claimed that the *Voice of Missions* and the Migration Society's propaganda were sufficiently seditious to be banned from the mails.[16] Middle-class blacks joined the white community in denouncing the emigration scheme, pointing out that only lower-class blacks paid any attention to Liberia. The affair ended with torrents of abuse for African emigration.[17]

The investigation revealed that although the International Migration Society had died quietly in 1899, its president, Daniel Flummer, had started a new emigration scheme called the Liberian Colonization Society. Its plan of operation was identical to that of the Migration Society except that passage to Liberia now cost $50 per person. Also, the new passenger contract contained an additional clause in which the would-be emigrants agreed to defer any legal action against the society for three years from the date of issue. Those who had paid money to the Migration Society could pay their lapsed dues and sail with the new group.[18]

An enterprising reporter from the *Times-Democrat*

14. *New Orleans Times-Democrat* and *New Orleans Picayune,* 25 July 1900.

15. *New Orleans Times-Democrat,* 29 July 1900.

16. Ibid., 5 August 1900. Needless to say, Flummer denied that his materials were intended to produce racial discord; "[they] were designed and calculated to convince the Negro reader of the utter hopelessness of any struggle by his race against the white man, and that the only security for his people is to be found in *separation*—not in strife, as you put it" (letter to *New Orleans Times-Democrat,* 1 September 1900). Cf. Bishop Turner's similar statement in *Voice of Missions,* September 1900.

17. *New Orleans Times-Democrat,* 5, 6 August 1900.

18. Ibid., 4 August 1900; *Birmingham News,* 26 July 1900.

visited Birmingham to learn more about the organization that had supplied New Orleans with "hate propaganda." He found Flummer, an athletic young man, in the process of moving crates of pamphlets, files, and records into a new office for the "new" society. Flummer stated that the Migration Society's failure to send regular ships to Africa and the distractions of the Spanish-American War had combined to end black interest in the society. "The payments kept decreasing in number and at last the thing simply dwindled out." Penniless immigrants did not suffer greatly in Liberia, he said, because fruit was plentiful, the natives friendly, and agriculture simple. Flummer claimed that thousands of blacks had already applied for reinstatement of their lapsed contracts. Many of them, he said, expressed dissatisfaction with Booker T. Washington's philosophy of racial accommodation and wanted to go where they could have equal rights.[19]

When the reporter asked about the newly formed Liberian Colonization Society, Flummer explained that, for all practical purposes, he was the society. The old network of agents would handle recruiting and the old propaganda would be reissued. Unfortunately, he said, because no regularly scheduled ships had been obtained, the campaign would have to rely on getting enough emigrants to warrant chartering a ship. "We are just starting up and haven't gotten things in shape as yet." The whites involved in the scheme were good men but had little money, Flummer said; so he was trying to get outside aid. For additional income, Flummer even offered to conduct African hunting trips for white sportsmen who would sail on his ships. "I hope to put this concern on a better footing, and I shall push it energetically from now on."[20]

In the months that followed the Liberian Colonization

19. *New Orleans Times-Democrat*, 4 August 1900.
20. Ibid., *Birmingham News*, 6 August 1902.

Society tried to follow the successful pattern its predecessor had devised in 1895 and 1896. Local agents pursued their lucrative calling as disfranchisement, violence, and poor crops made many blacks restless. Occasional bursts of emigration excitement occurred in various areas throughout the South but the interest was not sustained. In December 1900 Flummer announced that a ship with 250 black emigrants would sail on January 30, but only sixteen blacks showed up at the Birmingham headquarters on the appointed day. Recalling the publicity and momentum that had been generated by the small group of emigrants late in 1894, Flummer dispatched the sixteen to Liberia via New York and Europe. But the press and even Bishop Turner paid little attention, and the society failed to get publicity or start momentum.[21]

Trying to create new interest and seeking financial aid, Flummer visited Liberia early in 1902. The Liberians were still eager to receive new settlers, and President G. W. Gibson had even contemplated sending an ambassador to the United States to work up official and popular American interest in his country.[22] When Flummer arrived in Monrovia, he and his Liberian agent, Senator R. A. Wright, had little difficulty in getting the legislature to pass two bills granting aid to Flummer's society for buying a ship to transport emigrants. The society was required to put up $40,000 to obtain the $20,000 promised by Liberia. Neither the society nor the Liberians had the money to fund the project, but the appropriation made good propaganda and the trip indicated that Flummer was still serious about sending blacks to Africa.[23] But the long delay in transporting emigrants, (it had been six years since the

21. *Birmingham News,* 8 December 1900, 7 February 1901.
22. A. B. King to Wilson, 2 August 1901.
23. R. A. Wright to H. M. Turner, 17 March 1902 (published in *Voice of the People,* June 1902); J. C. Stevens to Wilson, 12 February 1902; *Acts, 1901–1902,* pp. 26 f, 37 f.

"Laurada" sailed) hindered the efforts of the Birmingham society. Moreover, there was evidence that Southern blacks no longer trusted Flummer's project. Even Bishop Turner stopped printing Flummer's advertisements and bulletins in his newspaper.

Even though Flummer and Turner could do little to stimulate a large-scale emigration movement in the years between 1897 and 1900, a number of blacks still considered going to Africa. Occasional reports from new settlers in Liberia stimulated the steady trickle of inquiring letters from Southern blacks. Some radical Southern whites also endorsed segregation of the races through the extreme measure of black deportation. From time to time individuals or groups tried to organize companies or clubs to facilitate getting to Liberia. Rumors maintained that Cuban blacks were going to the Congo Free State and that American blacks were,wanted in South Africa's mines.[24]

Tennessee, in particular, spawned emigration interest in 1900 and 1901. S. B. Turner, a Nashville businessman (who was not related to the bishop), announced in April 1900 that he was the leader of a group of black people that was saving its money to buy passage to Liberia.[25] The following year Bishop Turner's new journal, *The Voice of the People*,[26] and other black newspapers carried an advertisement for another Nashville organization, the Inter-

24. Cf. *Voice of the People,* May, October 1901.
25. S. B. Turner to Wilson, 15 April 1900.
26. The *Voice of Missions* had been not only Turner's paper, it was also the official organ of the A.M.E. missionary department. In 1900 Turner was replaced as president of that department, and his successor became editor of the paper after the December 1900 issue. Turner was out of favor with the other church leaders because of his implied connection with the Charles affair in New Orleans, his generally unpopular stand on race issues, his attacks on those who disagreed with his views, and his strident endorsement of William Jennings Bryan, a Democrat, for U. S. President in 1900. *The Voice of the People,* a nonchurch publication although it contained much church news, was edited by Turner from January 1901 until at least 1907.

national Migration and Steamship Company, headed by a black man, J. C. Bulis. The notice offered transportation to the fabulous land of Liberia for $52. The company also claimed to own 200 acres of land that had been donated by Liberia to help start an agricultural school, modeled on Tuskegee Institute. Bulis falsely claimed, furthermore, that his group owned a steamship, named "Liberia," that would regularly carry merchandise and passengers between New Orleans, Savannah, and Africa. Letters from "missionaries" described the wealth of Liberian agriculture in terms no dirt farmer could resist, if he believed them. Later notices contained letters from Liberians and the Liberian Consul General, a Boston white man, all praising the black republic.[27]

Notices for the Nashville company ran for three months in Turner's paper and then vanished with no comment. In their place appeared a summons for an "African emigration convention to be held in Nashville early in October."[28] Meanwhile, during the spring and summer of 1901 Secretary Wilson of the American Colonization Society received an increasing number of inquiring letters from interested blacks. Other evidence of renewed emigration sentiment convinced Bishop Turner that the time was ripe for another major attempt to found a shipping line between the United States and Liberia. He decided to take charge of the forthcoming Nashville emigration convention, hoping once more that he could launch a great African exodus.[29]

The emigration convention met in Nashville as sched-

27. *Voice of the People,* June, July, August 1901. Cf. *Colored American,* 20 July 1901.
28. *Voice of the People,* September, 1901.
29. Ibid. Cf. L. E. Fletcher to Wilson, 3 April 1901; *Morning Messenger,* April 1901, in ACS scrapbooks; *Southwestern Christian Advocate,* 28 March 1901; S. D. Mitchell to Wilson, 20 March 1901; S. B. Turner to Wilson, 1 July, 1 October 1901.

uled, in October 1901. No journal of the meeting was published and the local press took no notice of the event, but it appears that Bishop Turner dominated the proceedings, as usual. The only opposition faction insisted that emigration to places other than Africa also be considered. The convention resolved "to encourage, promote and advise emigration to any portion of the globe where a man's color will be no bar to his elevation and the enjoyment of his civil and political rights.[30]

The main achievement of the convention was to draw several minor, struggling emigration groups, including the Nashville International Migration Steamship Company and S. B. Turner's following, into one organization, the Colored National Emigration Association. Its primary goal was to raise $100,000 to purchase a used steamship for emigration and commercial purposes. "It is time for the Negro race to begin to help itself and wait no longer upon the white people or wealthy white men to put steamships between the United States and the countries where black men can have rights and be men in the full sense of the term." To raise the needed sum, the association would sell $5 shares to any who wished to invest in the scheme. Members of the association were not necessarily shareholders, but paid $4 each year for the privilege of belonging to it. There is no record of how many people attended the convention but, by including all the adherents of the component organizations, the association claimed a charter membership of 3,700.[31]

Delegates to the convention came from only eleven states but vice presidents for fifteen states and territories were named. A number of Nashville blacks were made

30. *Voice of the People,* November, December 1901, April 1902.
31. Ibid., H. M. Turner to B. T. Washington, 5 November 1901, in box 213, Booker T. Washington Papers, Library of Congress.

officers, and the president was William H. Heard. Heard
had been United States Minister to Liberia at the time the
"Horsa" and the "Laurada" landed their emigrants, and
in 1901 he served as pastor of an A.M.E. church in Atlanta
where he strongly endorsed Bishop Turner's nationalist
ideology. The chief officer, however, was not President
Heard but the chancellor and treasurer, Bishop Turner.
Because so many emigration plans had faltered for lack of
organization or honest leadership, and because the Birmingham society had lost the confidence of the blacks, the
convention convinced Turner that only he could generate
success. "He vowed to the convention that if the colored
people would half rally, he would have a ship or die." The
bishop promised that, as treasurer, he would guarantee
that every penny paid for investment in a ship would be
held in sacred trust, to be refunded if a ship was not purchased. The three-day meeting concluded with a call for
a larger convention in Chattanooga the following May.[32]

During the months between the conventions Bishop
Turner used his newspaper to spread the good news of the
Colored National Emigration Association. Local chapters
were formed throughout the South and as far away as Van-
couver, Canada, while the officers of the association took
the field to enlist support. *The Voice of the People* declared
itself the official organ of the association and carried reports that President Heard was negotiating with France
for shipping, that Liberia had given the association a ship
subsidy, and that money for shares was beginning to come
in, almost all of it from Northern blacks. Mostly, however, Turner publicized the Chattanooga convention,
where he expected the association to receive many new
members and much financial support. A rash of lynchings

32. *Voice of the People,* November, December 1901, January–June
1902.

in the spring gave him grounds to hope for a large convention to protest such violence.[33]

Only a hundred delegates appeared in Chattanooga on May 28, 1902. After they listened to Heard lambaste the United States and praise Liberia, they passed "amid much cheering" a petition asking Congress for 500 million dollars for emigration. But the meeting must have been disappointing for Bishop Turner. Although the delegates represented members throughout the nation, their number was small; money was slow in coming; and most black leaders simply ignored the movement. Nevertheless, as it adjourned, the association optimistically resolved to hold another convention in Charlotte, North Carolina, in October 1902.[34]

An unexpected visitor at the Chattanooga convention was Daniel Flummer of Birmingham. Just back from Liberia, where he had received a promise of a subsidy from the legislature, he circulated among the delegates telling them of his plans. In Liberia he had arranged with his agent, R. A. Wright, to settle a shipload of blacks at Greenville, a hundred miles south of Monrovia and hopefully in a more healthy climate. There, he promised, they would find a projected reception center complete with a hospital, houses, and an agricultural school. While Flummer had been in Africa his agents had begun to score successes in parts of Alabama and Arkansas, and he announced that he would soon have a ship plying between Savannah and Liberia.[35] Bishop Turner, however, was not impressed by

33. Ibid., January–May 1902.

34. Ibid., July, August 1902; *Chattanooga Times,* 28, 29, 30 May 1902. Bontemps and Conroy, *They Seek a City,* p. 167.

35. *Chattanooga Times,* 29, 30 May 1902; E. D. M. Wilson to John Hay, U. S. Secretary of State, 2 April 1902 (forwarded to the Colonization Society); W. S. Goss to J. O. Wilson, 26 April 1902; R. A. Wright to H. M. Turner, 17 March 1902 (published in *Voice of the People,* June 1902.

Flummer's report and did not mention the Liberian Colonization Society in his newspaper account of the convention. The bishop had other plans to boost emigration, and Flummer did not at that time figure in them.

Those plans centered around the person of J. H. Green, a printer and the editor of *The Christian League* at Jackson, Mississippi. Turner believed that reliable information from Liberia would serve as the best propaganda for emigration. On that assumption he persuaded Green to sail for Africa, equipped with a printing press and plans for a monthly newspaper that would circulate on both sides of the Atlantic. After the Nashville convention, Green made preparations to sail and formed the African League Publishing Company to support his venture. In his Jackson newspaper he asserted that a thousand people were ready to emigrate as soon as he could supply necessary information about prospects for founding "an American city of American Negroes." After a rousing send-off at the Chattanooga convention, Green proceeded directly to Liberia.[36]

The first issue of the *African League* appeared on July 30, 1902, just one month after Green arrived in Monrovia. Filled with news of Liberians and praise for the republic, it was calculated to attract settlers from the United States. Subsequent issues carried massive advertisements for "Liberia City," a planned, self-supporting community of black settlers "where lynching is not known and freedom reigns supreme!" Green promised that the city would be built on a healthy, fertile site in the interior "where gold and other precious metals abound. In taking up a farm you may fall heir to a gold mine—who can tell?" A considerable number of American subscribers received the *African League* with its glowing descriptions of Liberia. Bishop Turner, furthermore, quoted extensively from the "Liberia City"

36. J. H. Green to Wilson, 26 October 1901; *Christian League* (n.d., n.p.), quoted in *New Africa, 4* (July 1902), 195.

notices and announced that the "Colored National Emigration Association hopes to be ready to send over those who may wish to be pioneers of this manly movement."[37]

The response in the United States, however, was far from overwhelming. Turner's association received money for its ship, but only in small amounts and at a leisurely pace. Its October convention, scheduled for Charlotte, had to be canceled because the whites allegedly forbade such incendiary meetings in their city. The convention was re-scheduled for the following spring at Montgomery, Alabama.[38]

The Liberian Colonization Society, on the other hand, was having better success. By midsummer of 1902, Flummer felt confident enough to announce that a chartered steamer would sail from Savannah for Liberia on January 20, 1903. Bishop Turner ecstatically announced the forthcoming voyage in the *Voice of the People*. His Colored National Emigration Association would continue to work for its own ship but he welcomed transportation for emigrants under any auspices. "Glory be to God the Father, the Son and to the Holy Ghost, for the glorious tidings," the bishop cried. "God being our helper, we shall go on the same ship."[39]

Flummer's organization held the emigration spotlight during the late months of 1902. His agent at Liberia began preparations to receive the settlers at Greenville, in Sinoe County, Liberia, where the Sinoe Emigrant Relief Association planned to help the newcomers. Liberian merchants prepared to ship their products to New York via Flummer's ship, and Liberia's President, G. W. Gibson, happily antici-

37. *New Africa*, 4 (August 1902), 227; ibid., *4* (September 1902), 266; *African League,* 13 May, 12 September 1903; *Voice of the People,* December 1902.

38. *Voice of the People,* September, October 1902.

39. Ibid.

pated the arrival of "several thousands of industrious, intelligent, Christian Negroes from the United States."[40]

Late in November Flummer traveled to Savannah to plan for the departure of the steamship "Donald" with 250 emigrants. Just as his agent had done before the "Laurada's" departure, Flummer ordered supplies, arranged for temporary housing, and chartered a train that would again start from Memphis and pick up emigrants along the way.[41] Considerable interest among blacks in various parts of the South was manifest and Bishop Turner grew jubilant at the prospect of resuming the emigration that had almost stopped after the "Laurada" sailed in 1896.[42]

Despite all Flummer's planning and publicity, the "Donald" never sailed, nor did any other ship ever sail for Liberia under his direction. He claimed that the "Donald" had been found "not satisfactory." Turner's newspaper carried the announcement that its departure had been postponed: "The president has not informed us as to the date, but we are assured the ship will sail in March."[43] March came and went, however, but the "Donald" did not. Although Flummer and his agents had set several sailing dates the year before and failed to keep them,[44] this may have been only a disreputable tactic to gain new members. But having publicly proclaimed the "Donald's" sailing and then failed to produce the ship ended Flummer's work as an emigration operator. The owners of the "Donald" confided to Secretary Wilson of the Colonization Society that

40. *New Africa, 4* (December 1902), 361, 366; R. A. Wright to D. J. Flummer, 9 October 1902 (published in *Voice of the People*, January 1903).

41. *Atlanta Constitution*, 25 November 1902.

42. H. C. Thomas to Wilson, 18 November 1902; C. E. Owens to Wilson, 25 November 1902; *Voice of the People*, December 1902, January 1903; *Southwestern Christian Advocate*, 1 January 1903.

43. *Voice of the People*, February 1903.

44. See above, nn. 21 and 35, and J. C. Wood to Wilson, 26 October 1902; *Southwestern Christian Advocate*, 1 January 1903.

the real reason the ship had not sailed was that Flummer, after chartering the steamer, had been unable to pay the contracted amount.[45] Money, indeed, was his greatest problem. In an open letter later in 1903 he announced that a colony of up to 500 people would depart in February 1904 if the colonists received "financial aid from their Anglo-Saxon friends." The aid was not forthcoming, however, and Flummer apparently abandoned the emigration business under direct attack from the *African League* and the many Afro-Americans who had paid him their money. After the failure of the "Donald" expedition, Bishop Turner ignored Flummer.[46] So ended the Birmingham emigration organization, ten years after its founding. Its net accomplishments were the collection of thousands of dollars and the transportation of about 600 blacks to Africa.

Profit, rather than humanitarianism or even racist compulsion, seems to have been the main motive for Flummer and his associates, certainly after 1900. Although he apparently acted in good faith with most of the people who purchased tickets, it is clear that Flummer's profits came not from shipping but from the lapsed payments of would-be emigrants. Like others before and after him, he capitalized on the unfortunate blacks who believed the only way to be independent of white domination was to leave the country. Whatever emigration occurred under his auspices took place because Flummer knew that to keep his scheme working he had to show some results. In the end it was not lack of interest so much as lack of transportation that killed the plan.

Bishop Turner's Colored National Emigration Association, however, continued working to buy a ship. His disappointment over the cancellation of the Charlotte conven-

45. J. A. Donald to Wilson, 26 May 1903.
46. *Voice of the People,* December 1903, January 1904; *African League,* 13 May 1903.

tion in October 1902 was temporarily assuaged by the promise of Flummer's expedition in January 1903. Ill health kept the bishop from extensive activity in behalf of the association, but through the *Voice of the People* he repeated the call for more money. To give the organization legal status President Heard secured a charter from the State of Delaware, and to boost the slow-selling stock, Heard followed the example of Flummer and petitioned the legislature of Liberia for a $25,000 subsidy. The accommodating senator, R. A. Wright, secured the grant, at least on paper. During the long, disappointing winter, Heard and Turner looked forward to the 1903 convention, which would be held in Montgomery late in June.[47]

During the spring the situation deteriorated markedly. Anti-emigration blacks continued their attacks against Turner and his association and the bishop retorted in his usual vitriolic style. "You miserable black coons who are everlastingly trying to berate Liberia and speak of the country as nothing, should invest your thousands in the grandest move that the black man has inaugurated since his liberation."[48] Not only did the articulate leaders oppose emigration, the black peasants were growing apathetic. Turner complained that there had been "so many disappointments and failures about ships between the United States and Africa, and so many thousands of dollars have been lost by the people paying their way and the ships failing to go, that our people have literally lost confidence."[49]

The Montgomery convention, therefore, was to be a massive effort to rekindle the emigration flame. Senator John T. Morgan of Alabama, who had endorsed the Butler

47. *Voice of the People*, January, February, April 1903; *Acts, 1902–1903*, p. 11.
48. *Voice of the People*, April 1903. Cf. *Colored American*, 21 February 1903.
49. *Voice of the People*, March 1903.

bill in 1890 and spoken boldly for emigration on numerous later occasions, had recently called again for separation of the races. Heard therefore asked him to address the gathering in Montgomery and Bishop Turner went so far as to announce that Morgan would be the main speaker, but the senator declined.[50] To broaden the convention's appeal, its publicity stressed the commercial prospects of the ship project rather than the emigration. Bishop Lucius H. Holsey, furthermore, who advocated a separate black state within the United States, was named director general of the association.[51]

The 1903 convention could hardly be called a success. On the first day, June 24, although a number of local blacks attended, only twenty-seven delegates appeared. Eventually forty-five arrived. Copies of the *African League* were circulated and $150 worth of stock was sold after Turner announced that "over $26,000 worth of ship stock" had been subscribed. (This figure evidently included the promised $25,000 subsidy from Liberia.) The delegates voted to charter a ship in 1904 rather than wait for the full purchase price to accrue. After a number of rousing speeches the convention adjourned, having planned to meet again at Atlanta in 1904.[52] To his critics who minimized the convention, Turner replied: "We suppose it was nothing to human churls who haven't got an idea as big as a pea, but it will be something when the lynchers get you."[53]

Despite his bravado, Turner was displeased with the

50. Ibid., April 1903; *New York Age*, 8 January 1903; *Liberia Bulletin*, 22 (February 1903), 58–62; W. H. Heard to J. T. Morgan, 30 March 1903, cited in McStallworth, "Congo Question," p. 192.

51. Undated circular in ACS Papers; *Colored American*, 18 April 1903; Meier, *Negro Thought*, pp. 273 f.; Bacote, "Negro in Georgia Politics," p. 33.

52. *Voice of the People*, August 1903; *Colored American*, 21 February 1903; John F. Foard, *North America and Africa* (2d ed. Statesville, N.C., 1904), pp. 46-60.

53. *Voice of the People*, August 1903.

progress of the association. Concerning the sale of stock, he confessed: "We are making poor headway. . . . We very much fear that the Negro is an 'inferior animal' at best, and but very little account when it comes to helping himself." Even though the Donald Steamship Company, which had become interested in black emigration through Flummer, offered to lease him a ship for 300 emigrants, Turner was afraid to accept for fear the people would not show up at the port. During the summer of 1903 he received several letters from would-be emigrants who wanted to sail to Liberia. "All we can say to those who wish to go at once to Africa," he replied, "is that we are in no condition to promise anyone transportation yet."[54]

President Heard, however, saw matters differently. Acting on the Montgomery convention's decision to charter a ship rather than wait until one could be purchased, he wrote to editor Green of the *African League* that a ship would said early in 1904. The fare, he said, would be only $30 for adults, $20 for children, and owners of five shares of ship stock would be transported free. The rate obviously could not include support of the emigrants after their arrival in Liberia. It is doubtful, moreover, in view of Flummer's experience, that the transportation could be arranged so cheaply. But Heard cheerfully told Green to inform his readers and those who wanted to settle in yet unborn Liberia City to get ready. "The outlook is indeed bright. . . . Tell Liberia to get ready, for we are coming."[55]

Liberia did indeed get ready, much to the later discomfort of Green and Heard. The man who took it upon himself to alert Liberia to the dangers of such indiscriminate immigration was the new United States Minister, Ernest Lyon. Lyon, a Methodist pastor and a protégé of Booker

54. Ibid., September 1903.
55. W. H. Heard to J. H. Green, 9 July 1903 (published in *African League,* 26 September 1903).

T. Washington, had worked vigorously in Republican campaigns, and at Washington's suggestion had received the coveted Liberian post from President Theodore Roosevelt. Lyon was a vigorous, well-educated man who had successfully served large churches in New Orleans, New York, and Baltimore. His attitude toward emigration was realistic: only those who could support themselves and contribute to Liberia's welfare should go. Lyon sailed for Monrovia about the time that Heard and Turner were leading the Montgomery convention.[56]

Shortly after Lyon's arrival in Monrovia he was faced with the sad problem of dealing with the survivors of a group of fifty-three Georgia blacks who had come on their own to Liberia early in 1903. By midsummer, despite considerable aid from the local government, twenty of them had died and the remainder wanted to return to Georgia. Lyon and other charitable persons in Monrovia helped the struggling newcomers as best they could, but Lyon reported to his Washington superiors that funds were low and prices disastrously high. "Owing . . . to the agitation now going on in the United States, on the subject of Negro emigration to Liberia, by irresponsible persons whose literature has wide circulation among the innocent and poorer classes of Negroes, the question becomes one of gravity for the consideration of both governments."[57]

While the problem of what to do with the stricken Georgia immigrants was still current, Heard's letter to Green, promising more settlers in 1904, was published in the *Afri-*

---

56. *New York Age,* 9 April 1903. Lyon had earlier served as secretary of the West African Steamship Company in New Orleans but, apparently, the company never functioned. J. W. Pierce to Coppinger, 6 July 1891. Considerable correspondence between Lyon and Booker T. Washington can be found in the Washington Papers.

57. E. Lyon to J. Hay, U. S. Secretary of State, 23 September 1903, Dispatches from U. S. Ministers at Monrovia, U. S. Archives. E. J. Barclay to G. W. Ellis, 30 May 1906, in Post Records (Monrovia, box 39–18, U. S. Archives.

can League. Upset by the matter, Lyon began to inquire further about the problems of newcomers in Liberia. He discovered that the old facilities for helping settlers had long since been unusable. Not even temporary housing was available, and the cost of foodstuffs was greatly inflated. Prominent citizens of Liberia informed Lyon that, in their opinion, penniless Afro-Americans could not possibly help Liberia. The minister wrote to the American Secretary of State: "From my knowledge of the condition of affairs here, I beg to inform you that Liberia is not prepared for indiscriminate immigration in 1904."[58]

Lyon's letter received wide circulation both in Liberia and the United States, and most Liberians agreed with his views. However, Green printed the letter in the *African League,* along with a blast at Lyon himself, so wherever that journal was read in the United States, Lyon's letter also was read. Furthermore, the State Department circulated the letter and many newspapers reprinted it with editorial attacks against the Colored National Emigration Association. The *Pittsburgh Times,* for example, after describing the association's empty promises of African riches, concluded: "It is difficult to conceive of anything more pernicious."[59] Lyon and the State Department did their job well; their widespread adverse publicity hurt the emigration movement severely. President Heard wrote to editor Green in March 1904: "We should have brought out at least three hundred emigrants this spring in a chartered ship, but for this letter printed in your paper from United States Minister Ernest Lyon. It did us great injury and Liberia much injustice," he complained. "This letter

58. *African League,* 26 September 1903; Lyon to Hay, 7 October 1903 (published in *Liberia and West Africa,* 7 [December 1905]).
59. *Pittsburgh Times,* 5 December 1903; *New York Age,* 23 June 1904. Both in ACS scrapbooks.

was printed in all the leading southern newspapers, and almost killed our enterprise."[60]

Lyon's letter was important because the association had already badly degenerated. Money stopped coming in and Bishop Turner complained that "the way we are going on, we will not be able to purchase our contemplated ship in twenty-five years. We are almost becoming discouraged." He asked the members either to pay up or allow him to return the money to the shareholders. "There is a perfect lag in our association," he wrote. "Is it possible the American Negro can start and finish nothing?" As if to announce surrender, he began publishing announcements of commercial passage fares to Liberia via Liverpool. Because at that time an emigrant could reach Monrovia from New Orleans for less than $70 on a British ship, there seemed little reason for the shipline agitation to continue.[61]

Although President Heard continued to be more optimistic about affairs and the *African League* continued to circulate in the South, inviting Afro-Americans to "Liberia City," the Colored National Emigration Association was practically dead.[62] Bishop Turner lost interest in the project and became deeply involved with local politics, trying to stop Georgia from disfranchising her black citizens.[63] Finally, as he explained to Secretary Wilson of the Colonization Society, he just disbanded the association. "For some time you may have noticed I have not said or done very much in the interest of Liberian colonization," he wrote in 1906.

60. W. H. Heard to J. H. Green, 11 March 1904 (published in *African League* [n.d.] and quoted in *New York Age,* 23 June 1904).

61. *Voice of the People,* January 1904.

62. Cf. J. W. Fant to Wilson, 17 April 1905.

63. Bacote, "Negro in Georgia Politics," pp. 378 ff.

I attempted to organize an association that would raise
a hundred thousand dollars . . . but after raising a few
thousand dollars . . . a lethargy or seeming indifference
appeared to come over our organization. . . . As treasurer of the organization I just returned the money . . . to
those who had given it and invested it, and disbanded
the institution. I did this against the protest of our president, Dr. W. H. Heard and some of the most influential
members of the organization, for the reason that I did
not intend to have any one say they put money in my
hands and that I had spent it or robbed them of it.[64]

Thus ended Bishop Turner's last organized attempt to
move Afro-Americans to Africa. He nevertheless continued to advocate emigration as the only solution to
America's race problem.

During the first years of the twentieth century, the years
when Turner and Flummer were pushing their emigration
plans, a spate of radically anti-black books achieved best-
seller status. Charles Caroll published *The Negro a Beast*
in 1900 and *The Tempter of Eve* in 1902, both designed
to discredit blacks. William P. Calhoun echoed Caroll in
his 1902 book *The Caucasian and the Negro in the United
States,* which was followed in 1905 by William B. Smith's
The Color Line: A Brief in Behalf of the Unborn and in
1907 by Robert Shufeldt's *The Negro a Menace to American Civilization.* Most popular of all were the novels of
Thomas Dixon, Jr., *The Leopard's Spots* (1902), *The
Klansman* (1905), and *The Traitor* (1907). Dixon, like the
others, abhorred any thought of racial amalgamation and
insisted that permanent separation of the races was the only
remedy. Afro-American emigration to Africa was the rec-

64. H. M. Turner to Wilson, 28 March 1906.

ommended permanent solution.[65] Even Bishop Turner, who welcomed the endorsement of emigration from such white men as Senator J. T. Morgan and Atlanta editor John Temple Graves,[66] could not stomach the "irreligious, ungodly, hypocritical, blasphemous and sacrilegious prattle of Dixon and his kind." The bishop regretted only "that there will be a host of Negroes that will have to spend eternity in hell with Tom Dixon."[67]

Whatever the eschatological fate of Dixon, his books, and others like them, kept the idea of black emigration before the American public. Although Afro-American leaders were caught up in the debates between Booker T. Washington and his critics,[68] Bishop Turner still influenced many of the less sophisticated blacks. When in 1903 Washington had been shouted down by a group of "radical" Boston blacks who favored protest instead of accomodation, Turner wrote: "Washington's policy is not worth a cent. It accomplishes no racial good except as it helps a thousand students at Tuskegee." On the other hand, he continued, although "we agree with our Boston friends in spitting on everything that would appear to underrate the value of the Negro in every particular, they are doing no more good than Washington. . . . Nothing less than a nation owned and controlled by the Negro will amount to a hill of beans."[69]

Because of the popular racism fermented by the likes of Dixon and the emigration espoused by Turner, a number of small emigration schemes sprang up in the first decade of the century. Some individuals, like the fifty-six

65. Logan, *Betrayal of the Negro,* p. 354; Maxwell Bloomfield, "Dixon's *The Leopard's Spots:* A Study in Popular Racism," in Charles E. Wynnes, ed., *The Negro in the South since 1865* (University, Ala., 1965), pp. 83–102; *Liberia Bulletin, 28* (February 1906), 51 f.

66. *New York American and Journal,* 13 September 1903.

67. *Voice of the People,* March 1903.

68. Meier, *Negro Thought,* Part 5.

69. *Voice of the People,* September 1903.

Georgians whose plight in Liberia had so alarmed Minister Lyon, had quietly sailed for Africa without formal organization or support.[70] Others formed grandiose organizations but moved no one to Liberia. From such unlikely places as Los Angeles[71] and Arizona[72] came reports of blacks who had organized to go to Africa. W. H. Ellis, the black man who had tried in the mid-1890s to establish an emigrant colony in Mexico, visited King Menelek of Abyssinia in 1903, expecting to establish a refuge there for American blacks.[73] From New York in 1904 came word of the formation of the African Trading Company, intended to facilitate commerce and emigration.[74] About the same time the New York and Liberia Steamship Company announced its intention to start a ship for Africa.[75] The American and West African Steamship Company also existed for a time.[76] From Newark, New Jersey, came word of the Liberian Trading and Emigration Association of the United States of America.[77] The African Colonization Church opened its "Liberia Temple" in Washington early in 1906,[78] the same year that Captain Harry Deane of Chicago, who claimed six years' experience in Africa,

70. Ibid., April, May 1903; *Washington Star,* 8 January 1903; *Washington Post,* 25 November 1903; C. H. Adams to Wilson, 8 March 1904.

71. M. T. Williams to Wilson, 21 July 1899, 8 August 1901; J. R. Rayford to Wilson, 26 June 1899; E. W. Michaux to Wilson, n.d. (c. July 1903); A. Saunders to Wilson, 21 August 1908; John H. Washington, Jr., to Booker T. Washington, 8 July 1911, in box 446, Booker T. Washington Papers, Library of Congress.

72. D. R. Thomas to H. M. Turner (published in *Voice of Missions,* March 1900); *Voice of the People,* February, December 1903.

73. *Voice of the People,* October, November 1903, February 1904.

74. W. H. Butler to Wilson, 15 March 1904.

75. Prospectus in an unclassified packet of printed material in ACS Papers. J. R. Spurgeon, "The New York and Liberia Steamship Company," *Colored American Magazine,* December 1904, pp. 735–41.

76. *African League,* 30 September 1904.

77. W. H. Tinsley to Wilson, 7, 9 November 1905.

78. *Washington Star,* 14, 19 February 1906.

launched his Ethiopian Empire scheme.[79] Even Booker T. Washington helped dispatch several Afro-Americans as agricultural advisers to Togoland and the Sudan.[80] Numerous Southern local emigration clubs emerged in vain, but the shift of African emigration interest to the Northern cities was noteworthy.

The most interesting and sustained of the urban emigration schemes emanated from Detroit and gained adherents throughout the North. The most distinguished black man in Detroit, Judge D. A. Straker, had insisted during the 1890s that Afro-Americans should become politically and economically independent. In addition he had espoused the "single tax" ideas of Henry George, who advocated social and economic reforms in which the state would support itself exclusively on taxes on the increasing value of land.[81] One of Straker's disciples was a young Detroit intellectual, Francis H. Warren, who long after Straker had abandoned the single-tax idea was deeply involved in various schemes for economic reform. As president of the Michigan Co-Operative League, he was well known throughout the state. As editor of the *Detroit Informer,* he had a regular newspaper to espouse his racial and economic views, including the single-tax system.[82]

By 1901 Warren had conceived the idea of planting an autonomous colony in Africa that could experiment with the single tax. In a letter to Bishop Turner, he explained that he had chosen a place "300 miles southeast of Liberia

79. H. Deane to J. O. Wilson, 11, 21 June, 6 August 1906. Cf. Harry Deane, *The Pedro Gorino* (Boston, 1929), for Deane's embellished life story. Cf. *Living Chronicle* (Cape Palmas, Liberia), November, December 1906.

80. Louis R. Harlan, "Booker T. Washington and the White Man's Burden," pp. 442–47, Cf. T. Thomas Fortune in *Washington Post,* 20 April 1902.

81. Meier, *Negro Thought,* pp. 46, 57.

82. *Alexander's Magazine,* 2 (October 1906), 17. Unfortunately no file of the *Detroit Informer* has been found but a few clippings are preserved in the ACS scrapbooks.

and North of the Congo. It is in the heart of the wilderness, but communication can be easily opened with the coast trade. This part . . . has been selected principally because of its favorable climate and fertile soil."[83] Warren's naïve enthusiasm for Africa matched his utopian economic schemes. Turner, who probably did not take him very seriously, told him to go to Liberia instead of the wilderness. "We favor emigration from this hell-hole [of America]," the bishop wrote, "and care nothing about the tax, whether single or double."[84]

Warren persevered, nevertheless, and to expedite his plans he joined the Colored National Emigration Association. Because he was attending law school in May 1902, he could not attend the Chattanooga emigration convention; instead, he sent a letter to the delegates that reported his progress in Detroit. A number of people, including some whites, had expressed interest in the projected single-tax colony. Opposition was strong but the outlook was encouraging. Warren promised to address the next emigration convention on the merits of his economic scheme.[85] When his erstwhile mentor, Judge Straker, challenged his plans, Warren redoubled his efforts. "A great Negro republic in Africa with great commercial interests, would undoubtedly solve the race problem," he wrote, "and if grounded in the single tax, it would solve the universal problem of poverty."[86] In his speech at the Montgomery emigration convention in 1903, Warren again stressed the economic basis of the race problem.[87]

After 1903, of course, the Colored National Emigration Association deteriorated rapidly and Warren had to

83. *Atlanta Daily News,* n.d., quoted in *Voice of the People,* May 1901.
84. *Voice of the People,* February, March, May 1901, January 1902.
85. Ibid., September 1902.
86. Ibid., April 1903.
87. Ibid., August 1903.

continue his crusade alone. His *Detroit Informer,* however, gained a wide audience for his ideas. The newspaper, in addition to printing "all the race news of Michigan and Canada," declared itself "a fearless defender of human rights" and an advocate of "rational, systematic and progressive emigration of colored Americans to Africa and the West Indies [to form] an independent state with a single-tax constitution."[88]

By 1906 Warren had gained new allies in Boston, the heart of the radical black opposition to Booker T. Washington's ideas of racial accommodation. Charles Alexander, the editor-publisher of *Alexander's Magazine,* had been sent to Boston to start a journal in support of the Tuskegee attitude.[89] In the first few issues of his magazine, however, although they lauded Washington, Alexander included several articles on Africa, including one by Walter F. Walker titled "The Scientific Redemption of Africa."[90] Neither Walker nor Alexander endorsed emigration at first, but by October 1906 their conversion had begun. That month's issue contained a portrait of F. H. Warren and quoted from Bishop Turner, who after the Atlanta race riot of 1906 was again trying to stir up interest in emigration. The conversion was complete by January 1907, when, after glowing reviews of Sir Harry H. Johnston's new book, *Liberia,* Alexander advertised for young men, trained in agriculture and mechanics, "who would like to cast their lot in Liberia."[91] Henceforth *Alexander's Magazine* would be a vigorous exponent of African emigration.

Warren, meanwhile, had not been idle. He once advertised in the *Informer* for fifty retired army veterans who

88. *Alexander's Magazine, 1* (March 1906), 6.
89. Emma Lou Thornbrough, "American Negro Newspapers, 1880–1914," *Business History Review, 40* (Winter 1966), 467–90.
90. *Alexander's Magazine, 1* (August 1905), 3.
91. Ibid., *2* (October 1906), 5, 13, 25, and *3* (January 1907), 127.

would settle in Liberia and use their government pensions as capital.[92] He confidently began inquiring about chartering a ship to take "several hundred emigrants to Liberia."[93] His plan had further ripened by early 1907, when he announced that about 600 people were planning to depart the following September. The primary requirement for these emigrants was capital—certainly enough to support themselves for at least a year after arrival and hopefully enough to introduce new industries to Liberia. To meet the shelter problem in Africa, Warren advocated taking prefabricated houses in "knock-down bundles," and ship departures would be so controlled as to land the newcomers in the dry, healthy season. Although he was still vague about the financial arrangements for chartering the ship, Warren had the economics of the new colony fully rationalized. The single-tax system had been defeated in the United States, he said, because the highly developed American economy had too much to lose in the conversion process, but a colony in a less developed land could begin with the new system. And in time its success would spread to other areas and eventually throughout the world.

We propose to colonize the hinterlands of [Liberia] and ask the government for the privilege of raising our taxes according to our own plans [Warren wrote]. Herein lies a great opportunity for colored Americans with single-tax proclivities, to join us in civilizing that part of Liberia now occupied by semi-civilized tribes of natives and there work out a true civilization that we believe will eventually dominate the earth. And what a grand

92. Cited in *Liberia and West Africa*, 8 (November–December 1906), 4.
93. F. H. Warren to E. Lyon, 27 April 1906, quoted in Lyon to E. Root, 13 June 1906 (Dispatches from U. S. Ministers at Monrovia, U. S. Archives). Warren to Wilson, 29 December 1906; Wilson to Warren, 2 January 1907.

contribution to the cause of humanity Afro-Americans would thus give to the world![94]

Throughout 1907 Warren and Alexander did their utmost to publicize the plan. Walker, Alexander's assistant, was particularly excited about going to Liberia and wrote about it often. But his excitement was not contagious. Financial panic struck again in 1907, and November came and went without the departure of what had come to be known as the "rag-time colony." Warren and his allies, however, did not lose hope. Late in 1907 they organized the Liberian Development Association for "progressive emigration of American Negroes, the economic, industrial and social improvement of Liberia, and the cultivation of her hinterland." Warren, Alexander, and Walker headed the organization, whose executive board contained W. H. Heard of Atlanta and other blacks from Detroit, Providence, Kansas City, and the Republic of Panama.[95]

The association's first acts were done in desperation. It called on the moribund American Colonization Society for financial aid on the pretext of starting an "industrial school in the interior . . . along the lines of Hampton and Tuskegee." Secretary Walker asked for $2,500 to assist the emigrants who would conduct the school, but at its annual meeting the Colonization Society of course declined the request. Nor could it afford to give Alexander even a $25 subsidy for his magazine. The association had not begun well.[96]

The group nevertheless pursued its goal by sending its

94. *Detroit Informer,* 2 February 1907 (reprinted in *Alexander's Magazine, 3* [February 1907], 183–85).

95. W. F. Walker to Wilson, 31 January 1908.

96. Ibid., and ibid., 17 December 1907; Wilson to Walker, 19 December 1907, 3 February 1908; Wilson to C. Alexander, 12, 31 March 1908; *Alexander's Magazine, 5* (February 1908), 78.

secretary to spy out the land. "Walter F. Walker has gone to Liberia for me and the Liberian Development Association," Alexander wrote in March 1908. Walker was to advise the would-be emigrants on their preparations for Africa. For several months, however, there was no word from him. Readers of *Alexander's Magazine* must have wondered what happened to the young man who had left his studies at Boston University for the cause of African emigration.[97] In August, finally, his report appeared, but it was disastrous for the association. It contained a succinct, articulate, and accurate picture of affairs in Liberia, a picture that would stifle the desire of most men to emigrate there.

"Immigrants have never been told the truth about Liberia and the difficulties confronting emigration to this republic," Walker wrote. Most newcomers confessed that, had they known the truth before coming to Liberia or had money enough to return home, they would certainly be in the United States. "The motto of the republic, 'The love of liberty brought us here,' has been vulgarly expanded into: 'The love of liberty brought us here, And the want of money keeps us here.' " Walker elaborated on the nature of an undeveloped state, the problems of health and agriculture, the lack of roads, the high cost of living, the fact that local commerce was controlled not by blacks but by Europeans, and the opinion of Liberian government officials that they could not handle large-scale immigration. "I feel that it is only just to those whom I might have influenced, as well as to all American Negroes, that I now present conditions as I see them and not as they appeared to me 7000 miles away," he wrote. "Can the Negro ameliorate his environment by coming to Liberia? Emphatically, no!"[98]

97. C. Alexander to Wilson, 7 March 1908.
98. *Alexander's Magazine*, 6 (August 1908), 162–66.

Walker's report was the last item on emigration to appear in *Alexander's Magazine*. The only subsequent mention of Africa was in the form of occasional advertisements for the African Mining and Real Estate Company with headquarters in New York and "gold mines" in the Gold Coast Colony.[99] The Liberian Development Association quietly disappeared and Warren began stressing other kinds of economic reforms. W. F. Walker stayed in Liberia as a Methodist missionary.[100]

The amen to Walker's report appeared in newspaper accounts of Liberia's financial and diplomatic problems. In the summer of 1908 a Liberian commission arrived in Washington, hat in hand, asking for American aid. Things looked so grim that articles such as "Can the Black Man Stand Alone? Liberia as It Is Today" were common.[101] An American commission visited Liberia in 1909 and told the world essentially the same story Walker had reported:

In the present economic condition of Liberia, . . . the Commission is quite unable to recommend to the American Negro any extensive emigration to that country. It believes that there is a field there for a large body of civilized Negroes, but it is equally certain that under existing conditions the emigrant who carries thither little besides his physical strength and his willingness to work out his own salvation would encounter little but hardship. . . . Liberia has much to do before it can offer tempting prospects to the would-be settler.[102]

99. Ibid., 7 (March–April 1909), 209.
100. *Liberia and West Africa, 10* (February–March, July, November 1908).
101. E. A. Forbes, in *World's Work, 18* (October 1909), 12155–68.
102. *Report of the Commission of the United States of America to the Republic of Liberia* (Washington, 1910), p. 26. Harlan, "Booker T. Washington and the White Man's Burden," pp. 452–59; Raymond E. Bixler, *The Foreign Policy of the United States in Liberia* (New York, 1957), pp. 23–36.

Such adverse publicity for Liberia severely curtailed any serious emigration schemes. Although Bishop Turner continued to attack the United States for its racism and to advocate emigration, he was losing his vigor and his audience. A small Denver organization, "The Colorado African Colonization Company," which claimed to have been incorporated in 1902, tried to stimulate emigration in 1910. Nothing, however, came of its plans.[103] The first decade of the twentieth century ended, as it had begun, with emigration in the doldrums. Desire to flee the United States for an African utopia certainly was still alive but money and organization were missing. From time to time in succeeding years that sentiment would reemerge with new leaders and finances. The groundwork of agitation among black peasants, however, had long roots in the past, and during the two decades from 1890 to 1910 the man who had kept alive interest in emigration to Africa was Bishop Turner.

103. Henry E. Brundage to Wilson, 11 April 1910; J. N. Walker to Wilson, 25 May 1910; Wilson to Walker, 1 June 1910; President Arthur Barclay of Liberia to Walker, 4 March 1911, and Walker to President William Howard Taft, 21 April 1911 (both forwarded to the Colonization Society).

12

Epilogue and Conclusion

When Bishop Turner died in 1915, W. E. B. DuBois remembered him as the "last of his clan: mighty men, physically and mentally, men who started at the bottom and hammered their way to the top by sheer brute strength."[1] But it was for his personal ability and churchmanship that Turner was most remembered, not his black nationalism. Most black intellectuals disagreed with the bishop's solution to the American racial problem and were happy to forget his back-to-Africa schemes, which had excited many black peasants. Because black nationalism was overshadowed by the "accommodation" of Booker T. Washington and the civil rights protests of W. E. B. DuBois, contemporary observers took little notice of it. Even today it is difficult to evaluate Turner's movement.

It is clear that the African emigration movements of 1890–1910 were black in makeup and broad in extent. Some white men, such as those in the American Colonization Society and the International Migration Society, served as auxiliaries by providing transportation. But the leadership, money, and inspiration came from blacks. Just how broad the movement was is difficult to judge with precision, but signs of emigrationism appeared in all the deep South and Southwestern states, where the vast majority of Afro-Americans lived. Thousands were caught up directly in one or more of the emigration schemes and millions may

1. *Crisis, 10* (July 1915), 132.

have shared the black nationalists' pessimism about the United States. Although "African fever" reached its peak in the mid-1890s, it seems never to have died completely, as later movements attest.

Alienation and despair lay at the root of nationalism and emigration: despair of ever realizing the American dream and alienation from land, society, and self. Although the motives of would-be emigrants were vague, and hardly ever explicit, desire for land and economic security clearly played a major role. The 1890s juxtaposed the sharecrop and crop-lien system and a vicious depression, twin specters from which flight seemed the only chance of escape. The abrupt increase in violence while their civil rights rapidly disappeared convinced some of the more thoughtful black farmers that, despite the glorious verbal facade of freedom, liberty, equality, and democracy, the United States was no place for the black man. Bishop Turner drove home the fact that long years of slavery and subservience had subtly convinced the blacks themselves that black was evil and to be despised. Despite their fears to the contrary, Afro-Americans wanted to believe that they were as good as white men, and it appeared to some that the only way they could prove their worth was to establish a black nation.

Individual leaders played a crucial role in the emigration movement. Local organizers and advocates, indispensable but largely anonymous, served as emigration agents and nationalist spokesmen in country churches and lodge halls scattered throughout the South. Bishop Turner, on the other hand, used his high office in a national church to channel the basic peasant unrest and pessimism into African emigrationism. Black bitterness and despair could have led to violent anarchy, as it did with Robert Charles in New Orleans, if a nationalist leader had not provided a convincing analysis of the problems and a clear hope for success through emigration. It took a spokesman of national reputation, moreover, to dare to indict America's oppression of blacks. Much of Turner's popularity lay in his willingness to describe the racial situation as many blacks believed it to be but feared to state publicly.

Not least among Turner's functions was the portrayal of Africa as the promised land. Afro-American pessimism did not necessarily lead to nationalism, nor nationalism to emigrationism, nor emigrationism to Africa. When Turner first decided that Africa was the place to go, it was truly a dark continent, unknown to most of the world. By 1890, however, the Western world knew much more about it. Despite his four visits to "the fatherland," Turner never lost his romantic view of a potentially industrial land where the good life awaited Afro-Americans. By portraying it as such he could excite discouraged blacks into emigration. By describing his promised land in terms of the American dream, which Southern blacks also dreamed, he nurtured their desire for equality and self-government. By reminding them that Africa was their ancestral home and their promised land, Turner tried to prevail over advocates of emigration to other countries and continents.

Despite the popularity of Bishop Turner and Africa among Southern black farmers, middle-class blacks generally opposed nationalism and emigration. Despite their disabilities in the United States, they could see their progress up from slavery much more clearly than the sharecroppers, still in quasi-slavery. Even though Liberia cried for their talents and emigrationists urged them to go, few of the "black bourgeoisie" settled in Africa. They compensated for their refusal by sending missionary-teachers to Africa and by protesting against the excesses of European colonialism. Among black college students there was more respect for nationalism,[2] but after graduation the student radicals retreated to more "respectable" protests.

2. Cf. George Shepperson and Thomas Price, *The Independent African*, pp. 112–18.

The hallmark of the middle class was optimism, American optimism, which made the nationalist emigration movement appear to be folly. Many lower-class blacks joined their betters in rejecting emigration because they shared the aspirations, if not the successes, of the middle class. Quite probably, however, many more blacks approved Bishop Turner's bold, pungent attacks on American society, and perhaps endorsed his call for some kind of black separatism, than supported emigration.

The impact of African emigrationism upon white Americans was minimal. Only when actual migrations took place did most whites suspect that such black sentiment existed. On such occasions, furthermore, they were always caught unawares because customary "Negro spokesmen" had perpetuated the myth of the docile black peasant, content to stay at the bottom of society. While European immigrants by the millions entered the country, the very thought that anyone would want to leave the United States to look for better opportunities elsewhere seemed absurd to most Americans.

Within this general context, white reactions varied. Northern liberals like Tourgee rejected emigration because they believed the American love of justice would overcome the prejudice of race. More conservative whites endorsed the "gospel of wealth," as interpreted by Booker T. Washington, as the proper approach to race relations; they preferred the vision of industrious, uncomplaining workers to the prospect of radical malcontents who might upset the social equilibrium. The few whites who supported the American Colonization Society were either remnants of the pre-Civil War group that pictured emigration as a paternalistic solution to the race problem or representatives of a later generation that was concerned only for the welfare of Liberia. Although reactionaries like Thomas Dixon advocated deportation of blacks from the country, they found little support for the actual removal of Afro-Americans. Most whites simply wanted to keep the blacks at the lowest possible level of American society.

In Africa, however, the Afro-American emigration movement had considerable impact, although the thousand or so black peasants who sailed to Liberia between 1890 and 1910 helped that country but little. But the rhetoric of nationalism and the climate of protest among Afro-Americans reached far, and Bishop Turner's newspapers found avid readers in Sierra Leone, the Gold Coast, and Lagos. His visits to West and South Africa stirred the Africans, to the dismay of colonial officials. Just as important, African students who had studied in American colleges returned home with a newly militant attitude toward the colonial powers. If white Americans considered blacks passive and content, Africans learned otherwise.[3]

Perhaps the most important effect of Bishop Turner's campaign was to foster the hope for a better life in Africa in the memories of black Americans. For the African emigration movement did not stop in 1910; it has continued, in periodic outbursts, well into the twentieth century. The best-known movements were those led by Chief Alfred C. Sam and Marcus Garvey. But if the leaders and organiza-

3. For the impact of American black nationalism on Africa see, for example: Shepperson and Price, *Independent African;* Shepperson, "American Negro Influence on the Emergence of African Nationalism," *Journal of African History, 1* (1960), 299–312; idem, "Ethiopianism and African Nationalism," *Phylon, 14* (Spring 1953), 9–18; idem, "External Factors in the Development of African Nationalism, with Particular Reference to British Central Africa," *Phylon, 22* (Fall 1961), 207–25; idem, "The United States and East Africa," *Phylon, 13* (Spring 1951), 25–34; Mary Benson, *The African Patriots: The Story of the African National Congress of South Africa* (Chicago, 1963), pp. 28, 29, 47, 49, and passim; Sundkler, *Bantu Prophets*, pp. 38–64; Thwaite, *Seething African Pot*, pp. 36–39; Coan, "The Expansion of Missions," passim; Thomas Hodgkin, *Nationalism in Colonial Africa* (New York, 1957), pp. 81, 101, 108, 180 f.; David Kimble, *A Political History of Ghana* (London, 1963), pp. 537–44; Ruth M. Slade, *English-Speaking Missions in the Congo Independent State, 1878–1908* (Brussels, 1959), passim.

tions changed with time, the blacks who responded so
vigorously remained essentially the same.

Chief Alfred C. Sam, from Gold Coast Colony in West
Africa, suddenly appeared in Oklahoma in the summer
of 1913. He was selling stock in his company, Akim
Trading Company, Limited, and advocating Afro-American emigration to the Gold Coast, where he claimed to
own land. Sam appealed particularly to the residents of
several all-black towns, remnants of E. P. McCabe's settlement projects. Increasing prejudice and statewide disfranchisement had dashed all hopes for even local black independence; the blacks who fled to Oklahoma for refuge had
found none. In their despair they embraced Chief Sam's
nationalistic emigration scheme, invested their money accordingly, and prepared to sail to Africa. After purchasing
a steamship and christening it "Liberia," Sam confounded
his critics by sailing from Galveston with sixty emigrants
and a black crew. Indeed, several hundred black Oklahomans who had gone to Galveston in the hope of sailing
on Sam's first voyage were left behind, while hundreds
more waited in Oklahoma for Sam to return. Financial,
diplomatic, and political troubles cost Sam the ship, and
many of the emigrants eventually returned to the United
States. Like other schemes before it, Sam's efforts did little
more than demonstrate Afro-American dissatisfaction.[4]

Chief Sam could hardly have found a state more hos-
pitable to his scheme. In 1913 most of the blacks in Oklahoma had come from other states in their search for land
and security.[5] When Oklahoma proved to be just another
Southern state in racial matters, the blacks were bound to
be disillusioned, and candidates for emigration. National-

4. Bittle and Geis, *The Longest Way Home*, passim.
5. Oklahoma's black population multiplied almost sevenfold between 1890 and 1910; see U. S. Bureau of the Census, *Negro Population, 1790–1915* (Washington, 1918), p. 129.

ism, moreover, already had a strong foothold in Oklahoma, as evidenced by its separate communities and the attempt to build a black state in the territory in the 1890s. African emigration also had a strong local tradition. The blacks who traveled from Oklahoma to New York in 1892 and 1899, expecting to go to Africa, were solid evidence of that tradition. Samuel Chapman's emigration clubs helped keep it alive in the late 1890s, while Bishop Turner's newspapers and speeches fed the Afro-American desire to leave home for greener pastures. Chief Sam reaped what Turner had planted.[6]

The better-known Marcus Garvey came to the United States from Jamaica in 1916, just a year after Turner died. During the next ten years he built the largest mass movement in Afro-American history around his Universal Negro Improvement Association. Garvey's appeals to black nationalism and African emigration earned him the title "Black Moses," a designation bestowed earlier on Bishop Turner. The black masses who had moved to Northern cities responded to this ideology in astounding numbers and intensity. Lack of business skill, however, caused the downfall of Garvey and his movement, and he was imprisoned for mail fraud and eventually deported. Few, if any, in his legion of followers settled in Africa, but the Afro-American community was thoroughly aroused. Many white Americans realized for the first time that the myth of the docile, satisfied black Sambo was false.[7]

Garvey attributed the seed of his ideology to Booker T. Washington and the philosophy of black self-help.[8] But Afro-American solidarity and self-help were not exclusive-

6. See Chapter 5 and p. 250 above.
7. Cronon, *Black Moses,* passim; Frank Chalk, "DuBois and Garvey Confront Liberia: Two Incidents of the Coolidge Years," a paper delivered at the 52d annual meeting of the Association for the Study of Negro Life and History, 13–17 October 1967, Greensboro, N.C.
8. Cronon, *Black Moses,* pp. 15–19.

ly features of Washington's ideology; they were shared by integrationists and nationalists alike. It was only incidental that Washington had been able to make greater progress in building Afro-American businesses and encouraging black entrepreneurs; Garvey might just as well have learned the same ideas from Bishop Turner or W. E. B. DuBois.[9] Certainly Washington's autobiography inspired Garvey to become a race leader, but his nationalism was much closer to Turner's outlook than to Washington's scheme of accommodation, industrial education, and rural virtue. Whether he knew it or not, Garvey was part of a long tradition of black nationalism in the United States.[10]

Garvey's followers, moreover, were the same Southern black marginal farmers who had responded to the emigration appeals of Bishop Turner and his followers a generation earlier. During the boom times of the First World War many of them had moved north in "the great migration," seeking the promised land of economic opportunity and racial harmony. But postwar recession and race riots soon created the despair which bred pessimism. In the pattern of earlier African emigration movements, the lower-class blacks responded eagerly when flamboyant Marcus Garvey pointed the way. No longer isolated on scattered farms and restrained by southern conditions as Turner's followers had been, the black proletariat, crowded into urban ghettoes and disillusioned with their new homes, spread nationalism far and fast. Garvey himself may have been a foreigner but his millions of supporters manifested an old American response of black nationalism.

9. See, for example, W. E. B. DuBois' *The Conservation of Races* (Washington, 1897) for his view on the role of the black race in the world.

10. Cf. Eugene D. Genovese, "The Legacy of Slavery and the Roots of Black Nationalism," and the comments by Herbert Aptheker and C. Vann Woodward, with Genovese's rejoinder, all in *Studies on the Left*, *6* (November–December 1966), 3–65.

The same evaluation can be made of Turner that has been made of Garvey, whose "very success in selling an unrealistic escapist program to American Negroes throws into sharp relief the burning discontent and bitter disillusionment that he found in the Negro world."[11] Yet Turner did not achieve either the strong support or the notoriety of Garvey. A comparison of the two leaders and their movements reveals several reasons for this disparity.

Bishop Turner did not have the personal qualities that might have brought him more support. Instead of being devoted entirely to his emigration scheme, he was deeply involved in the affairs of his church. When in 1892 he had the opportunity to take personal charge of the American Colonization Society, he declined this option because of his church duties and pressure from the black middle class.[12] Garvey had no such ambivalent loyalties; his Universal Negro Improvement Association was his only commitment. Furthermore, as witnessed by Turner's political career during Reconstruction and his later church-building role, the bishop had the ability to organize his people into effective groups but failed to bring the same wholehearted effort to his nationalist campaign. Despite the unrest and discontent of Afro-Americans in the 1890s, the bishop was unable to bring to his emigration efforts the single-minded devotion that was necessary to make black nationalism function as an effective movement.

Despite the persistent interest in black nationalism during Turner's career, it was overwhelmed by other leaders and ideologies. At the height of the African excitement in the mid-1890s, Booker T. Washington captured the imaginations of blacks and whites with his "Atlanta Compromise" address of 1895. His success in capitalizing on this popularity brought him power and influence, and instilled

11. Cronon, *Black Moses*, p. 203.
12. See pp. 124–26, 128, above.

hope in many of the pessimistic blacks who might have followed Turner. Garvey, in 1919, was the only leader who was new and exciting; his movement collapsed because he was imprisoned, not because he was overwhelmed by other men with new ideas. Success for the emigration scheme was doubtful for many reasons; but if Booker T. Washington had not overtaken him, Turner might at least have become "notorious" for his black nationalism.

The black communities from which Turner and Garvey drew their support, although they shared the "lower-class black" label and all that this implied, were marked by important differences that help explain the contrasts between the two movements. Turner dealt with Southern rural blacks while Garvey's strength came primarily from the urban ghettoes. And urbanization provided a more compact community where ideas could spread—a critical mass in which nationalist excitement could sustain itself. The urban economy, which used cash for wages instead of crops for credit, made it easier to finance black organizations. The cities also protected blacks from the pressures experienced by Turner's followers in the South. Southern whites wanted blacks to remain placidly at work on their farms but most Northern whites would have been happy to see them depart from the cities. Furthermore, most of Garvey's urban followers had only recently moved from the farms. As the example of Oklahoma had shown, people who had already moved were likely candidates for further migration after the earlier promised land lost its promise. Clearly, the rural group that Turner sought to lead was more difficult to mobilize. But whether country- or city-based, in 1890 or 1920, the two movements shared a common nationalist response to American racial oppression.

Marcus Garvey also shared Bishop Turner's final failure to move American blacks to Africa; the difficulties in transporting large groups overseas stymied both leaders. A comparison of Turner's emigration scheme with the transatlantic migration of Europeans during the same years suggests a number of reasons for the failure of the bishop's plans.[13] In Europe, as in America, economic factors played a major role in spurring emigration; periodic depressions helped stir unrest, but even larger forces were at work. The collapse of the feudal system under the impact of agrarian capitalism and the industrial revolution had displaced the people who eventually came to America. Many peasants were thereby alienated from their land and traditional society; they became surplus people in their own homelands. Rather than accept landless status in agrarian countries or work at minimum wages in the new factories, they emigrated. Some—especially religious societies such as the Mennonites, Jews, and Armenians—chose emigration over massacre. Racial problems in the United States, though grim in those years, never approached the intensity of the Slavic pogroms against Jews or the Turkish slaughter of Armenian Christians. Blacks were alienated from American society but their alienation was a constant condition; they could stay in "their place" at the bottom of the economic and social order and still have access to work and food, minimal though this was. They were scarcely surplus labor, for land and employment were available in the West, and labor agents urged them to move north to the mines, railways, and factories. The depression of the 1890s stimulated African emigration but black peasants did not face such tremendous social and economic changes as challenged Europe. In short, the situation the would-be emigrants wanted to flee was not as bad as it may have seemed. Instead of starvation or large-scale slaughter, the

13. The following discussion of European emigration to the United States is based primarily on Maldwyn Allen Jones, *American Immigration* (Chicago, 1960), esp. pp. 177–206.

Afro-Americans faced only the shattering of their fondest, their greatest expectations.

Europeans chose to come to the United States primarily for economic reasons. Western farms, city factories, and sprawling railroads cried for labor, which the immigrants provided. America's industrial boom was common knowledge throughout Europe, and word filtered down to hard-pressed villagers that migration was the answer to their problems. Another major attraction was the strong pull of relatives and friends, who, having gone to America, wrote back to Europe and urged kith and kin to follow them. Some complained of hardships in the United States but most sent money to help their friends and family get to America. Compared with such a personal and economic magnet in North America, the appeal of Africa at the turn of the century seems feeble indeed. Although South Africa's mines were beginning to dazzle the world, West Africa, and especially Liberia, was mostly bush, which even when laboriously cleared yielded only a subsistence income not much greater than blacks already earned in the Southern states. Instead of a bustling industrial nation, they were being invited to a still very dark and primitive continent. Instead of relatives and friends sending back money to help them emigrate, Afro-Americans received requests for money to help the earlier emigrants return home. Despite strong mystical ties to Africa, many blacks could not overcome their notions of Africa as a savage, unhealthy land.

Emigrationist leadership in Europe was limited largely to steamship agents and occasional labor recruiters, and the ideas they employed to lure the peasants echoed the perennial American dream. The dream looked especially attractive when coupled with the success stories of friends who had emigrated earlier. Bishop Turner, on the other hand, had to use extensive propaganda to stimulate African emigration. He was constantly forced to rationalize away the reports of illness, disaster, and despair from former emigrants. His attempt to convert the American dream did not convince the middle-class blacks who had most thoroughly embraced that dream; they wanted no part of an African nightmare. Local agents for the International Migration Society had sporadic successes, but their task was more difficult than that of their European counterparts. Despite the efforts of Turner and other leaders to stimulate emigration, they could not consistently overcome inertia and start a steady, though small, stream of emigration which might eventually have made the movement successful.

Transportation was another crucial difference. Perhaps Bishop Turner was correct in arguing that steamships on a regular schedule between African and American ports would be filled with black emigrants, but the American commercial trade with West Africa could not support such traffic. Nor was there a long tradition of profitable passenger traffic, as in the case of Europe, which could justify ship companies' specializing in emigrant transportation. The International Migration Society tried this but failed. Had all the other factors been favorable, the lack of economical transportation would have severely jolted African emigration dreams.

The African emigration movement of 1890–1910 failed, then, for all these reasons. The troubles in the South were not sufficiently severe to drive the Afro-Americans out of the United States. Nor could the attractions of Africa draw the blacks away from home, especially while there were opportunities to move north or west within the United States. Emigrationist leaders, primarily Bishop Turner, could not generate enough push toward Africa to overcome the pull of the American dream. And, had he succeeded, transportation would have been lacking. Seen in retrospect, the African emigration movement never had much chance of success.

On the other hand, when viewed as a nationalist movement, Bishop Turner's campaign was more significant. The nationalist or separatist attitude toward race problems has appeared and reappeared frequently in Afro-American history but has not yet succeeded to the extent of establishing separate political units or unifying black Americans behind its objectives. Comparison of Turner's nationalist campaign with "successful" nationalist efforts in nineteenth-century Europe, especially in Germany and Italy, suggests that important nationalist elements were missing from the Afro-American movement.

Nineteenth-century nationalism had for its chief spokesmen the intellectuals and bourgeois leaders of Europe. They brought their talents as thinkers, writers, and teachers to the task of building a national spirit among their people as old empires were overthrown and old disunities mended. In the aristocratic societies of Europe, intellectuals were marginal men but they had abilities and aspirations that brought them success. The Afro-American middle class also consisted of marginal men, but neither they nor the educated black elite endorsed black nationalism; they were still caught up in American individualism. Their best minds protested discrimination, seeking inclusion in the American system, and did not plan or visualize a black nation. Bishop Turner was the only man in the movement who could be considered an intellectual—a leader whose supporters were inarticulate—and there grew up no dialogue within the movement between men who endorsed separation. Without such dialogue there was no sharpening of arguments, no clarification of strategies, no toughening of resolve. Although nationalists have always sought to unite the masses behind them, intellectual leadership has been indispensable. Black nationalism in the

1890s, as well as at other times, did not have that kind of leadership.[14]

Bishop Turner, who built his nationalist appeal not on the culture of black people but on an Africanized American dream, thereby lost one of the basic appeals that has strengthened other nationalisms, the call for a people with a distinct culture to establish a state in which that culture could flourish. European nationalists asserted their claims to political self-determination by delving into the primitive backgrounds of their people, finding tribal legends, fairy tales, mythical heroes, and linguistic origins. By asserting ancient grandeur, the nationalists could not only rationalize modern, self-determined states but could give the people a cultural identity beyond a mere linguistic or geographic identity. American blacks, cut off from most of their African memories and immersed in a nation that refused to acknowledge that blacks could have a cultural background, have had a difficult time fashioning a cultural identity other than the tradition of oppression. Bishop Turner was unable to find or create a mythical structure of the Afro-American past that would inspire his people. Because his African dream was essentially the American dream, he was unable to convince those who saw the discrepancies, particularly economic, between the two. His focus was still on the American goals of elite achievement rather than on the "soul" of the black masses.[15] His movement, to succeed, would have needed more internal cohesion in its vision—a uniqueness that only black folk could give, not just a dark imitation of the United States.

Geography also played an important role in nationalism. In most European and other nationalist movements the

14. Cf. Harold Cruse, *The Crisis of the Negro Intellectual* (New York, 1967), esp. pp. 451–98, for a discussion of black intellectuals and their problems with nationalism.

15. See Charles Keil, *Urban Blues* (Chicago, 1966), Chapter 1, for a vigorous discussion of the culture of contemporary Afro-Americans.

people who called for their own state occupied a specific territory on which their government could be based. They would throw off foreign kings, drive out alien residents, and gather in all the dispersed people who shared the national heritage. This, of course, has not been the case with Afro-Americans. Although in Bishop Turner's time the blacks were concentrated in the former Confederate states, they were not the majority element even there. There, more than elsewhere, blacks were continually reminded that they lived in "white man's country." Consequently a black nationalist movement could not realistically call for the independence of a black South. The attempt to make Oklahoma a black state met with no success at all. Therefore one of the basic elements of successful nationalism, a home territory sacred to its people and drenched in their national tradition, a land truly their own, was missing from black nationalism.

That Afro-Americans had no land to call their own explains why black nationalists have usually wanted to leave the United States. The lure of Africa as the ancestral home made it the emotional if not the logical choice for a modern black nation. The only nationalist movement to succeed in repatriating its members to a distant "homeland" has been Zionism. The parallels between Zionism and the black nationalism of Bishop Turner, Marcus Garvey, and other emigrationists are obvious, but the differences between them sum up the weaknesses of African emigration as a solution to the American race problem.[16] The foremost advocates of Zionism were Jewish intellectuals who, after 1896, met frequently to plan a strategy for founding a Jewish state. Without that intellectual leadership the Jewish peasants and refugees who might have wanted a state of their own would have had little chance of success.

16. The following discussion of Zionism is based primarily on Ben Halpern, *The Idea of the Jewish State* (Cambridge, Mass., 1961).

Not only intellectuals but at least a few wealthy and highly placed Zionists provided leadership, financial aid, and political pressure; without the aid of the Rothschilds or of affluent American Jews, Zionism would have had little success in creating a modern state of Israel. Black nationalists have had no such powerful support. Indeed, Bishop Turner found that financial crises did more to harm his scheme than ideological attacks. Although West Africa, as a potential homeland, was probably more blessed with resources than Palestine, its development needed capital and skilled entrepreneurs. Israel received those benefits, especially after the attempted genocide of European Jews by Nazi Germany. No such outpouring of skilled refugees followed by sympathetic investment capital went to Liberia.

Political Zionism was accompanied, even preceded, by a cultural Zionism whose goal was the revival of a national language and culture. Even though political and cultural Zionists did not agree on priorities, they nevertheless reinforced each other. Black Americans, as different from their surrounding populations as the Jews, and as oppressed, lacked the conscious cultural tradition based on religion and language that gave inner strength to Jews. Afro-Americans did indeed have a culture of their own, but in Turner's time it was not an object of pride. The bishop could urge his followers to "respect black" but the plea was based on elemental humanity and minimal achievements rather than on a unique tradition and cultural pride.

These comparisons between Bishop Turner's black nationalism and other nationalisms point up the serious problems that faced his movement. They also demonstrate that nationalism as a proposed solution to group friction is a widespread phenomenon. Moreover, there are enough similarities between the problems of Afro-Americans and other nationalist minorities to give black nationalists hope that their ideology may achieve similar success. Again, the persistence of black nationalism demonstrates the attractiveness of ethnic solidarity and self-determination as a means of fighting oppression.

Subsequent black nationalist movements have differed from Bishop Turner's in numerous ways, adding some features and shedding others, especially emigration. Still central, however, is the bitter protest against American hypocrisy and white nationalism. This has been accompanied by a call for blacks, who in an individualistic society are oppressed as a group, to face this collective aspect of their situation and to increase their solidarity and power as a group. Finding new ways to apply this principle to the American dilemma occupies many blacks, as it concerned Turner and his followers. The persistence of black nationalism suggests that, even though mass emigration has never been feasible, in his nationalistic reaction to American racism Bishop Turner transmitted an important but unrefined idea which may yet help solve the problems of Afro-Americans.

Bibliographical Note

The primary source for this study was the American Colonization Society papers, housed in the Manuscripts Division of the Library of Congress, Washington, D.C. This large collection contains correspondence, records, minutes, and reports dating from the 1820s. Letters received were divided into domestic and Liberian correspondence and bound into volumes shortly after receipt. The domestic correspondence remains in the original bindings, filed in chronological order and indexed. The staff of the Library of Congress has laminated the Liberian correspondence through 1892 and bound the material into sturdier, cleaner volumes which still maintain the chronological order and indexing. Outgoing correspondence, recorded and indexed in letter-press books, still remains in the original bindings without differentiation between domestic and Liberian letters. After 1892, when the Society underwent drastic reorganization, the filing system for letters received was changed. The new secretary classified correspondence as either "general" or "important," thus destroying the older categories. General letters, including correspondence from the many Southern blacks interested in emigration, were filed chronologically and indexed in bound letter books. "Important" letters, however, including correspondence from prominent men, foreigners, and successful applicants for emigrant passage, were placed in unlabeled manila folders where they still remain. Journals and minutes of the Executive Committee and the Board of Directors provided information about the operations of the society itself.

Although the society ceased to play a major role in the emigration story after 1892, its officers kept watch on other emigration and African developments. It received the publications and prospectuses of independent emigration organizations. Most of these books are now in the general collection of the Library of Congress. Smaller items such as circulars, broadsides, and announcements were filled in unmarked manila folders where they still reside.

Starting in 1892 with the published letters from Africa by Bishop Henry M. Turner, society officials kept a collection of clippings from American and African newspapers concerning emigration and Liberian affairs. Housed in ten scrapbooks, this collection provided invaluable leads to the activities of independent emigration movements after the society stopped sending large groups of emigrants to Liberia.

Until 1892 the society published the *African Repository*, a quarterly magazine carrying information about Liberia, emigration, and society business. In November 1892 the *Repository* was superseded by the semiannual *Liberia Bulletin* which published much the same kind of information until it ceased publication in 1909. The letters and news items published in the *Bulletin* were usually found also in the society's correspondence and scrapbooks. The society also published *Annual Reports* and the addresses of annual speakers, and these were included in the *African Repository* and *Liberia Bulletin*.

No papers of Bishop Henry M. Turner have been preserved other than a few personal items in the Moorland Collection at the Howard University Library and occasional letters in other manuscript collections. According to Josephus R. Coan, historian of the AME church in Atlanta and member of the Interdenominational Theological

Center there, a collection of Turner's papers was destroyed there some years ago.

The Booker T. Washington papers, also in the Library of Congress, provided mostly background information. Washington's staunch opposition to emigration was widely known and there was little communication between him and the advocates of repatriation. Nevertheless, he received occasional letters from semiliterate farmers who wanted to go to Africa. He also corresponded occasionally with educated Africans, and after 1903 his protégé, Ernest Lyon, was United States Minister to Liberia. Some of the correspondence between Washington and Lyon was useful in this study, but in general the Washington papers provided little that was not already known, especially after the publication of Louis R. Harlan's article, "Booker T. Washington and the White Man's Burden" *(American Historical Review, 71,* January 1966, 441–67), which detailed Washington's various relations with Africans and African affairs.

The papers of John Edward Bruce ("Bruce Grit"), housed in the Schomburg Collection of the New York Public Library, showed that Bruce, a prominent black journalist, had numerous contacts with Africans and eventually became a lieutenant of Marcus Garvey. Bruce's correspondence, however, added only peripheral information to the movement studied here.

In the United States National Archives, the diplomatic and consular correspondence and the post records yielded some useful information on Liberia, but most of the material was of a routine, background nature because until about 1905 Liberia considered the Colonization Society its most effective channel to American authorities. The archives of the Republic of Liberia are currently closed to foreign scholars.

Among the newspapers studied two were central: *The Voice of Missions* (1893–1900) and *The Voice of the People* (1901-c.1907). Professor Coan discovered the only known runs of these papers and has generously made them available on microfilm. Both papers were edited by Bishop Turner and provided indispensable information on the emigration movement, black nationalism, and Bishop Turner himself.

None of the numerous studies of the American Colonization Society carry the story into the 1890s. For the pre-Civil War period the most recent study is Philip J. Staudenraus' *The African Colonization Movement, 1816–1865* (New York, 1961). Staudenraus includes a bibliographical essay which evaluates the copious literature on the early years of the society. Willis D. Boyd carried the study of the society through 1870 in his dissertation, "Negro Colonization in the National Crisis" (UCLA, 1953). Both Staudenraus and Boyd deal primarily with the institution rather than with the blacks who accepted or rejected the emigration idea.

Liberia has no adequate history for the years 1890–1910. Of the numerous books called histories, most are memoirs, a few are based on published sources, almost none on archival evidence. For the formative years Staudenraus offers the best synthesis. For the later period the most useful are Harry H. Johnston's, *Liberia* (London, 1906), and Raymond Leslie Buell's, *The Native Problem in Africa* (New York, 1928), Volume II, Section XIV. Raymond W. Bixler's *The Foreign Policy of the United States in Liberia* (New York, 1957), is sketchy but outlines its subject. Several doctoral dissertations treat the history of Liberia and of American relations to that republic. The following provided useful background information: Hanna Abeodu Bowen Jones, "The Struggle for Political and

Cultural Unification in Liberia, 1847–1930" (Northwestern, 1962); John Payne Mitchell, "America's Liberian Policy" (Chicago, 1955). The annual volumes of *Acts Passed by the Legislature of the Republic of Liberia* and the various messages and addresses of the presidents of the republic provide the best available clues to the internal political history of Liberia during these years. These publications are most accessible in the Library of Congress and in the Dispatches of United States Ministers to Liberia, United States Archives.

Afro-American history in this period has been best recounted by August Meier in his *Negro Thought in America, 1880–1915: Racial Ideology in the Age of Booker T. Washington* (Ann Arbor, 1963). In this excellent work Meier concentrates on the emergence and later eclipse of Booker T. Washington and his racial ideas. In a short chapter on "Migration and Colonization," Meier discusses Bishop Turner's brand of nationalism only briefly, choosing instead to concentrate on the articulate blacks who followed Washington or W. E. B. DuBois. But Meier correctly described the nationalism of the time as a lower-class black movement and suggested that there was more interest in emigration among the less articulate masses than he could demonstrate. In the present study I have tried to provide evidence to support Meier's impressions.

Southern race relations for the period have been well surveyed by C. Vann Woodward in his *Origins of the New South, 1877–1913* (Baton Rouge, 1951), and *The Strange Career of Jim Crow* (New York, 1957, 1966). Woodward revealed the complexity of the race picture, the differences from state to state, and the political, economic, and social conditions which affected race relations. Rayford W. Logan in his *The Betrayal of the Negro* (New York, 1965), originally published as *The Negro in American Life and*

Thought: The Nadir, 1877–1901 (New York, 1954), surveyed race relations in national politics and white journals
of the period. Logan dealt with the North as well as the
South.

Two useful monographs on the Afro-American in this
period added significant background information. Carter
G. Woodson, in *A Century of Negro Migration* (Washington, 1918), touches on African emigration in the context
of general Negro restlessness. Clarence A. Bacote studied
"The Negro in Georgia Politics, 1880–1908" (unpublished doctoral dissertation, Chicago, 1955), and observed
Bishop Turner and his emigration activities in Atlanta.

Concerning Bishop Turner little has been written.
Mungo M. Ponton, in his biography, *The Life and Times
of Bishop Henry M. Turner* (Atlanta, 1917), is very un-
critical but does manage to convey some of the bishop's
personality. Ponton reprinted Turner's stirring speech to
the Georgia House of Representatives concerning the removal of black members in 1868. J. Minton Batten in his
early article, "Henry M. Turner: Negro Bishop Extraordinary" (*Church History, 7,* September 1938, 231–46),
provided an outline biography with stress on Turner's
ecclesiastical career. Josephus R. Coan's doctoral dissertation, "The Expansion of Missions of the A.M.E. Church
in South Africa, 1896–1908" (Hartford Seminary, 1961),
dealt with Turner's trip to South Africa in 1898 and its
stormy aftermath in both the United States and South
Africa. E. Merton Coulter wrote of Turner's active career
in Reconstruction politics in "Henry M. Turner: Georgia Preacher-Politician During the Reconstruction Era"
(*Georgia Historical Quarterly, 48,* December 1964, 371–
410). Coulter was very unsympathetic toward Turner but
he found important source material on the bishop's life at
the time when Turner was becoming embittered at white

American society. Turner was a complex man with many facets to his long career. Although African emigration was not his only concern, he was the man in this period who was most articulate in the nationalist cause.

Afro-Americans have had continuous ties to Africa, sentimental or otherwise, which have not yet been studied intensively. A number of historians touch on them in passing. George A. Shepperson has published a series of articles on black influences on African nationalism. Especially useful is his short survey of "American Negro Influence on the Emergence of African Nationalism," in the *Journal of African History, 1* (1960), 299–312. Howard H. Bell, in his excellent doctoral dissertation, "A Survey of the Negro Convention Movement, 1830–1861" (Northwestern, 1953), showed black antagonism to the ACS but confirmed concurrent attempts by various Afro-Americans to establish independent settlements in Africa. Hollis R. Lynch examined "Pan-Negro Nationalism in the New World, Before 1862," in *Boston University Papers on Africa,* II (Boston, 1966), 149–79. Lynch has also written a study of *Edward Wilmot Blyden, Pan-Negro Patriot, 1832–1912* (London, 1967), which is essential to the understanding of the emigration movements after 1890. Edith Holden has also written of Blyden in a less digested but more detailed biography, *Blyden of Liberia: An Account of the Life and Labors of Edward Wilmot Blyden, LL.D., As Recorded in Letters and in Print* (New York, 1966). St. Clair Drake has surveyed Afro-American relations with Africa in his "Negro Americans and the African Interest," in John P. Davis, ed., *The American Negro Reference Book* (2 vols. New York, 1966), 2: 629–66.

The International Migration Society left no known records. Some of its pamphlets and circulars are found in the ACS papers, but aside from a few letters to the ACS the

Migration Society must be studied from public newspaper accounts. The *New Orleans Times-Democrat* for August 4, 1900, contained a series of articles on the Migration Society, including one reportedly based on a reading of the society's monthly bulletins.

Black nationalism in general has received no satisfactory historical study. The earliest investigation was made by Ralph J. Bunche in his "Conceptions and Ideologies of the Negro Problem" (unpublished essay for the Carnegie-Myrdal study of the Negro in America, 1940, in the Schomburg Collection of the New York Public Library). August Meier pursued the study further in "The Emergence of Negro Nationalism (A Study in Ideologies)" *(Midwest Journal, 4,* Winter 1951–52, 96–104, and *4,* Summer 1952, 95–111). Marcus Garvey was well portrayed in Edmund David Cronon's *Black Moses: The Story of Marcus Garvey and the Universal Negro Improvement Association* (Madison, 1955). Howard H. Bell, in his study of the convention movement before the Civil War, found evidence of nationalism in the 1850s. Herbert Aptheker traced the terms "nation" and "national" in black rhetoric and presented his findings in "Consciousness of Negro Nationality to 1900," reprinted in his *Toward Negro Freedom* (New York, 1956). A useful study was presented by Howard Brotz in the introductions to documents in *Negro Social and Political Thought, 1850–1920; Representative Texts* (New York, 1966). But discussions of more recent black nationalist movements such as the Black Muslims have not been concerned with the pre-Garvey manifestations; and black nationalism—as a general response by Afro-Americans and as a historical phenomenon—requires further investigation.

Index